The Accountant's
Guide to
Peer and Quality
Review

THE ACCOUNTANT'S GUIDE TO PEER AND QUALITY REVIEW

R. K. McCABE

QUORUM BOOKS
Westport, Connecticut • London

657.06
M 121

Library of Congress Cataloging-in-Publication Data

McCabe, R. K.
   The accountant's guide to peer and quality review / R. K.
McCabe.
        p.   cm.
   Includes bibliographical references and index.
   ISBN 0–89930–685–3 (alk. paper)
   1. Accounting—Quality control.   2. Peer review.   I. Title.
   HF5657.M34   1993
   657'.068'5—dc20   92–34946

British Library Cataloguing in Publication Data is available.

Library of Congress Catalog Card Number: 92–34946
ISBN: 0–89930–685–3

First published in 1993

Quorum Books, 88 Post Road West, Westport, CT 06881
An imprint of Greenwood Publishing Group, Inc.

Printed in the United States of America

The paper used in this book complies with the
Permanent Paper Standard issued by the National
Information Standards Organization (Z39.48–1984).

10 9 8 7 6 5 4 3 2 1

Copyright Acknowledgments

The author and publisher gratefully acknowledge permission to use the following:

R.K. McCabe, ''Wanted: A Few Good Reviewers,'' *Journal of Accountancy* (August
1991): 109–14. Reprinted with permission from the Journal of Accountancy, Copyright
© 1991 by American Institute of Certified Public Accountants, Inc. Opinions of the
author are his own and do not necessarily reflect policies of the AICPA.

R.K. McCabe, ''A Quality Review Checklist,'' *Journal of Accountancy* (September
1990): 69–74. Reprinted with permission from the Journal of Accountancy, Copyright
© 1990 by American Institute of Certified Public Accountants, Inc. Opinions of the
author are his own and do not necessarily reflect policies of the AICPA. Portions of
chapter 8 in this volume are based on this article.

R.K. McCabe and K.W. Lantz, ''Selecting a Value-Oriented Reviewer,'' *The CPA
Journal* (July 1991): 74–75. This article was reprinted in part in ''Selecting the Right
Reviewer for Your Firm,'' *Tennessee CPA* (December 1991): 15. Portions of chapter 4
in this volume are based on the July 1991 article.

Lyrics from ''The Times They Are A-Changin' '' by Bob Dylan. Copyright © 1963,
1964 Warner Bros. Inc.; © renewed 1992 Special Rider Music. All rights reserved.
International copyright secured. Reprinted by permission.

This book is dedicated to the members of the accounting
profession and all the critters at McCabe's Arabians, including
Karen, Don, Dan, Irene, Casey, B.J., Rufus, Shataz, Montana,
and Rockette, without whom this book would not have been
necessary.

This book is also dedicated to the love of my life,
    my wife Carol.

Contents

Tables and Figures

TABLES

FIGURES

Preface

The Accountant's Guide to Peer and Quality Review does much more than what the title suggests. It shows firms how to develop a quality control system, prepare for the review, and earn an unqualified report. In addition, it tackles the problem of substandard quality head on. It examines the roots of review and discusses the undiscussable.

This book was written to be read from beginning to end. Firm members facing an upcoming review are certainly encouraged to do just that. In addition, reviewers and those considering the possibility of becoming a reviewer should read this book thoroughly.

This text also was written to be a useful reference. For those designing or amending their quality control systems, Chapter 5 should be especially helpful. For those about to have a review, the entire text is essential. Firms facing their first review will probably want to refer frequently to Chapters 4, 5, 6, and 7, which describe how to find a good reviewer, the quality control functional areas, the keys to a successful review, and what happens in a review.

Reviewers also should find this book interesting and important. For example, Chapter 7 includes important suggestions about questions to ask on reviews that are not on the reviewer checklists. Chapter 8 argues that the scope of peer and quality review ought to be expanded.

The book also is an excellent resource for some of my colleagues in academia. Quality control and quality review are two of the most important professional requirements, yet some accounting academics know little about them. In addition, other than a page or two in an auditing text, the issues of quality control and review are ignored in the accounting curriculum. As a result, entry-level professionals know little about controlling professional service quality. Without quality control and review, the profession could and would have ceased to exist.

The recommendations presented throughout this book, and in particular in Chapter 9, offer a fruitful basis for debate. The leaders of the profession, including those on the Auditing Standards Board and on the various AICPA committees, ought to read and consider these recommendations. So, too, should members of the various regulatory bodies such as the Public Oversight Board and the state boards of accountancy. Over the past several years a revolution has occurred in the accounting profession, but it is not complete. More needs to be done, and this book helps pave the way. Less than professional-quality service is no longer acceptable.

Many of the issues discussed in this book also apply to any organization attempting to control the quality of its product or services. Law firms and manufacturing companies will benefit by applying to their operations the concepts described here.

The book does not use such phrases as "total quality management." All too frequently this is simply a phrase that management does not understand and is not committed to, and, as a result, total quality management does not work. The quality system explained in this book does work. It works for CPA firms, and it will work for any company in any industry. All it requires is understanding and commitment.

Some describe the transformation of the accounting profession into the accounting business as a revolution and the beginning of widespread substandard service. The change from a profession into a business was completed with the repeal of the encroachment rules. Substandard service, however, existed well before these rules were abolished.

The repeal of the encroachment rules and the resultant increase in competition make accounting and audit services price sensitive. Price sensitivity can lead to substandard service. Substandard service also exists because the quality of what accountants and auditors do cannot be observed. Since inferior service may go unnoticed, some are tempted to perform at a level below professional standards.

Substandard service exists for several other reasons as well. Education in general and accounting education specifically are not adequately preparing tomorrow's professionals. Continuing professional education and licensing requirements need to be strengthened. Firms need to follow the policies and procedures outlined in their quality control documents and statements of philosophy. In addition, they need to reexamine the tone at the top. Firms that put profits and growth ahead of quality need to be admonished. These issues and others are addressed here.

The profession's leadership recognizes that substandard service threatens the profession's very existence. To reduce the instances of inferior-quality service, the profession requires firms to have a system of quality control and to conduct an annual internal inspection of that system. In addition, it requires firms to undergo a comprehensive triennial external review. In essence, unlike some other professions, the accounting profession is showing that it can provide a quality product and regulate itself. To eliminate incidences of substandard service much more must be done.

Chapter 1, "The Road to Peer Review," describes the revolution. The roots of review in substandard service are outlined. The chapter also describes society's perceptions of the profession's role and responsibilities. Government, society's spokesperson, has threatened, cajoled, and pushed the profession into regulating itself through peer and quality review. The profession's response has been both controversial and painful to many of its members. What accountant-auditors do has changed dramatically. Differences between the public's expectations and our perceptions of the role and responsibility of the profession have been narrowed. Serious expectation differences, however, remain.

The American Institute of Certified Public Accountants (AICPA) first experimented with quality review in the early 1960s. In 1977, it established a voluntary review organization, the Division for CPA Firms. The division has two sections: the Private Companies Practice Section (PCPS) and the SEC Practice Section (SECPS). Prompted partially by the continuing threats of Congress and by the success of the division, the AICPA's membership in 1988 approved mandated quality review for all firms. Firms must now design, implement, and adhere to a system of quality control in accordance with established quality control standards. This system is subject to a comprehensive triennial review.

Government's response to the profession's effort, mostly through the Securities and Exchange Commission, has been positive. The evidence to date shows that quality control and review do improve the caliber of professional practice.

Chapter 2, "The Choices," examines what accountants and auditors did just a few years ago when transactions were simpler and the world less complex. It also discusses issues that many in the profession disregard, perhaps in the hope that by ignoring them they might just go away. Issues such as staff signing off on audit procedures they did not do and charging significantly less time to an engagement than was expended cannot be overlooked.

Chapter 2 also compares the efficiency and effectiveness of audits today with those of audits in years past. In addition, it looks at how independence and confidentiality have decreased in importance. Neither is as sacred to the professional today as it was just a few short years ago.

It also examines some of the major influences on the profession, such as government and large CPA firms. As some things change, others remain the same. The large accounting firms are still very influential in the development of generally accepted accounting principles and auditing standards. Such is the cost of general acceptance.

The proposal by Senator Lee Metcalf's (D–Mont.) subcommittee to have government take over the accounting profession also is analyzed in Chapter 2. The subcommittee report, *The Accounting Establishment*, proposes that government set generally accepted accounting principles and auditing standards, and determine what services firms could and could not provide. This proposal did not receive broad support from Congress. The author argues that it is not in Congress's best interest to take over the accounting profession. Not only are the members of Congress ill prepared to do so, but also they would become the scapegoat when audit and business failures occurred. The fallout, however, from the savings and loan (S&L) catastrophe and the insistence by politicians, and especially those in Congress and the executive branch, that blame be placed elsewhere each contribute to an environment in which regulation can blossom. Add to this an uncertain economy with an overwhelming budget deficit, a deficit recommended by presidents and passed by Congress, and what we have is an environment perfect for government interference. In 1992, two bills were introduced in Congress that would have government set accounting principles and auditing standards. These measures are discussed in Chapter 9. To make self-governance work, the profession needs to improve relations with the regulators and become proactive. In addition, not only must peer and quality review limit instances of substandard service, it must also raise the service standard.

Chapter 3, "Division (Peer) or Quality Review," discusses the advantages and disadvantages of joining either the Division for CPA Firms or the AICPA quality review program. As a result of participating in either program, firm members are likely to perceive significant improvements in their quality control system. In addition, most will see review as providing the impetus to better comply with professional pronouncements. Further, they should notice an increase in firm member confidence in the firm's practices and procedures and enhanced firm member morale. They also are likely to experience other rewards. Research results of perceived review benefits and costs are discussed in this chapter as well.

The division and quality review programs are so similar that it is difficult to tell them apart. There are, however, two major differences. Division results are publicly available, whereas quality review results are confidential. Further, division reviews emphasize all nine quality control elements, and quality reviews emphasize only four. In division firms with ten or fewer professionals only five or six of the elements are emphasized, depending on which section the firm belongs to. Recommendations discussed in Chapter 9 would end these differences.

Chapter 4, "The Importance of Selecting the Right Reviewer and How to Do It," discusses the critical role of the reviewer and provides some practical advice on how to find the right reviewer. Research suggests that good reviewers frequently make suggestions that lead to improvements in firm efficiency and effectiveness. In addition, they directly bring about improvements to the firm's quality control system and in some instances help the firm improve its ability to detect material misstatements in client financial statements.

"Understanding + A Quality Control Document + The Proper Tone at the Top = Professional Quality Service" is the title of Chapter 5. It takes a detailed look at Statement on Quality Control Standards 1. It also discusses the characteristics of each of the nine quality control elements: independence, professional development, assignment of personnel, acceptance and continuance of clients, inspection, consultation, advancement, supervision, and hiring.

Because many have had difficulty following the AICPA's guidance on how to develop a quality control system, the appendix to Chapter 5 shows a quality control document that covers the nine functional areas. For each area there are several policies, and for each policy it provides guidance on developing one or more procedures. The appendix provides important guidance for those developing or amending their quality control system.

Chapter 6, "The Keys to a Successful Review: Preparation and Planning," presents a step-by-step approach to ensure a successful review. A firm should have little difficulty earning an unqualified review report if it follows these steps; designs, implements, and adheres to a quality control document as described in Chapter 5; and avoids the problems described in Chapter 8.

"The Review: What Happens and What to Do Afterward" is the title of Chapter 7. It describes how reviewers select engagements for review, what they look for, and how they document their review. It also examines how reviewers assess the firm's quality control system, including questions they ask staff. In addition, it examines the variables that influence the type of report to be issued. It also discusses the likelihood of receiving a letter of comments, which details the material deficiencies uncovered in the review. The chapter further explains how reviewers go about deciding what items to include in this letter. Finally, the exit conference is explained, and important advice is given on what the firm needs to do after the review.

"Problems to Avoid" is the subject of Chapter 8. It describes the common deficiencies found during peer and quality reviews. It also discusses the need for additional professional guidance in both accounting and audit areas. Finally, a thesis is developed that attributes the underlying cause of substandard service to the wrong tone at the top.

Chapter 9, "Summary, Conclusions, and Recommendations," offers suggestions for completing the revolution in the accounting profession. Some of the proposals will certainly be controversial because the end result would be to return the accounting business back to the accounting profession. Changes to professional standards are called for. The scope of quality and peer review must be expanded. Additional quality control elements are required. Education and accounting education in particular must be improved. These proposals and others will lead the business of accounting back to the accounting profession.

Twenty-five percent of the net royalties received from this book are going to the AICPA Benevolent Fund. This decision was based primarily on the belief that returning the accounting business back to the accounting profession is critical to the profession's survival. This book will help pave the way.

Those who read this book will understand that the profession's survival depends in part on understanding the roots of review and substandard service. Readers will also understand that limiting inferior practice quality depends on how well review works and on improving the review process. In addition, professional standards must be revised.

Another reason for making this donation is that it is a way of paying back a profession that has for nearly thirty years provided me with all the challenges and opportunities I could ask for. And in the main life has been good to me. Others in the profession have not been as fortunate.

ACKNOWLEDGMENTS

A book manuscript is seldom completed through the efforts of the writer alone. This book is no exception. I am particularly grateful for the exceptional effort and skill of Anita Dennis, editor extraordinaire. She is talented, hard working, and honest, and she cares about the accounting profession.

I am also indebted to a remarkable group of reviewers who took time out of their busy schedules to correct some of my glaring errors and omissions. They, in fact, made this a better book. The opinions expressed in this book are my own and were not necessarily supported by each of the reviewers. The reviewers were:

Charles Anderson, a shareholder with Anderson and Whitney, Greeley, Colorado. Mr. Anderson also is chairperson of the Colorado Society of CPAs' Quality Review Board and a former member of the SECPS Peer Review Committee.

Gerald H. Lander, Professor of Accounting, University of South Florida.

Keith Lantz, Professor of Accounting, California State University, Fullerton.

Andrew Luzi, Professor of Accounting, California State University, Fullerton.

Ronald O. Reed, Associate Professor of Accounting, University of Northern Colorado, Greeley.

Randy Stewart Watson, Shareholder Yanari, Watson, Lyons & Co., P.C., Aurora, Colorado. Mr. Watson also is a member of the PCPS Peer Review Committee.

Gerald J. Wenzel, Shareholder/Director of Audit and Accounting, Yale & Seffinger, P.C., Denver, Colorado.

Charles Williams, Attorney at Law, Williams and Trine, Boulder, Colorado.

The assistance of the AICPA is greatly appreciated. Several staff members were more than helpful. In addition, I am grateful to the AICPA for permission to cite from its published materials.

There are many who have influenced the author and also deserve recognition. The list includes Mr. Conley, my intermediate accounting teacher, who showed his love for accounting and fired my interest in it. It also includes Mr. Stein, my creative writing professor, who encouraged me to write, and Professor James P. Glispin, my philosophy teacher, who made me think.

In addition, there are many people who are now my cherished friends and who, as a result, have influenced me greatly. Some have helped to make me a better writer, and others have convinced me that the only limitations I have are the limits I place on myself. They include Donald Gorton at Wayne State University, John Tracy and Rudolph Schattke at the University of Colorado, Jerry Lander at the University of South Florida, and John Larson at the University of Michigan. The list also includes Anthony Robbins, who convinced me that we can make a difference.

Three invaluable student assistants at California State University, Fullerton (CSUF), did much of the photocopying in the library and did it with a smile and enthusiasm. They are Tamara Larson, Sherry Kollab, and Anne Marie Gabel. I also want to thank Dr. Ephraim Smith, Dean of CSUF, for his encouragement and support. To my colleagues at CSUF, it has been a joy to work with you.

To my hero Charles Williams, I cherish your friendship. In addition, the influence of my friends and former partners, Stacia Keller and David Laundy, cannot be overlooked.

This book could not have been done without the support of the three most important people in my life, my wife and two children. Dr. Carol has brought peace, love, and excitement to my life. Karen and Daniel have made me a better human being. This book was written for these people.

This book was also written for the memory and spirit of my Dad, my Mom, and my sister Beverly.

The Accountant's Guide to Peer and Quality Review

1

The Road to Peer Review

One of Bob Dylan's greatest hits is a song titled "The Times They Are A-Changin'." A similar lyric could be written about the accounting profession. In a little over ten years, the profession went from voluntary peer review to mandatory quality review. In the fall of 1977, the American Institute of Certified Public Accountants (AICPA) started a voluntary peer review organization. In January 1988, AICPA overwhelmingly approved mandatory quality review. Why did this happen? In short, because some Certified Public Accountants (CPAs), and there were more than a few, failed their profession by doing substandard work.

Peer review can be attributed to other factors as well. For example, we have not done a good job at all in defining our roles and responsibilities. Society has certain beliefs about our role in audit and accounting work. It also knows where to lay the blame when there is a failure, as shown by the explosive rise in litigation. Society's expectations seem to be changing as well.

The Securities and Exchange Commission (SEC) has played a major role in bringing about peer review. Much of the SEC's effort was at the urging of Congress, which has itself been influential.

The profession's leadership, after much pushing and prodding, realized it must do something to prevent substandard service. It recognized that society's expectations of the auditor's role and responsibility differed from those of the profession. The profession's leaders also saw that we needed to narrow this "expectations gap." In the 1970s and 1980s, the profession set about to examine itself. The response to these issues resulted in what can only be called a revolution.

This revolution involved a painstaking self-examination. It included a reevaluation of the standards for admission to and continuation in the profession. It involved a reassessment of generally accepted auditing standards (GAAS) and, in particular, those areas in which there were discrepancies between society's and the profession's expectations regarding the accountant-auditor role. The code of conduct was changed. The profession set up mechanisms to control the activities of firms. Previously, it could control only the activities of individuals. It designed quality control policies and procedures to which firms must adhere. Finally, it experimented with and then made mandatory a requirement for a triennial peer or quality review. The revolution was in essence a decision to better serve society's interests through self-regulation. An integral part of this self-governance process is peer or quality review.

It is these topics (substandard service, society's expectations, the SEC's and Congress's part in the creation of peer review, and the profession's amazing response) that form the focus of this chapter. The chapter concludes with a brief look at why peer review had to be part of the answer and whether it is working.

SUBSTANDARD SERVICE QUALITY—THE COMPELLING FORCE

Substandard professional service quality has existed in society since earliest times. It also has been severely punished. Evidence from 2000 B.C. shows physicians faced extreme penalties, such as the loss of a hand, for incompetent practice [Fine and Meyer, 1985]. Fortunately for some, substandard accounting service has been dealt with in a more genteel manner. The earliest instances are found in court records. In England, cases involving accountants' professional liability occurred well before 1900 [Ostling, 1986].

Inferior accounting service can occur in many different ways. The most conspicuous is audit failure. While audit failures may occur infrequently, they "can have a devastating impact on investors and creditors, on the audit firm, and on the public accounting profession" [Mautz and Matusiak, 1988: 56]. Audit and accounting failures have cost public accounting firms many millions of dollars in judgments, settlements, and legal fees, and have caused professional liability insurance premiums to skyrocket. The cost of the cases being litigated today may confirm the opinion of Robert Levine, former CEO of the now bankrupt Laventhol & Horwath, who said, "it is theoretically possible that the accounting profession could go away—simply vanish" [Stevens, 1991: 252]. Unfortunately, Laventhol, which had about $2 billion in liability claims, did vanish [Lochner, 1992: A10]. "The profession probably faces an additional $15 billion in liability claims now, with more to come" [Lochner, 1992: A10]. A more recent estimate fixes the claims at $30 billion [AICPA, "Large Firms Unite in Fighting Liability Crisis," October 1992: 4]. The judgment of $338 million against Price Waterhouse in connection with its audit of United Bank of Arizona is alarming because the award is far in excess of the claimed losses ["Accountant Hit," 1992: D1]. Perhaps Mr. Levine understated the situation and should have said that "it is *very* possible that the accounting profession *will soon* go away." Further, accounting and audit failures also cause many talented men and women to leave the profession and persuade bright young graduates to seek careers elsewhere.

The audit failure best known to many of us in the profession was the case of McKesson & Robbins, in the 1930s. This case has been followed by more than a few additional embarrassing instances. It is difficult to forget at least the highlights of Continental Vending, National Student Marketing, and Equity Funding. Possibly more recent cases, such as ZZZZ Best, Regina Vacuum Cleaner Company, ESM Government Securities, and MiniScribe, are even more unforgettable. Each of these suits, as well as others, has brought criticism to the profession and embarrassment to each of its members.

Business failures also have brought the profession public criticism. Certainly the fall of Penn Square Bank and the near demise of Chrysler inspired distrust of the profession. An unqualified report was issued just three months before Penn Square was declared insolvent. Business failures cause doubts about audit quality. Business failures accompanied by allegations of lack of independence cause doubts about the entire profession.

It is not just audit and business failures that cause criticism of the profession. Substandard service occurs with compilation and review services, too. The 1136 Tenants Corporation case is one of the more unforgettable court cases. It involved an engagement in which the accounting firm performed some limited auditing procedures, but did not follow up on some of its findings. As this was not an audit engagement the firm should not have performed any audit procedures. Since it did, the procedures needed to be followed up. The court decided in favor of the plaintiffs because the accounting firm's performance of audit procedures contradicted its claim that this was not an audit engagement. The plaintiffs were awarded over $200,000 [Arens and Loebbecke, 1991: 114].

The *Ryan v. Kanne* case is not as well known as the 1136 Tenants case, but its implications are more alarming. In the 1136 Tenants case, the accountants did not follow professional standards. In the *Ryan* case, one could say the firm did follow professional standards. However, the compiled financial statements were, as in 1136 Tenants, misstated. The "court was unwilling to accept the accounting profession's concept of unaudited services, a rejection which was probably attributable to the court's perception of the public expectation of accountant's responsibility in both audit and non-audit engagements" [Ostling, 1986: 15]. The lesson here is that it does not make much difference how the profession defines its role and responsibility. At least in the opinion of this court, society defines our role.

The cases cited are well known, but they are not uncommon. More suits were filed against accountants between 1972 and 1987 than in the entire history of the profession [Mednick, 1987]. The volume of cases is certainly partially a result of our litigious society. It also is a function of a failure to follow professional standards. These oversights have not gone unnoticed by others. Legislators (including those in Congress), the press, the profession, and the public at large are well informed of the accounting profession's failings. An influential AICPA committee, the Anderson Committee, issued a report titled *Restructuring Profes-sional Standards to Achieve Professional Excellence in a Changing Environment* [AICPA, 1986], which indicated it also understood that substandard work oc-curred far too frequently and that change was needed.

As a result of the Anderson Committee report, the AICPA developed and presented to its membership for approval the Plan to Restructure Professional Standards. Included among the several proposals was a recommendation re-quiring mandatory quality review. It was approved by 76 percent of the AICPA's membership in January 1988 [Huff and Kelley, 1989]. Five other proposals were considered in that ballot and passed by different percentages.

The Anderson Committee's recommendations were, for the most part, not new. Many are similar to those contained in a 1977 report from the Commission on Auditors' Responsibilities (CAR) [1977]. The Anderson Committee recom-mendations also were reflected in a 1987 report, *Report of the National Com-mission on Fraudulent Financial Reporting* (the Treadway report) [National Commission on Fraudulent Financial Reporting, 1987].

Until it approved the Plan to Restructure Professional Standards, the account-ing profession had not taken any consequential initiatives to prevent substandard work. Like the medical profession, it tended to react only when there was pressure from outsiders [Egan, 1985]. Pressures to improve the quality of professional accounting practice were a result of adverse publicity from audit, accounting, and business failures. These failures challenged the public's perceptions and expectations about the auditor's role and responsibility. They also led to inves-tigations by various governmental agencies, such as the SEC and congressional committees.

SOCIETY'S EXPECTATIONS

Over the past several years, business publications regularly have included articles about the accountants' role and responsibility in the collapse of the savings and loan (S&L) industry. Many of these reports categorically place the blame on the accountants. Recently, Ernest & Young's made a $400-million deal with federal authorities to settle its role in the nation's savings and loan collapse [Telberg, 1992: 1]. As a result, the public's confidence in the profession is being diminished.

The public holds certain opinions about the accountant's role in society, and some of these beliefs are contrary to how the profession defines its role and responsibility. Society believes the accountant-auditor's primary responsibility is to financial statement users. The profession does not disagree with this position, but its situation is awkward because an accountant's contractual relationship is with the client. It is difficult for many to understand how an accounting firm can serve financial statement users' interests and yet be paid by the client. Occasional allegations and actual instances of loss of independence challenge society's belief that the accountant is independent.

History shows that accounting services have changed in almost every way. For example, accountants formerly served primarily management's interests. Today, auditors serve a diverse number of groups outside the entity. These groups include present and potential investors, creditors, and, in the language of the courts, foreseen, foreseeable, and unforeseeable users.

The public also believes the accountant-auditor certifies the accuracy of financial statements and the completeness of disclosures. Further, it believes the accountant is a guarantor of the entity's ability to continue as a going concern.

Representative Ronald Wyden (D–Oreg.) described the S&L crisis as a textbook example of the expectations gap between accountants and society [Stevens, 1991]. While the public believes the independent auditor's report means that the financial statements and related disclosures are totally accurate and complete and that the entity is financially viable, the report itself conveys a quite different message. Going-concern paragraphs occur only when there is substantial doubt about the entity's short-term viability, which is perhaps too shortsighted. The going-concern question is, however, difficult to explain to financial statement users. Should we as accountants and auditors include a going-concern reference when there is less than substantial doubt and, as a result, possibly increase the likelihood of the entity's demise? Should a going-concern paragraph be included when there is substantial doubt about the entity's viability over a longer time horizon, a step that could seal and perhaps hasten its dissolution? Wouldn't this harm the client and its investors? Certainly, a going-concern reference in a report on an S&L would cause an institution's depositors a great deal of anxiety and probably guarantee its closure.

Accounting and audit failures, regardless of how infrequent, defy society's expectations. Business failures also challenge these expectations, especially when the prior audit report contained no going-concern paragraph.

The profession's conception of what the auditor does, or should do, is changing as well. Perhaps the "theory of rising expectations," developed in the political and social science areas, also applies to the accounting profession [Ertel and Aldridge, 1977]. For example, rising expectations led to the so-called "expectation gap standards." The Auditing Standards Board (ASB) approved nine Statements on Auditing Standards (SASs 53 through 61) in 1988. In the main, they reflect the profession's attempt to bridge the gap between what financial statement users thought the auditors did and what professional standards required. Some of these statements reflect changes made to accommodate the public's expectations. They also reflect the profession's "duty to continually assess auditing standards in light of the expectations, concerns and criticisms of others" [Guy and Sullivan, 1988: 8]. For example, SAS 53, The Auditor's Responsibility to Detect and Report Errors and Irregularities, increased the auditor's responsibility to detect unintentional and intentional misstatements or omissions of amounts or disclosures in financial statements. SAS 54, Illegal Acts by Clients, established the same burden for violations of laws or governmental regulations. SAS 59, The Auditor's Consideration of an Entity's Ability to Continue as a

Going Concern, requires auditors to evaluate in every audit where there is substantial doubt about the entity's ability to continue to exist. The public's expectations then, often represented by the SEC, do influence the development of professional standards. In 1985, for example, the SEC in its report to Congress was urging the profession to reconsider the auditor's responsibility to detect and report fraud [Wallace, 1989: 29].

GOVERNMENTAL INFLUENCES

Government, through its legislators and its agencies, serves as a watchdog over the activities of its citizens. We have ceded power to government and in return expect it to serve our best interests. However, "watchdogs tend to be suspicious of established enterprises and persons" [Benston, 1985: 45]. One of those established enterprises is the accounting profession, which Congress views with great skepticism. Mistrust has led Congress to persuade the SEC to increase its oversight of the profession. To a great extent, the SEC serves as the watchdog's watchdog.

The SEC

The Securities Act of 1933 and the Securities and Exchange Act of 1934 gave the SEC the power to determine accounting principles and procedures. The SEC has relied mainly on the private sector to establish and maintain generally accepted accounting principles (GAAP) and GAAS. It is, however, far from silent about GAAP or GAAS and does make its power known. SEC representatives regularly attend Financial Accounting Standards Board (FASB) and ASB meetings. Also, the SEC's views are sought before a new FASB statement of financial accounting standards (SFAS) is released.

In addition, the SEC has been instrumental in bringing about peer review. Several business failures put the accounting profession in the spotlight in the early 1960s. As a result, the SEC, at the urging of Congress, pressed for regulation of the profession [Pattillo, 1984].

In the early 1970s, the SEC started making peer review a requirement in settling disciplinary proceedings against firms. For example, Laventhol and Peat Marwick were the first of twenty or so SEC-mandated peer reviews [Wallace, 1989].

After the profession made a more earnest effort to prevent substandard service quality through the AICPA Division for CPA Firms, the SEC became more supportive. In its 1980 *Report to Congress on the Accounting Profession and the Commission's Oversight Role*, the SEC said the profession's efforts "deserve the continued support of the Congress and the Commission" [SEC, 1980: VI].

The SEC was not then and still is not satisfied with all aspects of the profession's efforts [Mautz and Evers, 1991]. Disputed issues included the SEC's access to peer review workpapers, the voluntary nature of peer review, and the necessity for sanctions. The SEC also was displeased by the secrecy that surrounded the activities of the Quality Control Inquiry Committee (QCIC), a committee of the Securities and Exchange Commission Practice Section (SECPS) of the Division for CPA Firms.

By 1982, an agreement was reached to allow SEC staff access to selected workpapers. As a result, the 1982 SEC report to Congress was more supportive [SEC, 1982].

Disagreement over peer review's voluntary nature remained unresolved for some time. As a result of the AICPA membership's approval of mandatory review in 1988, this disagreement was at least temporarily tabled. The question of sanctions or remedial action still is not resolved.

The SEC's positions are not without support in the professional accounting community. For example, the 1977 CAR report criticized the secrecy surrounding the profession's disciplinary process, and the 1987 Treadway report called for increased criminal prosecution and a mandatory quality assurance program.

On April 1, 1987, the SEC developed a proposal for monitoring firms that audit public companies. This proposal required that all firms auditing SEC registrants be reviewed under the auspices of the Division for CPA Firms or by a CPA firm under SEC supervision. Besides making peer review mandatory for firms that audit public companies, this proposal also would have given the SEC access to the reviewer's workpapers and perhaps even access to the records of firm audit clients. It was this last possibility that was most feared. Some believed that putting the SEC in control meant that it could and would go to the firm's clients when questions arose during a review. The 1989 vote of AICPA members to require SECPS membership for firms that audit SEC registrants persuaded the SEC to let its proposal lapse into inactive status [*Accounting and Auditing Developments*, 1991: 29].

Disagreement continues about whether firms should face sanctions or remedial actions. The SEC, in its 1982 report to Congress, said that "the true test of any self-regulatory organization is whether it appropriately sanctions members that do not meet its standards" [SEC, 1982: 16]. Division for CPA Firms members are subject to sanctions, which can include suspension or expulsion from membership, monetary fines, reprimands, and so on [Committees of the SEC Practice Section, 1992: 1000.33]. Some division firms have been expelled from membership. The usual action, though, is to require the firm to take remedial steps. These steps include requiring firms to reassign staff, including partners; accelerating the date of the next peer review; and compelling a firm to have its staff complete certain professional education courses.

The SEC would like to see more stringent sanctions imposed, but division members have in almost all cases agreed to take corrective measures, so there is little need to impose penalties. Also, as Wallace [1989] points out, the issue is mostly one of semantics. Isn't the profession imposing sanctions when it orders an accelerated peer review? Perhaps if the division used the term "sanctions" in connection with its "corrective measures," some of this disagreement would disappear.

Some have argued that the division should sanction CPAs for deficient service quality by punishing them in some way. It seems "one CPA in jail is worth all the peer reviews ever made" [Mautz and Evers, 1991: 9]. The division does expel firms from its membership, but some would call for more punitive actions in certain instances. These instances are probably best handled by the AICPA ethics process, state boards of accountancy, and the courts.

The SEC, an independent regulatory agency of the U.S. government, is strongly influenced by members of Congress. Congress has been critical of the profession and the SEC.

Congress

The Securities Act of 1933 and the Securities and Exchange Act of 1934 gave the accounting profession, and CPAs in particular, the claim to the attest function. "Increasingly complex and extensive reporting requirements have made the securities statutes a guarantee of employment for many accountants and lawyers" [Benston, 1985: 55]. The securities acts, however, are a double-edged sword for the accounting profession. While they may operate as a full employment act, they also impose much greater liabilities on the profession than does the common law. These laws also subject the profession to a much higher level of public scrutiny that focuses on the quality of professional service [McNair, 1991].

Under the direction of Senator Lee Metcalf (D–Mont.), the Subcommittee on Reports, Accounting, and Management issued a report titled *The Accounting Establishment: A Staff Study* [1976]. This report severely criticized the accounting profession and recommended governmental control over many of its activities. It called for the federal government to establish auditing standards, set accounting principles, and define auditors' responsibilities. Further, the report called for a periodic federal government inspection of auditors of public companies. Senator Metcalf made an alarming suggestion in a 1977 speech: "Who should audit the auditors? I believe that governmental authorities responsible solely to the public should perform that task" [Benston, 1985: 37]. Fortunately, Senator Metcalf's attitude did not represent the overall feelings of Congress. He did, however, have supporters. The senator's report made the profession realize it needed to address the underlying problem of substandard service quality.

Representative John Moss (D–Calif.) was one of Senator Metcalf's supporters. He kept pressure on the profession by introducing legislation to establish a National Organization of SEC Accountancy in 1978. Under that legislation, firms in SEC practice would have had to undergo periodic peer review. Further, the legislation called for an expanded SEC role in the standard-setting process.

This legislation would have removed any hope for continued self-regulation. It was not, however, enacted into law.

In response to the Metcalf report, the AICPA created the Division for CPA Firms in 1977. The purpose of this voluntary organization is to improve the quality of professional practice. The response of the AICPA could well be called modest, but it was, at least, a beginning. Ostling's [1986: 1] comment seems most fitting: "Legislative overseers lambast the profession, often inaccurately and unjustifiably, but the associations often seem timid by comparison in their response." To expect a voluntary organization like the Division for CPA Firms to solve the profession's underlying problem of substandard service is, indeed, an imaginative stretch.

Consistent with expectations, the division did provide the profession with experience at regulating itself. It also provided evidence that peer review is one effective way to improve the quality of firm accounting and auditing practices. It further showed that review is an instrument for achieving accountability in the accounting profession, as in other professions [Ertel and Aldridge, 1977]. Peer review, if effective, also will deter those interested in pursuing the course of greater governmental regulation [Wallace, 1991: 53].

In 1977, the AICPA created the Quality Control Standards Committee (QCSC), which two years later issued Statement on Quality Control Standards (SQCS) 1, System of Quality Control for a CPA Firm. Statement 1 requires firms that perform auditing, accounting, or review services to design and implement a system of quality control that will provide reasonable assurance that the firm is complying with professional standards.

With the aid of hindsight, the AICPA's responses were not sufficient. For example, they did not deter those interested in further governmental regulation. Also, and perhaps most important, they did not sufficiently limit instances of substandard service. Congressional scrutiny continued, most notably under the direction of Representative John Dingell (D–Mich.), chair of the House Energy and Commerce Committee. From 1985 through 1990, his Oversight and Investigations Subcommittee conducted twenty-three hearings on the profession [AICPA, 1990: 1]. Other congressional committees have been investigating the profession as well. In 1985, the Legislation and National Security Subcommittee of the House Committee on Government Operations requested a report from the General Accounting Office (GAO) about its review of CPA audit quality. This report, *CPA Audit Quality: Inspectors General Find Significant Problems* [U.S. GAO, 1985], was, to say the least, derogatory. It claimed that one out of four audit reports did not follow professional standards and that one in five audits had problems in substantiating whether sufficient audit work was done. Similar charges are found in a 1988 report, *Office of Inspector General Report to the Congress* [1988]. These continuing agency and congressional misgivings and assertions about substandard work were well supported and were, as a result, instrumental in the decision to implement a mandatory quality review requirement for all firms as an integral part of the profession's self-regulation effort.

THE PROFESSION'S RESPONSE

The AICPA

The AICPA has led the profession's effort to maintain self-regulation through peer review. Charles Kaiser, former chair of the AICPA's board of directors, said, "self-regulation provides credibility, generates public trust and reduces unnecessary, costly governmental intervention" [Kaiser, 1989: 41].

AICPA efforts to maintain self-regulation have a long history. In 1962, the AICPA established a voluntary program of report review through its practice review committee. This initial experience was the seed for peer review [Sperry, Spede, and Hicks, 1987]. In 1972, it cooperated with the SEC in the commission's disciplinary proceedings by providing lists of peer reviewers for SEC-mandated reviews.

As noted earlier, the AICPA in 1977 established the Division for CPA Firms and the QCSC, its first serious effort to deal with the issue of inferior service within firms. Prior to 1977, the AICPA dealt with the problem of substandard service at the individual level. In 1983, the AICPA appointed the Anderson Committee to make recommendations about professional standards. One of these recommendations, as discussed above, was for mandatory quality review, which the membership approved in 1988. In 1989, the AICPA led an effort to approve another Anderson Committee recommendation to require firms that audit public companies to be members of the SECPS. The membership approved this amendment in January 1990.

Professional Requirements

Section 2, Admission To, and Retention of, Membership and Association, of the AICPA bylaws spells out the requirements for admittance to and continuance of membership. Section 2.2, Requirements for Admission to Membership, requires members in public accounting to practice in firms enrolled in approved AICPA practice-monitoring programs. This section became effective in January 1988. Section 2.3, Requirements for Retention of Membership, was approved in January 1990. It requires that when a member works for a firm with one or more SEC audit clients, the firm must be an SECPS member.

AICPA members also are required to comply with the AICPA Code of Professional Conduct. Article I of the Principles of Professional Conduct states, "members have a continuing responsibility to cooperate with each other to improve the art of accounting, *maintain the public's confidence*, and *carry out the profession's special responsibilities for self-governance*" (emphasis by author) [*AICPA Professional Standards*, Volume 2, 1992: ET§ 52.01]. (The principles are ideal tenets of professional conduct and are not, as a result, enforceable. They are, instead, a guide to AICPA members.) Article I then urges members to do what is necessary to maintain public confidence and self-regulation. To maintain public confidence, inferior service quality must be prevented. Peer review is one effective way to limit substandard-quality service. Peer review by one's fellow professionals is also crucial to maintaining self-regulation.

The Rules of Conduct of the Code of Professional Conduct are enforceable and apply to all AICPA members unless stated otherwise. The Rules of Conduct set a minimum standard of conduct. Rule 201 of the General Standards requires compliance with certain standards that encompass issues related to quality service [*AICPA Professional Standards*, Volume 2, 1992: ET§ 201]:

A. Professional Competence. Undertake only those professional services that the member or the member's firm can reasonably expect to be completed with professional competence.

B. Due Professional Care. Exercise due professional care in the performance of professional services.

C. Planning and Supervision. Adequately plan and supervise the performance of professional services.

D. Sufficient Relevant Data. Obtain sufficient relevant data to afford a reasonable basis for conclusions or recommendations in relation to any professional services performed.

Further, Rule 202, Compliance with Standards, requires members who perform auditing, review, and compilation services to comply with standards designated by bodies appointed by the AICPA's governing board. Interestingly, this does not include the QCSC, which issued SQCS 1 and related interpretations.

SAS 25, The Relationship of Generally Accepted Auditing Standards to Quality Control Standards, says, "a firm should establish quality control policies and procedures to provide it with reasonable assurance of conforming with generally accepted auditing standards in its audit engagements" [*AICPA Professional Standards*, Volume 1, 1992: AU 161.02]. GAAS then requires that firms design, implement, and maintain appropriate quality control systems.

The professional requirements are clear. AICPA bylaws, the principles and rules of the Code of Professional Conduct, and GAAS together require AICPA members to subject their practices to peer review as evidence of maintenance of high-quality service so the public's confidence may be maintained.

The Division for CPA Firms

The profession's first serious effort to improve the quality of professional service and thus curb firms from practicing below minimum standards occurred in 1977 with the formation of the Division for CPA Firms. Two characteristics of the division were particularly notable. First, all professional organizations are made up of individuals and not the entities within which the members operate. The division allowed the AICPA to control the activities of firms in addition to those of individuals. Second, to become and remain a member, a firm has to undergo a comprehensive triennial peer review. The expectation behind this grand experiment was that, if successful, the profession would show it could regulate itself and thus dissuade those interested in increased governmental control.

The division has two sections: the SECPS and the Private Companies Practice Section (PCPS). Firms can belong to one or both. SECPS membership is required for firms that audit SEC clients. PCPS membership is voluntary. Each section has an executive committee to govern its activities.

The two sections' objectives are similar and are designed to achieve the following:

1. To improve the quality of accounting and auditing services provided by CPA firms.

2. To institute and maintain a system of quality control appropriate for the firm.

3. To improve the public's confidence in the services provided by CPA firms through the peer review process.

4. To impose corrective measures or sanctions on members for failure to maintain an effective quality control system.

5. To provide a medium for members to participate in establishing professional standards.

The requirements of each section also are similar and include:

1. Submission to a triennial comprehensive peer review.

2. Adherence to the quality control standards issued by the QCSC.

3. Completion of 120 hours of continuing professional education over a three-year period by the professional staff. This includes CPAs and non-CPAs. A minimum of 20 hours is required each year.

In addition, there are specific SECPS requirements, such as partner rotation and concurring partner review.

To entice firms to join, the PCPS acts essentially as an association of CPA firms. It provides a variety of member services to help firms manage their practices and market their services. It has a TEAM-PLUS (TEn professionals At Most Plus slightly larger Firms) program for firms with up to ten professionals and a SET (Size Eleven to Twenty) program for larger firms. These programs cover such issues as tax season strategies, personnel decisions, marketing, and profitability.

The PCPS has an important committee called the Technical Issues Committee (TIC). Its objective is to review and comment on proposed standards from the perspective of local practitioners and their clients. It was instrumental in getting the AICPA Accounting and Review Services Committee to issue several interpretations of Statement on Standards for Accounting and Review Services (SSARS) 1. It has promoted, where appropriate, the use of other comprehensive bases of accounting (OCBOA) as an alternative to GAAP.

Recent evidence shows that the TIC has been successful in obtaining the approval of the standard-setting bodies. For example, the FASB has asked the TIC to develop samples it can publish to provide advice to practitioners about financial instruments, post-employment benefits, and accounting for income taxes [*The Practicing CPA*, 1991].

Public Oversight Board

The SECPS is subject to oversight through the Public Oversight Board (POB). It is important to note that the PCPS has no such oversight organization, nor does the quality review program. One has to wonder about the logic of providing oversight only over a select few firms.

The POB is an independent body made up of five prominent individuals. The board elects its own chair and members. It also hires its staff and sets its own compensation and agenda. The POB's purpose is to represent the public interest, but apparently just some of the public since it only oversees SECPS activities. It also serves as a liaison among Congress, the SEC, and the profession.

The POB examines the public interest implications when the SECPS alters its membership requirements or changes its standards. It monitors SECPS peer review results and litigation alleging audit failure. It takes the view that the public interest can best be served by identifying the causes of audit failure. The POB had much to do with the formation of the SECPS' QCIC, which is charged with gaining "assurance in the light of adverse allegations whether a firm's quality control system is adequate and being complied with" [Mautz and Evers, 1991: 1].

Quality Control Inquiry Committee

The QCIC investigates audit practices following allegations of audit failure. The POB oversees all of the QCIC's inquiries into alleged audit failures.

The QCIC was called the Special Investigations Committee (SIC) until December 1988, but its name was changed because it was felt that the word "investigations" implied that its purpose was to pass judgment. Because of its work, it has been the most controversial committee in the self-governance process. One obvious fear was that the QCIC could prejudice the case of a firm in litigation. Another concern was that the QCIC might be ineffective and, as a result, cause renewed criticism of the profession's self-regulatory effort. Since inception, neither position has proved to be correct. There is no evidence that the QCIC's investigations have prejudiced firm cases. Also, the SEC, while withholding a complete endorsement of the QCIC's activities, does believe it provides additional assurance to the self-governance process [Mautz and Evers, 1991].

SECPS firms must report to the QCIC within thirty days any litigation that alleges an audit deficiency when an SEC client or a regulated financial institution is involved. They also are required to cooperate with QCIC investigations by supplying information about the alleged audit deficiency. Such information might include audit planning and audit issues memoranda as well as other audit documentation. Further, the firm under investigation is required to authorize its peer reviewers to cooperate with QCIC inquiries.

Currently, the QCIC follows a highly structured approach in its investigations into alleged audit failures, but this has not always been the case. In its early years, investigation quality depended on the assertiveness and experience of the person assigned to the case. At the POB's urging, the QCIC adopted a more structured approach.

The QCIC begins an investigation into an alleged audit failure with an analysis that includes a review of the allegations, related financial statements, and other materials to determine whether the case has quality control implications. If so, the case is held open and goes to the inquiry stage. In this phase, the firm is contacted about the quality control issues. It is asked to respond to the allegations. In addition, the firm is asked if the particular audit was included in the last peer review or inspection. If the QCIC is still concerned, the case goes to the investigative step. No case is closed until the QCIC is satisfied that the alleged deficiency did not involve a quality control matter or, if it did, that corrective actions have been taken.

During the investigative phase the QCIC also examines questions raised by the media. This may result in an interrogation of the audit team and discussions with the firm's peer reviewers. The firm's inspection reports are examined, and regulatory reports, if available, are reviewed. If the QCIC representative is still not satisfied, then a special review is conducted. In a special review, the adequacy of a firm's quality control system and the extent of its compliance with that system are reviewed. The special review might be conducted by the firm's peer reviewers under QCIC supervision or by a team the QCIC selects. It might encompass audit engagements done by the personnel who worked on the allegedly failed audit or audit engagements conducted by the same office or in the same industry. The QCIC's work is totally confidential to avoid prejudicing the defenses of firms in litigation.

Mautz and Evers [1991: 63–64] analyzed 349 cases reviewed by the QCIC from its inception in November 1979 through June 30, 1990. They report that the QCIC took 141 actions in connection with these cases. In 38 cases, it recommended a special firm review or an expansion of the regular review. In 53 cases, the firm responded appropriately. These responses can take many forms. Mautz and Evers [1991: 29] cite one case in which serious quality control deficiencies were found in one office of a firm. The corrective actions taken included reassigning and terminating audit personnel (including partners), appointing a new partner in charge, and requiring concurring review by partners outside of this office. In 36 cases, the AICPA technical bodies were asked to provide additional guidance or change professional standards. Also, in 14 cases, the AICPA Ethics Division was asked to investigate specific individuals.

The evidence, while sketchy due to its secrecy, does suggest that the QCIC plays an important role in improving the quality of professional practice. At the same time, it suggests that review is not as successful as we would like in limiting instances of substandard service. Substandard service continues even with review.

Quality Review Division

Starting in 1988, firms whose members desire to retain their AICPA membership were required to belong to the Division for CPA Firms or have their practices reviewed under the AICPA quality review program. The quality review program is governed by an executive committee, which has senior technical status. The quality review executive committee has the authority to establish and conduct a review program in cooperation with state CPA societies that elect to participate. The goals and requirements of quality review are essentially identical to those of the SECPS and PCPS described previously. Perhaps the major difference between SECPS and PCPS peer reviews and quality review is that the results of peer reviews are publicly available.

As mentioned above, the quality review program does not have a technical issues committee or a public oversight board. It also does not have a quality control inquiry committee. Further, secondary benefits available from PCPS membership, such as the aids offered to help firms practice more efficiently or develop more effective marketing programs, are not available in the quality review program.

THE SEC'S RESPONSE TO PEER REVIEW

The SECPS is subject to SEC oversight. Because of this oversight responsibility, the SEC is allowed and does have access to selected peer review and POB workpapers. "The SEC staff's review has resulted in acceptance of the quality of the peer review process and a strong endorsement of the peer review program by the SEC in its report to Congress each year" [Mautz and Evers, 1991: 9]. This endorsement does not include QCIC activities because these are conducted in strict secrecy. For the most part, the SEC has been allowed to review only QCIC summaries to which the SEC has taken exception. "By refusing to let the commission see these papers, the profession has made it clear that it wants to package the information in neat summaries all tied up in red ribbons" [Stevens, 1981]. Considerable progress has, however, been made in improving the documentation quality, such that the SEC was persuaded to say in its 1990 report "the Commission believes the QCIC benefits the public interest" [SEC, 1990: 68].

WHY MANDATORY PEER OR QUALITY REVIEW?

Given the SEC's satisfaction with the profession's self-regulation effort and its overwhelming focus on audits of public companies, why should the profession require mandatory review? Mandatory peer review is necessary for several reasons. It undoubtedly will improve the quality of professional practice and, as a result, decrease instances of accounting and audit failure. Also, some CPAs are simply taking a free ride on the reputation of others. For many years, the CPA designation implied a standard of excellence in performance. The profession's growth, the complexity of the business environment, the inability of accounting education to keep up, and society's increased expectations changed that designation's meaning. The free riders could and do provide accounting and auditing services without regard for the professional care standard of the profession. These individuals and firms do assume a greater risk of accounting and audit failure, but they do not bear the total costs. The profession shares these costs through increased malpractice insurance premiums and loss of reputation. The profession, in order to maintain some semblance of self-regulation, had to develop a means to control these behaviors, and mandatory quality review is a suitable response.

It is also essential to make quality review a condition of licensing. The free riders are dropping their AICPA membership, thus avoiding quality review. They are continuing to avoid the cost of providing professional-quality service. Since membership in the AICPA is voluntary, so is review. Those proposing increased regulation to protect the public interest should take note that a practice-monitoring program should be required of all firms.

A third argument on behalf of mandatory review is, therefore, that it serves the public interest. *The Accounting Establishment: A Staff Study* took this position when it argued that auditors' effectiveness in carrying out their responsibilities is a matter for public oversight [Subcommittee on Reports, 1976: 2].

There were, of course, other influences in making quality review mandatory. Certainly the allegations and threats of certain members of Congress riveted the public's attention because of the strongly worded charges of wrongdoing. This attention attracts others, such as business journalists and accounting academics. Adverse notoriety probably was key to bringing about mandatory peer review. Regardless of the underlying influences behind mandatory peer review, it is clear that if the profession is to survive as a self-regulating group, substandard service quality has to be reduced; otherwise, there is little need for our services.

DOES PEER REVIEW WORK?

There is substantial evidence that peer review works. "Since 1979, almost twice as many actions have been brought against firms that have not had SECPS peer review" [Kaiser, 1989: 43]. The GAO found in a review of 150 governmental audits that peer-reviewed firms were charged far less often with standards violations. "The Securities and Exchange Commission studied its 48 enforcement actions against accountants from 1981 to 1986 and reported that the incidence of such actions was 11 times higher for accounting firms which had not undergone a peer review" [Wallace, 1989: 38]. The author's study of 167 peer-reviewed firms showed that peer-reviewed firms believed such review provides the impetus to maintain the highest degree of compliance with professional standards [McCabe and Lantz, 1991: 74].

Peer review is notably effective in limiting instances of accounting and audit failure. Human failure cannot, however, be totally prevented, no matter how effective the systems of peer review and quality control.

One predominant factor in accounting and audit failure is not adequately addressed, however, within either the quality control policies or the peer review process. This factor was identified many years ago by the AICPA's Commission on Auditors' Responsibilities [1977: 164–66]. The CAR analyzed seventeen alleged audit failures and concluded that "excessive time pressures are the most pervasive cause of audit failures." Filing deadlines and other client demands do result in unrealistic time budgets. This, in my opinion, is not the major reason for "excessive time pressures." "When a firm's primary goals switch from excellence to efficiency—and when the quest to retain clients and maximize partner earnings supersedes all other objectives—the time-consuming steps of corroborating management assertions and following up on red flags planted by federal regulators are often eliminated from the process" [Stevens, 1991: 68]. The major reason can be simply stated in one word: mismanagement. Some accounting firms, automobile companies, and many others are mismanaged and will continue to be until quality becomes a goal equal in importance to profits and growth.

Peer or quality review does and will continue to have a major impact on the prevention of substandard service, but it cannot stop it entirely. Only when we as members remember that we are a profession, with a duty to the public, will inferior accounting and auditing services cease to be provided.

A revolution in the accounting profession has indeed occurred. The profession is demonstrating that it can regulate itself. It is no longer entirely possible to perform substandard service with no negative consequences. High-quality service is again the professional standard. Mechanisms for dealing with the free riders, further professional sanctions, and the greed of some still need to be developed. The journey on the road toward peer review and self-governance continues. Some might argue that the profession should just return to the "good old days" and forget about review. Others might argue that government should take over the accounting profession. These choices are examined in Chapter 2.

REFERENCES

"Accountant Hit with Judgment of $338 Million." *Los Angeles Times*, 20 May 1992, D1, D3.

Accounting and Auditing Developments 1991. New York: Deloitte & Touche, 1991.

American Institute of Certified Public Accountants. *Digest of Washington Issues: 101st Congress, Volume 2.* Washington, D.C.: AICPA, December 1990.

———. *Restructuring Professional Standards to Achieve Professional Excellence in a Changing Environment.* Report of the Special Committee on Standards of Professional Conduct for Certified Public Accountants. New York: AICPA, 1986.

AICPA Professional Standards, Volume 1. "The Relationship of Generally Accepted Auditing Standards to Quality Control Standards," AU 161. New York: AICPA, June 1992.

AICPA Professional Standards, Volume 2. "Code of Professional Conduct," ET §§ 50–57. New York: AICPA, June 1992.

———. "General Standards," ET 201. New York: AICPA, June 1992.

———. "Admission to, and Retention of, Membership and Association," Bylaws of the AICPA, BL 200. New York: AICPA, June 1992.

Arens, A., and J. Loebbecke. *Auditing: An Integrated Approach.* 5th ed. Englewood Cliffs, N.J.: Prentice-Hall, 1991.

Benston, G. J. "The Market for Public Accounting Services: Demand, Supply and Regulation." *Journal of Accounting and Public Policy* No. 4 (1985): 33–79.

Commission on Auditors' Responsibilities. *Report, Conclusions, and Recommendations of the Commission on Auditors' Responsibilities.* New York: CAR, 1977.

Committees of the SEC Practice Section. *SEC Practice Section Reference Manual,* edited by K. Jones and V. Zielinski. New York: AICPA, 1992.

Egan, J. "The Politics of Peer Review." In *Psychiatric Peer Review: Prelude and Promise,* edited by J. M. Hamilton, 71–78. Washington, D.C.: American Psychiatric Press, 1985.

Ertel, P. Y., and M. G. Aldridge. *Medical Peer Review: Theory and Practice.* St. Louis: C. V. Mosby Co., 1977.

Fine, D. J., and E. R. Meyer. "Quality Assurance in Historical Perspective." In *Psychiatric Peer Review: Prelude and Promise,* edited by J. M. Hamilton, 1–33. Washington, D.C.: American Psychiatric Press, 1985.

Guy, D. M., and J. D. Sullivan. "The Expectation Gap Auditing Standards." *Journal of Accountancy* (April 1988), Reprinted in *Implementing the Expectation Gap Auditing Standards,* 1–8. New York: AICPA, 1988.

Huff, B. N., and T. P. Kelley. "Quality Review and You." *Journal of Accountancy* (February 1989): 34–40.

Kaiser, C. "The Mandatory SECPS Membership Vote." *Journal of Accountancy* (August 1989): 40–44.

"Large Firms Unite in Fighting Liability Crisis." *The CPA Letter.* New York: AICPA, October 1992, 4.

Lochner, P., Jr. "Black Days for Accounting Firms." *Wall Street Journal,* 22 May 1992, A10.

McCabe, R. K., and K. W. Lantz. "Selecting a Value-Oriented Reviewer." *The CPA Journal* (July 1991): 74–75.

McNair, C. J. "Proper Compromise: The Management Control Dilemma in Public Accounting and Its Impact on Auditor Behavior." *Accounting, Organizations and Society* 16, No. 7 (1991): 635–53.

Mautz, R. K., and C. J. Evers. *Evolution of the Quality Control Inquiry Committee.* New York: Public Oversight Board, 1991.

Mautz, R. K., and L. W. Matusiak. "Concurring Partner Review Revisited." *Journal of Accountancy* (March 1988): 56–63.

Mednick, R. "Accountants' Liability: Coping with the Stampede to the Courtroom." *Journal of Accountancy* (September 1987): 118–22.

National Commission on Fraudulent Financial Reporting. *Report of the National Commission on Fraudulent Financial Reporting*. New York: AICPA, 1987.

Office of Inspector General Report to the Congress, No. 20. Washington, D.C.: U.S. Government Printing Office, 1988.

Ostling, P. J. "Under the Spreading Chestnut Tree—Accountant's Legal Liability—A Historical Perspective." In *Auditing Symposium VIII, Proceedings of the 1986 Touche Ross/University of Kansas Symposium on Auditing Problems*, edited by R. P. Srivastava and N. A. Ford, 1–23. Lawrence, Kans.: School of Business, University of Kansas, 1986.

Pattillo, J. W. *Quality Control and Peer Review—A Practice Manual for CPAs*. New York: John Wiley & Sons, 1984.

The Practicing CPA. New York: AICPA, November 1991.

Securities and Exchange Commission. *SEC Annual Report*. Washington, D.C.: U.S. Government Printing Office, 1990.

———. *Report to Congress*. Washington, D.C.: U.S. Government Printing Office, 1982.

———. *Report to Congress on the Accounting Profession and the Commission's Oversight Role*. Washington, D.C.: U.S. Government Printing Office, August 1980.

Sperry, J. B., E. C. Spede, and D. W. Hicks. "The Evolution and Current Status of Peer Review." *Journal of Accountancy* (May 1987): 81–82.

Stevens, M. *The Big Six*. New York: Simon & Schuster, 1991.

———. *The Big Eight*. New York: Macmillan Publishing Co., Inc., 1981.

Subcommittee on Reports, Accounting, and Management of the Senate Committee on Governmental Operations. *The Accounting Establishment: A Staff Study*. Washington, D.C.: U.S. Government Printing Office, December 1976.

Telberg, R. "Ernst Deal Marks New Era." *Accounting Today* 6, no. 23 (December 7, 1992): 1.

U.S. General Accounting Office. *CPA Audit Quality: Inspectors General Find Significant Problems, Report to the Chairman, Legislation and National Security Subcommittee, House Committee on Government Operations*. Washington, D.C.: U.S. Government Printing Office, 1985.

Wallace, W. A. "Peer Review Filings and Their Implications in Evaluating Self-Regulation." *Auditing: A Journal of Practice & Theory* (Spring 1991): 53–68.

———. "A Historical View of the SEC's Reports to Congress on Oversight of the Profession's Self-Regulatory Process." *Accounting Horizons* (December 1989): 24–39.

2

The Choices

Enormous changes have occurred in every aspect of the accounting profession in the last two decades. What accountant-auditors do and how they do it have changed dramatically. The profession's role and responsibility in society have been reshaped as well. This transformation, this revolution, happened for many reasons. One obvious reason was the recurrent threats of increased governmental regulation. It also happened because of joint and several liability combined with the class-action doctrine and contingent fee arrangements. The elimination of the encroachment rules played a role, too.

The encroachment rules essentially prevented competition. Their elimination helped change the accounting profession into the accounting business. Accounting and auditing services became, in large part, a commodity because of competition. Commodities are price and quality sensitive. Since the quality of what it is accountants and auditors do is difficult to measure, accounting and audit services are unusually price sensitive. This price sensitivity leads to pressures to reduce costs, which can hamper service quality.

A primary goal in sponsored audit research has been to increase efficiency. In response to the temptation to reduce service quality, the profession requires that firms design, implement, and maintain a quality control system. This system and the firm's adherence to it are subject to a comprehensive triennial review. This review requirement has been one of the most controversial changes in the profession.

Some argue that quality review is too costly and dream of a return to the "good old days." An attempt to eliminate quality review probably would bring about further governmental regulation, if not governmental takeover. Let's review how backtracking and greater governmental involvement would affect the profession.

THE GOOD OLD DAYS

About thirty years ago, public accounting was much simpler. Those were the days when the form of the transaction often took precedence over its substance. For example, as a junior accountant, I questioned whether a twenty-year building lease with a $1 purchase option should be handled as an operating lease. The senior not so gently explained that since the agreement was called a "lease agreement," then indeed it was rent expense.

GAAP was much simpler then. Deferred income taxes, fully diluted earnings per share, capital lease obligations, and segment disclosures did not exist. A statement of changes in working capital, rather than a statement of cash flows, was prepared. Little acknowledgment was given to the fact that many client officers had no grasp of what a current asset was, or a current liability, let alone working capital.

A Simpler World

The national and international environments were simpler, the business structure was simpler, and, thus, the transactions between and among businesses were simpler. The reason fully diluted earnings per share did not exist was because convertible securities did not generally exist. Also, there were few sale lease-backs, deferred compensation agreements, and product financing arrangements. The world was larger then, so we seldom dealt with foreign currency translation. The globalization of business as we know it had not occurred. Some industries were infants or had not been born yet. Equipment leasing and cable television companies existed, but these industries were miniscule in comparison to their sizes today. Biotech, microcomputer, and computer software companies did not yet exist.

GAAP consisted of a "bag of rules." Today, it is a very much bigger bag. Passing the CPA examination today is a formidable task. Practicing accounting today is a close-to-impossible task.

GAAP is being influenced by the FASB's six statements of financial accounting concepts. These concept statements provide a framework of fundamentals on which to base financial accounting and reporting [Financial Accounting Standards Board, 1988: i]. They have influenced several SFASs and are particularly evident in the statements on deferred income tax, leases, and post-retirement obligations.

The Straw That Broke the Camel's Back and Other Taboo Subjects

Those also were the days when encroachment on the practice of our fellow professionals was prohibited by the Code of Professional Ethics. It was unacceptable to solicit another firm's clients or its employees. The profession believed "encroachment causes enmity, and the organized profession is fully justified in stamping it out in the interests of the group as a whole" [Carey and Doherty, 1966: 152]. But then, in the late 1970s, the U.S. Department of Justice, at the urging of many members of Congress, demanded that the profession drop its trespass rules because they limited competition and, thus, made audit and accounting services too costly. By vote of the AICPA membership, the encroachment rules were repealed. What happened as a result? Something close to chaos. The profession was turned upside down, and a revolution began. Indeed, the camel's back was broken.

Public accounting quickly became the home of the slick marketing executive. Because what accountants and auditors do is in many respects unobservable, firms attempted and still attempt to differentiate themselves from others in the profession. Firms develop marketing brochures, newsletters, proposal presentations, databases, and mailing lists. In just a few short years, the accounting profession verily became the accounting business. To maintain or increase their client bases, many firms "lowball" their audit fees and particularly the initial fee [DeAngelo, 1981]. They hope to recoup expenses and profits later by increasing fees or by providing management advisory and tax services [Simon and Francis, 1988; Turnpen, 1990]. Audit service fees became and remain for many firms a loss leader for some categories of clients. Further, firms began prizing "rainmakers" for their skill at bringing in new clients. Partners who had risen to the top because of their technical skills found they had to take a back seat to their more marketing-oriented partners.

This new emphasis on growth and the use of audit services as a loss leader made audit engagement time budgets even more unattainable. Success in public accounting, now more than ever, depends on one's ability to meet and ultimately to beat the time budget [Covaleski et al., 1989]. Since this often cannot be done, the staff person resorts to behaviors that are undiscussable in the profession [McNair, 1991]. While referring to certain behaviors as undiscussable is a bit strong, it does help make the point that many in the profession choose to think that they do not exist because they are generally not discussed. Also, choosing not to confront these behaviors is a decision to forgo quality. These undiscussable behaviors include underreporting on time reports, switching time between budget categories, and charging time to another client [Kelly and Margheim, 1990; Margheim and Pany, 1986]. Firm managers and partners ban or at least strongly discourage such behavior, even though many of them once did the same. Of an even more serious nature, based on survey data, staff also resort to other strategies to meet or beat the budget, including accepting weak explanations in response to audit inquiries, making cursory reviews, and signing off on audit procedures they did not do [McNair, 1991; Marxen, 1990]. These behaviors can and do cause accounting and audit failures.

Of course, some will argue that these last behaviors do not exist, and others will say that they occur very infrequently. Those who say they never happen either have not worked in public accounting or have very selective memories. The frequency of these behaviors is unknown. Research studies, though, suggest fairly high rates. For example, McNair [1991: 648] reports that in a survey of 150 audit staff members, over 60 percent reported accepting weak explanations to inquiries. Specifically, 24 said they frequently accepted weak explanations, and 66 said they rarely did it. As for signing off on audit procedures that were not done, perhaps the most serious dysfunctional behavior, over 20 percent said they had done it. Specifically, 7 said they frequently signed off on audit procedures they had not done, and 24 said they rarely did it. These behaviors must be blamed in part on the fact that the profession chooses to ignore their existence and even worse, chooses not to discuss them. The result is that substandard service will continue in spite of quality review.

Efficiency and Effectiveness

In the good old days, audits were fairly effective, but they were also definitely inefficient. They were inefficient because the sample tests of transactions and controls tended to be very large compared to current practice. Statistical sampling had not yet been introduced to the profession. Often, the tests of details consisted of a 100 percent examination of balance sheet accounts. This was often done even when controls were found to be strong. As a result, there was no need to extrapolate adjustments from the sample because the entire population was examined. This "oversampling," had to result in at least moderately effective audits because sampling error was avoided. However, nonsampling error caused by boredom and fatigue may increase as the number of test items increases. Also, there was not the same level of pressure to meet unrealistically constructed time budgets. Yes, there was pressure because firms did emphasize profits over quality. It was understood that the road to the top required technical competence and the ability to beat the time budget, but, on the other hand, the audits were not given away. On average though, engagement budgets were generous compared with those used today.

Independence and Confidentiality—Two Commandments

Independence and confidentiality were two standards that one never considered breaching. Much of the profession's reason for being was and is its independence from the client, both in mental attitude and in appearance. A practitioner was asked to "avoid relationships which would be likely to warp his judgement even subconsciously" [Carey and Doherty, 1966: 19]. To many accounting professionals, independence did not allow for developing close friendships with clients, let alone furnishing client advisory services. Staff were advised to "avoid any appearance of being overly friendly" [Mautz and Martin, 1953: 57]. (Being independent also was easier then because of the prohibition against encroachment.)

Client names were always kept secret. A client's file was carried so the name was hidden lest anyone learn the client's identity and ask questions about the engagement. Staff were told not to reveal client names to others, including their own family members. In fact, spouses were not given client names or telephone numbers, either of which were necessary to reach their mates during the day. In a family emergency, the firm office relayed the message. Perhaps we were overly zealous about protecting client confidentiality, but clients probably appreciated it. A continued focus on confidentiality, however, might have prevented the possibility of quality review.

Who Ran It and What Did We Do?

Personnel from the then Big Eight firms largely ran and still run the accounting establishment. They do this in spite of the fact that they represent less than 25 percent of the AICPA's membership [Magill and Previts, 1991: 119]. Then, their influence on the development of accounting principles and auditing standards was close to absolute. Representatives of these firms were on the Committee on Accounting Procedure, which issued fifty-one accounting research bulletins from 1939 to 1959. They also were on the Accounting Principles Board (APB) (active from 1959 to 1972), which issued thirty-one APB Opinions. These statements make up a great part of what is described as GAAP. Between 1939 and 1972, the Big Eight also made their presence known on the Committee on Auditing Procedure, which formulated much of what is called GAAS.

The influence of the Big Eight (now Six) remains great, but today it is more indirect. The big firms do contribute large sums to the Financial Accounting Foundation (FAF), which oversees the FASB. They do respond to FASB proposals and actively participate in AICPA and state association committees. While some might argue that the large firms are too influential, it still must be admitted that their support is crucial to general acceptance. These firms audit an overwhelming majority of the public companies, and, thus, to some extent, they determine what is generally accepted.

Less than two decades ago, there was no such thing as a review engagement. Either financial statements were audited and included an auditor's report, or they were published with an "unaudited" report. In the 1960s, Management Advisory Service (MAS) was just beginning and consisted for the most part of accounting system design and implementation. Many practitioners, dinosaurs perhaps, were suspicious of all the talk about MAS and wondered out loud what the nonaccountants were doing in the office. Accounting firms were not yet designing compensation systems or providing actuarial and recruiting services.

Accounting and Auditing Failures?

Accounting and audit failures did occur in the good old days. There are more failures today, but business and the profession have grown tremendously. As a percentage of engagements completed, the ratio of audit and accounting failures today is probably about the same or even less than in the past, and, at that, proportionately small. Because of the increased time pressure to complete underbid audit engagements and the enormous increase in transaction complexity, this is quite an accomplishment.

The number of accounting and audit failures then and now is unknown. To be sure, these failures almost always come to light with a business failure. However, audit and accounting failures may occur more frequently than we know because if the business does not fail, they probably go undiscovered.

Can We Return?

Many things make a return to past practice impractical and undesirable. First, the chances of reinstating the encroachment rules are close to zero. Such a proposal sounds anticompetitive, even though it might go a long way toward improving accounting and audit service quality, and, thus, reduce society's costs of substandard service. Second, the world has become smaller, and business transactions have become much more complex. The FASB has its hands full keeping up with the explosion in financial instruments and industries, the globalization of business, and Wall Street's inventiveness in structuring transactions. More and more, practitioners have had to become specialists. Those who have not become specialists are subject to being criticized as "jack of all trades, master of none."

Also, society's expectations have changed dramatically. Its demands will not allow us to turn the clock backward. We can no longer claim that the audit is not designed to detect fraud. Society demands it, and our professional standards require it. While our hesitancy to take on responsibility for fraud detection is understandable, it is amazing we were able to avoid that burden for so long. The public believes and has believed for some time that the auditor's unqualified report implies an absence of management fraud. This added responsibility for designing an audit to detect irregularities is long overdue.

While the average person would find it difficult to understand, the detection of management fraud is, at best, mystifying. GAAS and standard audit procedures are not very helpful in uncovering fraud. In fact, there is little professional guidance to help the auditor in the detection of irregularities and illegal acts. The capacity to uncover management fraud depends as much on the auditor's personal characteristics as on anything else. One important characteristic is the ability to establish rapport with client personnel at all levels of the organization. While the SASs regularly call for inquiries of management personnel, it is as important, if not more so, to be able to establish rapport and talk with nonmanagement personnel. Often, lower-level employees have a very accurate sense of what is going on. The auditor also has to have an intuitive awareness about a person's character and the ability to think like a thief. Research in this area is critically needed.

Society also expects to be reimbursed for losses incurred, regardless of the extent, if any, of its reliance on financial statements. CPA firms are the "deep pockets.'' Often the sole survivor in a business failure is the CPA firm, so regardless of how deep the pockets are, there is still a pocket to be picked, and pick it clean they will. The sheer number of civil suits suggests not only that the profession has quality problems, but also that the "innocent" investors or creditors should not be held accountable for their own greed. For example, individuals who bought S&L certificates of deposit yielding 12 percent when the going rate was 9 percent are not innocent or misinformed. The rate of return among other things is a function of risk. Investors from all walks of life know this and should not be compensated for their greed.

The legal profession has certainly influenced society's expectations about who deserves blame in a business failure. Perhaps there are simply too many lawyers, each scavenging for new revenue sources in order to survive. These lawyers are being helped by expert witnesses, some of whom may not be qualified. Unfortunately, "evidentiary standards have declined the most, even as standards for liability itself have grown more strict" [Huber, 1992: 132]. "If courts aspire to maintain high standards of performance among professionals summoned to court as defendants, they must find ways to maintain equally high standards among the professionals who accuse them. Otherwise, there is a real risk that the least competent fringes of a scientific community will end up, through the courts, prescribing standards for the rest" [Huber, 1992: 132].

The courts are simply not doing their job. Experts are testifying even though they have questionable expertise. For example, more than a few accounting academics supplement their income by providing litigation support services. Some even take pride in testifying against CPA firms. In the main, academic accountants are very bright, well-trained researchers who also teach accounting. Some have significant practice experience, and others have little or none. Strong research training, a passing score on an entry-level examination, and little or no experience are not a sufficient basis to qualify as an expert. The courts need to assess whether the expert has sufficient academic and practice experience before determining that the person is in fact an expert. On the other hand, academics with significant practice experience must participate in the legal system. We have, I believe, a moral obligation to help justice prevail.

The doctrines of joint and several liability, foreseeable and unforeseeable third parties, and class-action privileges have been expensive for the profession and the public it serves. These doctrines, like the prohibition against the encroachment ethics rules, are not likely to be overturned. The legal principles outlined and contingent fee arrangements, as well as the requirement that firms practice fundamentally as partnerships, threaten the profession's very existence.

While Rule 505 of the AICPA Code of Professional Conduct, Form of Practice and Name, has been changed to allow firms to use the corporate form, it will be some time before related state laws are changed. Some states, you can be sure, will still be debating this issue long after we have ceased to care.

There is evidence that legal liability, the class-action doctrine, and contingent fee arrangements have had a positive effect on the profession. Basically, this research argues that these doctrines have provided the impetus to improve accounting and audit service quality [DeJong, 1985]. This argument makes some intuitive sense. It relies, however, on the assumption that the firm's legal liability persuades it to perform more audit tests, which then results in a better audit. Whether higher-quality audits actually occur, however, is still a question.

Firms do assess the legal consequences of failing to detect a material misstatement along with assessing audit risk. It is not known, however, whether and how the severity of the potential consequences affect the nature, amount, and timing of the substantive tests because many other variables also influence those decisions.

It can be shown that the profession does respond to specific court findings. For example, the then Auditing Standards Executive Committee issued Statement on Auditing Procedure 41, Subsequent Discovery of Facts Existing at the Date of the Auditor's Report, in direct response to a court's decision [Davies, 1983: 14]. The same could be said for some of the expectation gap standards.

Yes, the good old days are gone. We cannot return to a time when transactions were not nearly so complex and when accounting principles were not as concerned with economic substance. Returning to the days when the only fee pressure was from the client and when professional competence was more esteemed than marketing ability just is not possible. People have changed as well. They used to take responsibility for their losses and their gains. Now they brag about their brilliance when they earn a profit and hire a lawyer when they incur a loss. There are an abundance of lawyers who, because of contingent fee arrangements, are in a feeding frenzy in order to survive. Government, too, has changed. While the accounting profession has become the accounting business, public service has become the business of politics.

Would We Want to Return?

In reality, the good old days were not really all that good. We wore hats long after the rest of the business world gave them up. "A clean hat, neat business suit, harmonizing ties and socks are expected" [Mautz and Martin, 1953: 54]. Our Frieden calculators did not hold a candle to today's personal computers. There was a seamy side to those days, too. Discrimination against minorities of every kind was the rule of the day. Young Jewish graduates could choose only from Jewish-owned firms. Women did not consider accounting as a career. Minorities of any kind were neither invited nor welcomed into the profession. Alcohol abuse was common and even expected. Fortunately, the profession, like society, has made some progress, but still needs to go further.

On the positive side, we did have rules on encroachment, and independence was valued. Individuals became partners based, for the most part, on their technical competence. The world was less hostile, a glut of attorneys had not left them lurking around every corner, and people took responsibility for their own decisions. Today, however, financial statements present a more realistic picture of an entity's economic condition than they did before. For example, recognition of lease obligations, deferred taxes, and post-retirement obligations have done much to present a truer picture of the company's liabilities. Much of the credit for this goes to the FASB. Yes, the FASB has come up with an even bigger bag of rules, which makes taking and passing the CPA examination an even more formidable task. It also makes practicing accounting more difficult, what with the myriad rules one has to know under GAAP. Yes, much of what the FASB has produced can be characterized as industry accounting guides. Yes, not much, if anything, has been done to make financial statements more comparable. In spite of these failings, though, the FASB has made progress. It now compels us to consider the substance of transactions. Deferred tax, lease, and post-retirement benefit obligations are no longer ignored. There is still a long way to go in transforming the balance sheet into a statement of financial condition, but it is closer than it has been in fifty years.

Great strides have been made in increasing accounting and audit efficiency. The use of microcomputers has had much to do with gains in accounting service efficiency. While micros are used in auditing, it is debatable whether they have actually increased audit efficiency. The delay seems to be related to the typical auditor's lack of skill in statistical and analytical techniques. Improvements in these areas could do much to increase analytical procedure effectiveness and, therefore, audit efficiency. For example, multiple regression analysis could, in some instances, be very helpful in providing evidence that substantiates income statement account balances.

Advances have been made in audit planning and in evaluating the sufficiency and competency of the audit evidence. To be sure, some of these procedures seem like smoke and mirrors. For example, the procedure for calculating attribute sample sizes seems unbiased. Upon inspection, however, the procedure loses much of its impartiality because it is based on the auditor's "professional judgment" about the tolerable deviation rate and the auditor's "estimate" of the population error rate. The benefit of this procedure is not in its seeming objectivity, but rather in its requirement that the auditor consider tolerable deviation rates, control risk, sampling risk, and so on in planning the audit. Similarly, the audit risk model is not nearly as quantifiable as some might pretend. Again, the main benefit is that the model specifically address the major influences on audit risk: inherent risk, control risk, and detection risk. It also permits the auditor to make some defendable judgments about the amount of detection risk as a guide in determining the nature, timing, and amount of the substantive tests. These advances have resulted in much greater audit efficiency and perhaps greater effectiveness. They also have made professional judgment less of a mystery and, thus, provide some protection against litigation.

Where Are We Headed?

The onslaught of lawsuits from every sector and threats from governmental agencies and Congress will continue. Somehow we have faced this onslaught and not only survived, but often prospered. As long as there are investor losses, too many attorneys, and contingent fee arrangements, the legal assault will continue.

The threats from regulators and governmental officials, we hope, have been and will be well intentioned. Congress, the SEC, state boards of accountancy, and the like have, along with accountants, a responsibility to protect the public interest. A reading of the transcripts of some congressional hearings does make one wonder, however, about politicians' intentions. To describe some of the questioning at these hearings as hostile would be an understatement.

A new era has begun in which government again has the itch to regulate. "In fact, students of regulation agree, the nation is heading for another era of regulatory activism, if it isn't here already" [Miller, 1988: 70]. "The trend toward reregulation is evident in the increasing numbers of government workers employed by federal regulatory agencies and in the rising budgets of these agencies" ["Don't Retreat," 1990: 23]. In November 1991, members of Congress and even the president made statements about caps on credit card rates that suggested renewed eagerness to regulate. The Bush administration made efforts to get bank examiners to ease up. It seems only yesterday that "weak bank examiners" were blamed for the crash of S&L institutions. Congress continues to refuse to recognize that the true villain was not weak or tough bank examiners, deregulation or bad auditors, but, rather, the government's unquestioning guarantee of the decisions of corrupt or incompetent bankers.

Renewed interest in governmental regulation suggests that the recommendations of the late Senator Metcalf may have renewed life. In fact, two bills introduced in Congress in 1992 would do much of what Senator Metcalf sought. A brief review of these bills is provided in Chapter 9.

The fallout from the S&L catastrophe and the insistence, especially in Congress, that blame be placed elsewhere each contribute to an environment in which regulation can blossom. Add to this an uncertain economy due to an overwhelming budget deficit, the result of legislation recommended by presidents and passed by Congress, and what we have is an environment perfect for governmental interference. That leaves the accounting profession's efforts to regulate itself vulnerable to attack. "There does appear to be general agreement that self-regulation has failed" ["Medicine," 1991: A25]. If government is to set standards for professions, let's consider how regulation of the accounting profession might be accomplished.

GOVERNMENTAL REGULATION

Senator Metcalf's *The Accounting Establishment: A Staff Study* [Subcommittee on Reports, 1976] provides the most comprehensive view of what governmental regulation of the accounting profession would look like. Some mistakenly claim that the staff study only criticized the then Big Eight firms. It went much further than that.

Criticisms of the Big Eight

The criticisms of the Big Eight were indeed acrimonious. While it is not my purpose to defend large firms, a review of these allegations provides insight into some of the regulators' biases. One of these, and a recurrent theme throughout the subcommittee's report, is that big is bad. It is interesting that politicians seldom level the same criticism at government.

Perhaps if these firms had been more cooperative with the information requests of the subcommittee, the report might have been less cantankerous. Whatever the reason, the senator clearly decided not to hide his ill will toward the Big Eight. Among the many allegations against them were the following:

1. There is little evidence to support the view that they serve the public [4].

2. There is little evidence to support the belief that they are independent from their clients [4].

3. They exercise too much influence on the formulation of accounting practices approved by the federal government [4 & 5].

4. They are too large and, as a result, service too many industries [7].

5. The individual firms serve too many clients within the same industry [7].

6. Providing management advisory services is inconsistent with the responsibilities of independent auditors, and, as a result, the firms cannot be independent in fact and in appearance [8].

7. Representatives of these firms have advocated increased investment tax credits, more liberalized depreciation rules, and so on. This shows that they represent the interests of corporate clients [8].

The first two allegations about the evidence to support the views that the Big Eight serve the public and are independent are peculiar in their wording. In research, a hypothesis has certain desirable attributes, such as whether it is testable and quantifiable. It also uses the "if-then" format. In the first two allegations, the hypotheses that the Big Eight or any firms serve the public and are independent cannot be proven because they are neither testable nor quantifiable as they were framed in the report. The fact that they found "little evidence" can just as reasonably be interpreted as proving Big Eight firms serve the public interest and are independent.

The allegations in statements 3 through 5 (too much influence, too large, and too many clients) rely on the premise that being large is inherently wrong. Perhaps it is fortunate the senator did not see the 1991 *Forbes* magazine listing of the 400 largest private companies; all six of the now Big Six firms are among the top thirty companies.

An assertion that large accounting firms exercise a great deal of influence in the development of accounting principles is probably supportable. The report, however, said it was too much influence. It is not clear how much is too much. It also is not clear from the report why their influence is undesirable. These firms do respond to proposed standards, and their employees are active on AICPA and state society committees. It is probably true that their employees are more active than the average AICPA member. But what is the basis for concluding that this is too much or not in the public interest? Certainly, if accounting principles are to be generally accepted, they require the support of firms that audit over 90 percent of public companies.

The allegation that these firms serve too many industries is problematic as well. Realistically, only large accounting firms can competently serve companies across many industries. It is no longer practical or desirable for the small and medium-sized firm, let alone the sole practitioner, to claim expertise in all industries.

The fifth allegation suggests that industry specialization is inappropriate. Apparently the writers did not believe specialization leads to a better understanding of an industry and, thus, to a better inherent risk assessment and more efficient substantive audit procedures. Presumably, the more efficient the firm, the lower the audit fees. Specialization also might result in greater audit and accounting effectiveness.

The sixth allegation in the report expresses legitimate concern over the effect that providing MAS has on the fact and appearance of independence. As to the former, there is little evidence to substantiate claims that auditors are not independent in fact when they provide client advisory services. It is reasonable to expect, though, that an auditor's judgment about control risk and reportable internal control conditions will be affected when the auditor also has assisted in accounting system design and implementation. Auditors may very well overlook weaknesses in an internal control structure that they helped design. However, evidence substantiating such a relationship is miniscule. It is equally logical to concede that some auditors, no matter how few, are unethical and that lack of independence stems not from MAS, but rather from human frailties.

It has been argued that providing MAS results in a better audit [Burton, 1980]. This may be true in certain instances. It also is true that, in many firms, the audit and the MAS staff are quite separate. Because of this separation, the knowledge gained in a MAS engagement may not be available to audit personnel. Also, the "audit effectiveness argument" does not address the real issue, and that is the effect a MAS engagement has on users' perceptions of auditor independence. The bottom line is that accountants are perceived to be less independent when they provide services other than audit and accounting services. Perhaps firms must follow the lead of Arthur Andersen and others and set up a separate entity to provide MAS.

The appearance of independence has not been given the consideration it deserves. Without independence there is little reason for the attest function. Apparently oblivious to the criticism it could engender, the AICPA Professional Ethics Executive Committee [1991] proposed a revision to Rule 175 to allow members to serve on the boards of directors of banks that have loaned clients material amounts. It also proposed a revision of Rules 302 and 503 to allow a member's spouse to receive contingent fees or commissions from clients, provided the member is not actively involved in the spouse's activities. One can imagine two-inch headlines that read "CPA Bank Board Member Responsible for Bank Failure" or "CPA Linked to Exorbitant Commissions." When it happens, we will again wonder why the public is so misinformed. It is time for the profession to acknowledge that the appearance of independence is as important as, if not more important than, independence in fact.

The Metcalf committee's last allegation criticizes members of large firms for testifying before Congress on tax policy issues. Without doubt, CPAs are much better informed about tax issues and policy than are most members of Congress. Perhaps some elected officials feel that the country's abdication of governmental responsibility to career politicians will not be complete until they also eliminate input from its citizens.

The Accounting Establishment

The Metcalf report's title, *The Accounting Establishment*, implies that the entire accounting profession is to blame for accounting, auditing, and business failures. The study attacks the AICPA, the FAF, the FASB, the SEC, the then Auditing Standards Executive Committee, the CAR, and independent accountants in general. Among its many allegations, three are particularly notable:

1. The accounting establishment allows too many accounting methods to report similar business transactions. Using alternative accounting methods selected from the collection of acceptable methods can result in drastically different financial results [6].

2. Current auditing standards permit great discretion in determining the extent of audit testing [6].

3. Doubts about the accuracy and reliability of corporate financial information are a result of continual revelations of corporate misconduct which was overlooked or not reported by independent auditors [7].

The allegation about alternative accounting methods reveals a second underlying theme in the report: the necessity to eliminate alternative practices. The report's view, as one might expect from a governmental representative, is simple and pragmatic. It repeatedly criticizes these practices without acknowledging that, in some cases, the alternative principles have, according to their proponents, strong theoretical support. While the profession has not achieved basic uniformity and it must make a concerted effort to do so, Congress must accept part of the blame. It, for example, encouraged general acceptance of the last-in, first-out method.

The profession cannot, however, blame anyone except itself for the overabundance of alternatives. FASB 106, Employers' Accounting for Post-Retirement Benefits Other Than Pensions, for example, allows a company to amortize the cost of post-retirement benefits against earnings over a twenty-year period or to take the entire amount against earnings on the implementation date. Acknowledging that this may cause drastically different results may, in this case, be an understatement. While there may be no effect on stock prices because the cash effect of post-retirement benefits should have been recognized long ago by the market, the different income results will fuel renewed criticism of the profession.

Regarding the second allegation, auditors do have a great amount of discretion in determining the nature, amount, and timing of substantive tests. Since the senator's report, several new SASs have provided auditors with important guidance. For example, SAS 31, Evidential Matter, offers significant guidance about the amount of evidence to accumulate [*AICPA Professional Standards*, Volume 1, 1992: AU 326]. Also SAS 47, Audit Risk and Materiality in Conducting an Audit, and SAS 55, Consideration of the Internal Control Structure in a Financial Statement Audit, provide important direction in audit planning.

But there will always be differences in judgment about the amount of evidence needed to support a particular financial statement assertion. These differences occur for several reasons that certainly include variations in auditors' detection risk perceptions and attitudes about risk (i.e., whether auditors are risk adverse, risk seeking, etc.).

Differences in auditors' perceptions about detection risk are partially a result of experience differences. Unfortunately, most states require only a short internship period. A few jurisdictions require no experience if the candidate has appropriate advanced education. "The professional auditor acquires a complex network of knowledge over his or her years of experience, knowledge which simply cannot be obtained in the classroom" [Waller and Felix, 1984: 383]. Many states require two years of audit experience before a candidate can become licensed. Two years is probably adequate to learn how to apply various attribute and substantive tests, but it is entirely inadequate to plan an audit engagement or to evaluate audit test results. If the CPA designation implies professional expertise, a reevaluation of the profession's experience requirement is long overdue.

The third allegation, about disclosure of corporate misconduct, reflects an honest difference of opinion about the independent accountant's role. Many believe the auditor should be a whistle blower. For example, "democratic Congressman Ron Wyden of Oregon wants to force accountants to blow the whistle on lawbreaking clients" [McCarroll, 1992: 49]. In fact, Representative Wyden introduced legislation in 1990 to force accountants to do just that. His bill did pass the House. The profession, however, categorically rejects this role of being the public accuser. Its position is described in SAS 54, Illegal Acts by Clients, which says "disclosure of the illegal act to parties other than the client's senior management and its audit committee or board of directors is not ordinarily part of the auditor's responsibility, and such disclosure would be precluded by the auditor's ethical or legal obligation of confidentiality, unless the matter affects his opinion on the financial statements" [*AICPA Professional Standards*], Volume 1 1992: AU 317.23]. It also would make the audit function much more difficult. While some might disagree, audits are in the main conducted very expeditiously. One of the major reasons is management's knowledge that the information it shares with its auditors is confidential. If auditors were cast in the role of guardians of the public interest, audits would become much more difficult, and much more expensive. The day, however, may soon come when auditors will have to tell what they know because society believes we should. In the meantime, a requirement that all audit clients have functioning audit committees with outside directors and sufficient resources should be instituted.

Governmental Regulation in Action

The heart of *The Accounting Establishment* report lies in the recommendations it made to the Senate Committee on Governmental Operations. The following seven deserve special comment:

1. Congress should abolish "creative accounting" techniques, such as the percentage of completion income recognition method and other potentially misleading accounting methods [21].

2. Congress should amend the fraud provisions of the federal securities laws to restore an individual's right to sue independent auditors for negligence. Such legislation is necessary to overturn the U.S. Supreme Court decision in *Ernst & Ernst* v. *Olga Hochfelder* [21].

3. Accounting standards for publicly owned corporations should be established by the federal government [21].

4. Auditing standards should be established by the federal government [22].

5. Periodic quality reviews of independent auditors should be conducted by the General Accounting Office, the SEC, or a special inspection agency [22].

6. The federal government should promulgate and enforce strict standards of conduct for auditors, and nonaccounting work should be prohibited [22].

7. Auditors' responsibilities should be defined by the Federal government so that the expectations of Congress, the public, and courts of law are met [23].

The first recommendation about creative accounting has caused a great deal of controversy in the profession. Let's deal with that issue first.

Creative Accounting

The phrase "creative accounting" can be attributed to the various statements of the distinguished professor of accounting from the City University of New York, Abraham J. Briloff. Dr. Briloff has been an eloquent critic of the accounting profession and has appeared before several congressional committees. He is repeatedly quoted throughout the Metcalf report and other congressional reports since. His influence on Congress and elsewhere cannot be underestimated.

Professor Briloff was a consistent critic of the misapplication of the percentage of completion method. "Professor Briloff described problems resulting from the use of this method of income recognition by Stirling Homex Corp and Four Seasons Nursing Homes" [Subcommittee on Reports, 1976: 189]. More recently, in 1985 testimony before the House Subcommittee on Oversight and Investigations, when commenting on the FASB, he said, "most certainly such a putative scholar would have proceeded with all deliberate speed to limit that [percentage of completion] exotic accounting procedure" [1985: 113]. While Dr. Briloff cites many examples of accounting gone bad and, in particular, the misuse of the percentage of completion method, it is not fair to say he was recommending its elimination. He was, it seems, simply objecting to what he saw as inappropriate applications of the method based on the facts as he understood them.

The report's second recommendation would make the auditor even more liable. Let's examine that point next.

More Liability

The Supreme Court's *Hochfelder* decision has not been overturned. In that case, "the Court held that scienter—the intent to deceive, manipulate, or defraud—is a necessary requirement of any private action for damages under the fraud provisions of the Federal securities laws" [Subcommittee on Reports, 1976: 182]. Many in the profession believed this case would significantly reduce exposure to liability. However, plaintiffs are successfully suing firms, thanks to the inventiveness of some few attorneys, under Rule 10b-5 of the Securities Exchange Act of 1934. Under this rule, it is unlawful to issue misleading financial statements. The burden of proof, however, is essentially on the auditor to show that the statements were not misleading. So, while *Hochfelder* has not been overturned, other ways have been found to hold the accounting firm liable.

The remaining five recommendations (items 3 through 7) deal with the takeover of the accounting profession.

Governmental Takeover

The prospect of the federal government setting accounting and auditing standards (recommendations 3 and 4) is frightening. Senator Metcalf believed the evidence "indicates that government agencies are capable of setting standards competently and more efficiently than private organizations" [Subcommittee on Reports, 1976: 19]. The report offered no significant evidence to support this claim. Perhaps, the Cost Accounting Standards Board (CASB), an agency of Congress that was very active at that time, served as the committee's example of competency and efficiency. In fact, the committee did recommend that a board similar to the CASB develop accounting standards. While CASB members have been very competent, it is a challenging task to judge the efficiency of a governmental agency. The report does mention that the CASB's budget was about half that of the FASB. How comparable these entities are is open to question.

More important, CASB standards have been criticized on several counts [*Cost Accounting Standards*, 1976: 36]. Some claim they are too detailed and rigid, and do not allow for alternatives. The subcommittee, however, believed "the Cost Accounting Standards Board has benefitted from its specific statutory mandate to achieve uniformity and consistency in cost accounting standards used by the federal government" [Subcommittee on Reports, 1976: 20]. This also supports the second theme in the report, the unacceptability of alternative practices. Further, it has been alleged that CASB standards favor the government by not allowing companies to charge the full cost of government contracts. In addition, some companies, including a few former clients of the author, claimed the standards require a third set of books. Further, the standards do not clearly distinguish between direct and indirect contract costs, which is possibly the most serious weakness in the standards. What we have now are numerous letters of understanding between the grantor agency and the grantee that detail what costs are direct and what are indirect. Problems arise, of course, when federal auditors ignore these letters of understanding.

There are other examples of governmental competence and efficiency in standard setting. These include, but are not limited to, the Internal Revenue Code, the Single Audit Act of 1984, and the Standards for Audit of Governmental Organizations, Programs, Activities, and Functions. Based on abundant experience, it is ludicrous to assert that government is more competent or efficient than is the private sector at anything other than fighting wars. Since only governments find it necessary to declare and carry out wars, even that is debatable.

The report's fifth recommendation would have governmental employees perform quality review. This recommendation was the basis for the bill introduced by Representative Moss, which would have set up an accountancy commission in 1978 to review the work of individual accounting firms every three years.

The spirit of this recommendation still lives and today would be based on an assertion that quality review is nothing more than an exercise in mutual back scratching because the reviewed firm is permitted to select the peer reviewer.

Personal experience as a managing partner of a division firm, as a reviewer for a state society and the AICPA, and as a member of the Colorado Society of CPAs Quality Review Board has shown this was not the case. In every instance that I know of, reviews have been done with integrity. Those who believe review is an exercise in mutual back scratching should examine the Division for CPA Firms public files. For example, on September 28, 1989, Peat Marwick issued an unqualified peer review report on Ernst & Whinney and a letter of comments criticizing Ernst regarding its adherence to the supervision element of its quality control system. Similarly, on January 23, 1989, Arthur Young issued an unqualified report with a letter of comments criticizing Coopers & Lybrand's documentation of issues related to long-term debt covenants. In addition, the files show that very few firms get through review without criticism. Research also shows that review is working in the private sector. For example, Wanda Wallace investigated certain assertions about the "moral hazard" in the peer review process. Specifically, she addressed the following concerns:

- If CPA firms are permitted to select other firms to perform a peer review, then they can exercise control over the resultant reports and a back-scratching result will be observed.

- Since the voluntary nature of the program creates a self-selection bias, no substantive findings will appear in the public record.

- Due to regulatory demands to demonstrate the effectiveness of self-regulation and the desire to attract additional CPA firms into the voluntary program, the findings will be diluted over time. [Wallace, 1991: 57]

She concluded that "the evidence is consistent with the premise that the SECPS has overcome moral hazards inherent in any selection biases, timeliness of completing peer reviews, and the substantive nature of the findings both in the initial years of the program and over time" [Wallace, 1991: 53].

An assessment of whether quality review should be taken over by government should include a comparison of each side's effectiveness, competence, and efficiency. Significant evidence exists that peer review of accounting firms under the AICPA's auspices is effective [McCabe, 1991; Public Oversight Board, 1991; Wallace, 1991]. Whether government could be as effective is not determinable because it has never done it.

As to competence, there is no question that the leadership of the AICPA quality review program, its reviewers, and members of the profession are competent. An equivalent conclusion could probably be drawn about those who administer reviews for the GAO. The private sector may be more competent overall because public accounting, unlike other industries and government, makes a more concerted effort to hire the very best. Their presence on most campuses is very strong. Whether they do hire the very best is debatable, but it is reasonable to think that they do. For example, they certainly seem to hire the students with the highest grade point averages.

As to efficiency, the following quote is, I hope, not representative of government's concern in this area. "In September 1985, OMB (Office of Management and Budget) asked the inspectors general to supplement the provision of OMB Circular A–128, 'Audits of State and Local Governments' by developing a quality control program for single audits. Some of the areas for consideration were desk reviews on 100 percent of the audit reports" [U.S. GAO, 1985: 32]. How can a 100 percent review even be considered?

On balance, the evidence suggests that the AICPA's review effort is effective. While the competence of each sector's leadership and staff may be equal, the private sector is always in my opinion more concerned with efficiency issues. Every effort, then, needs to be made to keep review within the profession. While Stevens' [1981] comment in his book titled *The Big Eight* is a little strong, it does deserve mention. He said, "Surely the nation needs no further proof that the bureaucratic influence is a stultifying one—a negative force that drains energy, imagination, and innovation" [215].

The sixth recommendation would have an organization like the SEC develop and enforce standards of conduct prohibiting activities that impair independence either in fact or in appearance. Specifically, it would bar firms from performing client advisory services and from testifying before Congress on matters of tax policy.

The subcommittee's seventh recommendation would redefine the auditor's role and greatly increase his or her responsibilities. Specifically, the auditor's unqualified report would be understood to "mean that financial information is presented fairly and that corporate records are complete and accurate" [Subcommittee on Reports, 1976: 23]. Note the absence of the phrase "in conformance with generally accepted accounting principles." The auditor apparently would be required to select accounting principles that accomplish the fair presentation objective. Such a position is certainly in line with Professor Briloff's proposals. The requirement that the auditors attest to the completeness and accuracy of the corporate records makes no allowance for considerations about materiality. Cost-benefit concerns seem to be beyond government's mastery.

The subcommittee report does give us a comprehensive view of what governmental regulation would look like. It looks too much like a governmental takeover. It is difficult to know how serious these proposals were. Certainly, it is in government's best interest to let others develop and maintain accounting principles, auditing standards, and codes of conduct. If government were to take over these functions, whom would it blame for its failures? Certainly, government does not want to take over the accounting profession and face the inevitable business, accounting, and audit failures. If nothing else, the profession serves as a whipping boy that Congress can beat to deflect criticism from itself.

It is also in the profession's best interest to let government beat the drum of dissatisfaction. Realistically, the quality of professional practice might not have been improved without the threats of Senator Lee Metcalf and Representatives John Moss, John Dingell, and Ronald Wyden. Quality review does improve firm adherence to professional standards and, thus, the quality of professional practice. Accounting and audit failures will be reduced through quality review.

The relationship between the profession and government can and should be improved. Perhaps we can convince the leaders of the profession and members of Congress to work together. After all, we share the same objectives. Let's now look at how the profession's leadership might better guide us into the twenty-first century.

LEADERSHIP FOR TOMORROW

To make self-governance work, the profession needs to improve relations with congressional committees, the SEC, and other regulators. The present relationships are cautious and, in some instances, acrimonious. To improve them the profession is going to have to drop its veil of secrecy. Keeping quality review results from the public is indefensible. The public relies on the independent accountant's report and, as a result, has a right to know the quality of the firm that prepared the report. In addition, the profession is going to have to become more responsive, proactive, and receptive [Prager and Cala, 1990].

Being responsive to the scrutiny of a congressional committee, SEC staff member, or other regulator means answering questions quickly and candidly. Members of Congress, SEC staff, and other regulators, as well as any of us, want to be well thought of and feel important. Being responsive makes people know they are important. Some of the obvious acrimony in *The Accounting Establishment* might have been avoided had some of the Big Eight firms been more forthright. The large accounting firms now realize that "big business" is subject to continuing public scrutiny. In addition, there seems to be significant support for opposing anything that is large. This is part of the reason people are dissatisfied with government.

The profession also needs to take the initiative with regulators. A proactive profession would provide information before it is requested. The AICPA leadership should be requesting committee hearings to offer updates on the profession's self-regulatory efforts. This would surely convince at least some members of Congress that the profession is in good hands. The AICPA's efforts have been commendable, considering that it is essentially a voluntary organization. Proactive leadership will come with commensurate costs. We should be prepared to pay the bill.

Proactive leadership will need to address several unresolved issues. The appearance of independence is an important one. It will mean more than a program to educate consumers of accounting information. It will require us to change our behavior. Professional failures need to be discussed and the causes corrected. Where possible, the number of alternative accounting practices should be narrowed. State laws governing licensing need to be amended to require more experience and quality review.

We also need to be more receptive to the regulators' suggestions. While much of *The Accounting Establishment* is irritating at best, we have to admit that some of its allegations and recommendations are correct. To respond as we have in the past, by denouncing the entire effort, is less than ethical. Mandated quality review happened for one reason: governmental dissatisfaction with substandard service quality. Many of the expectation gap standards happened for the same reason. Accounting principles also have been influenced and, as a result, reflect economic reality better than ever before.

For the foreseeable future, peer and quality review are here to stay. Firms with public clients must belong to the SECPS. Others must choose between the PCPS and the AICPA quality review program. This choice is discussed in Chapter 3.

REFERENCES

AICPA Professional Ethics Executive Committee. *Exposure Draft: Omnibus Proposal of Professional Ethics Division Interpretations and Rulings*. New York: AICPA, 8 November 1991.

AICPA Professional Standards, Volume 1. "Illegal Acts by Clients," AU 317. New York: AICPA, June 1992.

———. "Evidential Matter," AU 326. New York: AICPA, June 1992.

Burton, J. C. "A Critical Look at Professionalism and Scope of Services." *Journal of Accountancy* (April 1980): 48–56.

Carey, J. L., and W. O. Doherty. *Ethical Standards of the Accounting Profession*. New York: AICPA, 1966.

Cost Accounting Standards: A Guide to the Background, Objectives, Operations and Pronouncments of the Cost Accounting Standards Board. New York: Price Waterhouse & Co., 1976.

Covaleski, M., M. Dirksmith, and J. Heian. "Formal and Informal Management Control in Professional Bureaucracies: An Extended Institutional Theory Perspective." Working Paper, The Pennsylvania State University, University Park, 1989. Cited in McNair, C. J. "Proper Compromise: The Management Control Dilemma in Public Accounting and Its Impact upon Auditor Behavior." *Accounting Organizations and Society* 16, No. 7 (1991): 635–53.

Davies, J. *CPA Liability: A Manual for Practitioners*. New York: John Wiley & Sons, 1983.

DeAngelo, L. "Auditor Independence, Low Balling, and Disclosure Regulation." *Journal of Accounting and Economics* (August 1981): 113–27.

DeJong, D. V. "Class-Action Privileges and Contingent Legal Fees: Investor and Lawyer Incentives to Litigate and the Effect on Audit Quality." *Journal of Accounting and Public Policy* (1985): 175–200.

"Don't Retreat on Deregulation." *Nation's Business*, September 1990, 23–26.

Financial Accounting Standards Board. *Statements of Financial Accounting Concepts*. Homewood, Ill.: Irwin, 1988.

Huber, P. "Junk Science in the Courtroom." *Scientific American* (June 1992): 132.

Kelly, T., and L. Margheim. "The Impact of Time Budget Pressure, Personality, and Leadership Variables on Dysfunctional Auditor Behavior." *Auditing: A Journal of Practice & Theory* 9, No. 2 (Spring 1990): 21–42.

McCabe, R. K. "Predicting Satisfaction of Division for CPA Firms' Members." *Atlantic Economic Society Best Paper Proceedings* 1, No. 1 (January 1991): 102–105.

McCarroll, T. "Who's Counting?" *Time*, 13 April 1992, 48–50.

McNair, C. J. "Proper Compromise: The Management Control Dilemma in Public Accounting and Its Impact upon Auditor Behavior." *Accounting, Organizations and Society* 16, No. 7 (1991): 635–53.

Magill, H., and G. Previts. *CPA Professional Responsibilities: An Introduction.* Cincinnati: South-Western Publishing Co., 1991.

Margheim, L., and K. Pany. "Quality Control, Premature Signoff, and Underreporting of Time: Some Empirical Findings." *Auditing: A Journal of Practice & Theory* (Spring 1986): 50–63.

Marxen, D. A. "A Behavioral Investigation of Time Budget Preparation in a Competitive Environment." *Accounting Horizons* (June 1990): 47–57.

Mautz, R. K., and J. C. Martin. *Duties of Junior and Senior Accountants.* New York: AICPA, 1953. Cited in Buckley, J. W., and M. H. Buckley. *The Accounting Profession.* Los Angeles: Melville Publishing, 1974.

"Medicine: Regulations Lacking in Lucrative Field." *Los Angeles Times*, 23 December 1991, A1, A25–A26.

Miller, H. M. "What's Ahead in Regulation." *Industry Week*, 17 October 1988, 70–74.

Prager, A. J., and J. J. Cala. "Coexisting with Regulators." *The Journal of Business Strategy* (January/February 1990).

Public Oversight Board. *A Special Report: What Is the QCIC? What Is Peer Review? What Is the POB? What Is Self-Regulation?* New York: POB, 1991.

Simon, D. T., and J. R. Francis. "The Effects of Auditor Change on Audit Fees: Tests of Price Cutting and Price Recovery." *The Accounting Review* (April 1988): 255–69.

Stevens, M. *The Big Eight.* New York: Macmillan, 1981.

Subcommittee on Oversight and Investigations of the House Committee on Energy and Commerce. *SEC and Corporate Audits.* Washington, D.C.: U.S. Government Printing Office, 1985.

Subcommittee on Reports, Accounting, and Management of the Senate Committee on Governmental Operations. *The Accounting Establishment: A Staff Study.* Washington, D.C.: U.S. Government Printing Office, December 1976.

Turnpen, R. A. "Differential Pricing on Auditors' Initial Engagements: Further Evidence." *Auditing: A Journal of Practice & Theory* 9, no. 2 (Spring 1990): 60–76.

U.S. General Accounting Office. *CPA Audit Quality: Inspectors General Find Significant Problems, Report to the Chairman, Legislation and National Security Subcommittee, House Committee on Government Operations.* Washington, D.C.: U.S. GAO, 1985.

Wallace, W. A. "Peer Review Filings and Their Implications in Evaluating Self-Regulation." *Auditing: A Journal of Practice & Theory* 10, no. 1 (Spring 1991): 53–68.

Waller, W. S., and W. L. Felix, Jr. "The Auditor and Learning from Experience: Some Conjectures." *Accounting Organizations and Society* 9, no. 3/4 (1984): 383–406.

3

Division (Peer) or Quality Review

The AICPA has led the profession's effort to develop and maintain self-regulation through peer and quality review. In 1977, it established the Division for CPA Firms and the QCSC. The division has two sections: the PCPS and the SECPS. SECPS membership is mandatory for firms that audit public companies, provided one or more AICPA members are associated with the firm.

In 1988, the AICPA membership approved mandatory practice monitoring for all firms. Two approved practice-monitoring programs exist: the AICPA Division for CPA Firms and the AICPA quality review program. The division refers to its reviews as peer reviews, while the quality review program refers to its reviews as quality reviews. Firms can fulfill their review requirement through either program. Firms without SEC clients must decide whether to join the PCPS or the AICPA quality review program. This chapter's focus is on that decision and its influencing variables. Specifically, this chapter examines the similarities and differences between the two programs. In addition, it looks at certain division membership advantages.

SIMILARITIES AND DIFFERENCES

The objectives and requirements of the division peer review and the quality review programs are so similar that it is difficult to tell them apart. They are both designed to improve the quality of accounting and auditing services provided by CPA firms. Both require a triennial review and adherence to the standards in SQCS 1. The AICPA Division for CPA Firms can terminate firm membership or impose sanctions on the firm. The quality review program, however, can only terminate the firm's enrollment in the program.

There are additional differences between the two programs. To join the PCPS, a majority of the firm partners must be CPAs, and each partner eligible for

AICPA membership must be a member. For the quality review program, only one owner must be an AICPA member.

Division firms must file annual reports with information on their professional staff, office locations, and number of SEC clients. The report also must include the name of the managing partner, firm fiscal year, and information about pending litigation. This report is publicly available. There is no similar reporting requirement for the quality review program.

Division firms have more stringent continuing professional education (CPE) requirements. The division requires firm professionals, both CPAs and non-CPAs, to complete a minimum of twenty hours of qualifying professional education every year. In addition, each professional is required to complete at least 120 hours every three years. The quality review program requires only 120 hours for AICPA members. Under the quality review program, then, firms may find it more difficult to defend their personnel assignment decisions, a quality control element, if they do not provide CPE to all professional staff.

The SECPS has, as explained in Chapter 1, a POB and a QCIC. The quality review program has neither this additional oversight nor an investigative committee. The sanctions imposed on division firms can include mandatory corrective actions, additional CPE, accelerated follow-up reviews, and admonishment. They also can include monetary fines and suspension or expulsion from membership. The quality review program does not have this same range of penalties, nor does it need it, since its primary mission is educational. It must, when persuasion fails, rely on the threat of expelling firm members from the AICPA.

Division reports are publicly available, so when a review report is modified, it certainly is in the firm's interest to agree to an accelerated follow-up review. In instances of report modification accompanied by appropriate monitoring, it should always be in the firm's best interest to request an accelerated review so that the report is removed from the public file.

This public availability of review results is the most important difference between division and quality review membership. Any division firm's review report, letter of comments, and comment responses are available through a telephone call to the AICPA. The AICPA also will send, if requested, the firm's membership application, its annual report, and information about peer review committee actions. Information on sanctions is available only if the executive committee approves making it available.

Results of quality reviews are confidential. Only the review team and those administering the review know the results. Under the confidentiality rules they cannot reveal their findings to anyone. After acceptance by the administering organization, firms can and should publicize their reports since they have earned the right to boast, and some firms do so. Receiving an unqualified report is a major achievement, and firms should broadcast their success.

In choosing between division peer review and quality review, firms must consider the implications of having their review results available for the asking.

Firms that provide quality service should consider joining the division since, at the moment, it offers secondary benefits not available from quality review.

It is doubtful that any firm managers believe their firms provide inferior quality service. There are, I'm sure, many who believe that quality, like beauty, is in the eye of the beholder and are not sure if they should risk making their review results public. A modified or adverse report that is made publicly available would be devastating to most firms. A careful reading of the recommendations contained in Chapters 5 and 6 should more than adequately prepare firms for peer and quality review. Chapter 7 covers what happens in the review, and this should be read as well.

The objectives and requirements of both programs are very similar. The public availability of review results is, however, an important difference. Nevertheless, division members have access to worthwhile secondary advantages, so let's discuss those next.

SECONDARY DIVISION MEMBERSHIP ADVANTAGES

The division's PCPS has more than 6,500 member firms and claims its membership has tripled since mandatory peer review began. Its membership is large, but it is substantially less than 10 percent of U.S. practice units. There must, however, be sound reasons that about 4,000 firms have joined this section rather than the AICPA quality review program since both choices have been available. When the quality review program began, there were about 2,200 firms in the PCPS.

The PCPS says firms have joined because it has "an established peer review program and significant other benefits" [PCPS, *Why You Should Join*]. There is something to be said for both assertions.

The PCPS, begun in 1977, does have a comparatively long history. Its program is established and seems to work well. An established program does give the division a comparative advantage because it is a recognized symbol of quality service. This was acknowledged in 1986 when the Rural Electrification Administration (REA) required that its borrowers have audits by firms participating in an approved practice-monitoring program. The GAO soon afterward followed with a requirement that firms doing audits under government auditing standards have external quality control reviews. This recognition probably resulted from evidence that quality control and review reduce incidences of substandard service. Also, the division did carry out a public relations campaign designed to persuade businesses of the quality of its members. It will take some time before the business community recognizes that quality review program members earning unqualified reports deserve the same level of esteem.

The quality review program benefited from the division's experience and based its materials on peer review checklists and procedures. It also was able to draw upon an experienced pool of reviewers when quality review began.

There are other differences between peer and quality reviews, but probably only reviewers can distinguish them well. For example, peer review emphasizes all nine quality control elements. These elements are discussed in detail in Chapter 5. However, for small firms, defined as those with ten or fewer professionals, fewer elements are tested. Small firm members of the PCPS have five elements—independence, consultation, supervision, professional development, and inspection—substantively tested. These elements plus acceptance and continuance of clients are tested for small firms that are members of the SECPS. In the quality review program, the elements of independence, consultation, supervision, and professional development are tested, regardless of the firm size.

The division publishes a brochure titled *Why You Should Join the Private Companies Practice Section* which cites a variety of other member benefits and services. It argues that the PCPS is committed to quality and excellence. It does not acknowledge, however, that all firms enrolled in approved practice monitoring must show they provide quality service.

The brochure also points out that the "peer review program was the prototype for the AICPA's practice monitoring requirement. It allows your firm to benefit from a process that has proven itself over time" [PCPS, *Why You Should Join*]. As already pointed out, the quality review program did benefit from the peer review experience. Peer and quality review processes are, however, almost identical. The major difference, public availability of review results, is perhaps the reason that PCPS membership stood at only a little more than 2,200 firms before the passage of mandatory review.

A genuine advantage to division membership is the section's similarity to a CPA association with the associated benefits. Like other CPA associations, it provides a means for its members to fulfill their review requirement. In addition, it has management of accounting practice programs to help members improve their practices. In these sessions, members share ideas on marketing, tax season strategies, profitability, and the like. Its TEAM-PLUS programs are designed for firms with up to ten professionals; it also has set programs for larger firms. While all firms are invited to attend these programs, they are frequented for the most part by division firms.

Not long ago the division published a very helpful marketing manual. For some reason it no longer does so. It provided many examples about how to inform bankers, attorneys, and clients of peer review's significance. The AICPA ought to consider publishing it again and making it available to quality review members as well.

The AICPA Division for Firms does produce and distribute brochures that speak to PCPS member excellence. One such brochure, *Recommending a CPA Firm: How to Pick a Leader*, is distributed to bankers and lawyers. It says, "Since your referral is as good as your word, you need to know you're recommending a CPA firm that's a leader in quality, integrity and services. That's why many bankers and attorneys turn to the members of the . . . PCPS of the American Institute of CPAs" [PCPS]. Much to the chagrin of Eli Mason and others, it clearly implies that PCPS member firms are better than other firms. (Eli Mason, a former AICPA vice-president objected strongly to the division's message that its members were the profession's elite. [See, e.g., Bremser, 1986.])

PCPS members also "can participate in a program that provides exclusive use of newsletters and other materials for clients and business acquaintances" [PCPS, *Why You Should Join*]. My experience with these materials generally was positive. They are well written and, best of all, current. They are not, however, as good as what firms themselves could produce, but small firms find it close to impossible to find the time to write them. The PCPS also publishes a directory of firms that it distributes to bankers, educators, and others. There is clearly a strong effort to demonstrate the superiority of PCPS firms.

The division provides additional services that benefit its members and others in the profession. The PCPS sponsors the newsletter *The Practicing CPA*, which provides timely advice on how to practice more efficiently. It also has the TIC, whose purpose is to review and comment on proposed standards from the perspective of local practitioners and their clients. The TIC was influential in bringing about acceptance of statements prepared on a basis other than GAAP. Also, it works closely with the FASB, ASB, and other AICPA committees.

The PCPS also organized the AICPA consulting review program, which is now administered by the quality review program and state societies. A consulting review is a confidential, high-spot review. Obtaining a consulting review is an important step in a firm's preparation for quality or peer review, and it is discussed in Chapter 6. Firms that join the PCPS and get a consulting review receive a discount of up to $350 on consulting review charges.

The PCPS does, then, offer secondary benefits to its members that are not available under the quality review program, as well as important services to the profession. The rationale for having two almost identical programs escapes me, however.

The critical question for practitioners is whether the PCPS benefits exceed the possible cost of an embarrassing review report that is publicly available. Before answering that question, let's examine anecdotal evidence of other benefits available from the PCPS.

OTHER PCPS BENEFITS

W. Robert Thompson cites several intangible benefits of undergoing peer review. These include: "(1) A feeling of achievement. (2) Confirmation of our belief that we do quality work. (3) Conveying this recognition of quality to staff . . ., clients and others" [Bremser, 1986: 92]. These benefits also should accrue to firms successfully undergoing quality review. While this is a speculative conclusion, the feelings of achievement may not be as great in quality review since the review results are not publicly available.

Thompson also cites certain direct benefits, including increased respect from clients, more referrals, and lending institution approval [Bremser, 1986: 92]. All these benefits should accrue to quality review members as well, but firms must make them happen. My firm experienced tremendous growth after its review because we let everyone know the meaning and import of peer review and how we did. So many firms ignore this golden opportunity to change client perceptions about the quality of the firm with which they are doing business.

"Overall, peer review and PCPS membership has a positive impact, both with regard to client retention and the morale of our personnel" ["News and Views," 1987: 6]. The same article maintains that peer review has led to staff retention, too. It is logical to conclude that if clients and staff understand the review process, they are more likely to stay with a firm that has proven it provides quality service.

My research on division members shows some interesting results [McCabe and Brennan, 1992]. A questionnaire was sent to a random sample of 254 division firm managing partners. Replies were received from 167 firms, a response rate of 68 percent after adjusting for undeliverables and responses received too late for inclusion. Managing partners were asked, among other things, about their perceptions of certain peer review incentives. The responses were scored on a five-point scale, with 1 representing a "strongly disagree" response and 5 a "strongly agree" response. Table 3.1 shows selected results.

The response to question 1 shows that review is perceived as a mechanism for encouraging better compliance with professional pronouncements, a necessary condition for improving professional service quality. The replies to question 3 suggest that a firm's ability to comply consistently with professional standards has been enhanced because its quality control system has improved. Question 9 shows that in some instances review is seen as increasing the quality of some firms' practices through increased ability to detect material misstatement. Together these responses indicating better compliance with professional standards, improved quality control, and increased ability to detect misstatements suggest that review is succeeding.

Improved confidence and morale, questions 2 and 4, are a result of successfully meeting the peer review challenge. This finding was not surprising since research shows that satisfaction is increased by feedback and certainly a review provides that [Argyle, 1989: 235]. Earning an unqualified report from a peer or quality review should do much to improve firm members' confidence and morale.

Most division firms believe membership has increased their professional standing in the CPA community. Also, many respondents (47 percent) believe membership is prestigious. Perhaps meeting the challenge of public review gives firms bragging rights.

Only a small, but still significant, percentage felt that membership helped attract top-quality employees and that they benefited from division services. Maybe the minimal effect on recruitment is due in part to the fact that some faculty are unaware of the import of review. Because accounting faculty do influence the decisions of students, it is imperative that they be advised of the significance of earning an unqualified review report.

Table 3.1
Perceptions of Peer Review Incentives (*N* = 167)

		Percentage that	
	Mean	Agree	Disagree
1/ Peer review provides the impetus to maintain the highest degree of compliance with professional pronouncements.	3.97	86.2	7.8
2/ Our experience with review has given us more confidence in our practices and procedures.	3.92	81.3	10.9
3/ Quality controls over the accounting and auditing practice have improved since becoming a division member.	3.83	77.7	18.1
4/ The firm's morale has improved.	3.31	45.7	21.1
5/ Division membership increased our standing among CPA firms in our community.	3.30	53.6	21.7
6/ The prestige from membership has been gratifying.	3.23	47.0	22.9
7/ Division membership helped us attract top-quality employees.	2.87	31.3	38.6
8/ We have benefitted from division services, such as brochures and FASB representation.	2.86	32.5	42.8
9/ Our ability to detect material misstatement in client financial statements has increased because of division membership.	2.68	30.7	48.8

Note: Managing partners responded to questions using a five-point Likert scale. The scoring was based on a continuum from "strongly disagree" (1) to "strongly agree" (5). The questions were balanced to guard against response set.

The study also asked managing partners about their attitudes toward peer review. Admittedly, this question is somewhat like asking Ford owners how well they like Fords. Only three firms (1.8 percent) expressed a negative attitude, so firms that have undergone review are very favorable toward it. Any car manufacturer would be pleased with this level of satisfaction. This finding should allay some of the anxiety of firms about to undergo their first reviews.

The study also found that the variables shown in Table 3.1 relate significantly to the partners' attitude toward peer review. Specifically, positive perceptions of quality rewards, such as increased compliance with professional pronouncements, an enhanced quality control system, and an increased ability to detect misstatements, were highly correlated with the partners' positive attitudes toward peer review. Also, positive perceptions of membership rewards, such as standing in the CPA community, prestige, and division services, were found to relate significantly to the positive perception of peer review.

The most important finding was that 98.4 percent of the respondents planned to stay in the division. Only one firm planned to switch to quality review, and two firms were uncertain. This high approval rating shows a strong level of organizational commitment.

WHAT'S BEST?

Deciding between the PCPS and the quality review program is not easy. The choice becomes confusing because of the large number of similarities. Their objectives and requirements are hardly distinguishable. Perhaps the following summary of advantages and disadvantages might be helpful.

A. *PCPS membership advantages*

  1. A recognized symbol of quality

  2. The value of division services, including

    a. Sessions designed to improve firm efficiency and profitability

    b. Brochures and directories touting member superiority

    c. Exclusive use of topical, current newsletters and single-subject flyers

  3. A consulting-review fee discount for firms joining the PCPS

  4. Enhanced self-esteem and standing in the CPA community after successfully facing the challenge of a public review

B. *PCPS membership disadvantages*

  1. Additional costs of

    a. AICPA membership, required for each partner eligible for membership

    b. CPE for all professional staff

    c. Membership and review

  2. Disclosure of

    a. Review results

    b. Pending litigation

Firms that design and set up quality control systems following the guidelines contained in Chapter 5 should not have any difficulty with a peer or quality review. A properly designed and installed quality control system is an absolute necessity to prevent substandard service. Also, if firms follow the ten steps to a successful review outlined in Chapter 6, they should not have any difficulty passing a peer or a quality review.

The only drawbacks that remain, besides review result availability, are the additional costs of AICPA membership for all eligible partners and CPE for all professional staff, and possibly a difference in membership dues and review costs. I doubt if there are many firms in which all partners are not already AICPA members. The AICPA's life insurance program makes membership a bargain for many of us. As to providing CPE for all professional staff, I do not know how a firm in good conscience could do otherwise.

PCPS annual membership dues are $25 per CPA, including partners, up to a maximum of $500. SECPS firms pay $16 per professional staff member, with a $100 minimum. There is a $500 maximum for firms with less than five SEC clients, but no maximum for SECPS firms with five or more SEC engagements. The annual dues for the quality review program are set by the state societies. Overall they appear to be somewhat less than PCPS dues.

There may also be a difference in review costs between peer and quality reviews. Peer reviews test more elements than do quality reviews, so their review charges are probably higher. The AICPA, however, has decided to publicize the costs together rather than separately, so it is not possible to know. The author was unsuccessful at setting current average PCPS review costs versus quality review costs, though this information is probably available to those at the AICPA.

The decision to join the division's PCPS or the quality review program comes down to commitment. Certainly my study found a high level of commitment to the division. Social scientists say the following about commitment: "Conceptually, it can be characterized by at least three factors: (a) a strong belief in, and acceptance of the organization's goals and values; (b) a willingness to exert considerable effort on behalf of the organization; and (c) a strong desire to maintain membership in the organization" [Porter et al., 1974: 604]. This commitment to the division also is a commitment to the profession.

The profession has faced and will continue to face severe criticism for the secrecy that surrounds the review process. For example, in 1986, U.S. Comptroller General Charles A. Bowsher, in testimony before Subcommittee on Oversight and Investigations of the House Energy and Commerce Committee, called for a reduction in the secrecy that surrounds the peer review process ["Washington Update," 1986: 60]. Further, some CPAs certainly believe review results should not be shrouded in secrecy. The AICPA passed a resolution requiring firms that audit public companies to be SECPS members in order for the individuals in the firms to retain their AICPA memberships. The SECPS, like the PCPS, requires public availability of review reports. I strongly doubt this resolution passed because AICPA members believed that a public investor has a right to more information about the quality of the company's accountant-auditor than does an investor in a nonpublic company. Admittedly, its passage was certainly influenced by the SEC proposal to require practice monitoring and public disclosure of review results, which if enacted would have been a major step toward eliminating self-regulation. It also passed because some members believe that the public has a right to know about the quality of the professional services it pays for. Firm managers facing the decision on whether to join the Division for CPA Firms or the quality review program need to decide if they, too, favor public availability of review results. Perhaps those firm managers who are apprehensive about making their firm results available should first undergo a few quality reviews and then join the division.

Review is an integral part of maintaining and improving firm quality. The value obtained from a review depends in large part on the quality of the firm's reviewer. The importance of selecting the right reviewer and how to do it is the focus of the next chapter.

REFERENCES

Argyle, M. *The Social Psychology of Work*. London: Penguin Books, 1989.

Bremser, W. G. "Peer Review: What's Happening and What's to Come." *The Practical Accountant* (July 1986): 87–98.

McCabe, R. K., and T. Brennan. "Self-Regulation: Can It Be Preserved?" Paper presented at the Western Regional Conference of the American Accounting Association, San Jose, Calif., 1 May 1992.

"News and Views." *The CPA Journal* (September 1987): 4, 6.

PCPS. *Why You Should Join the Private Companies Practice Section*. New York: AICPA.

————. *Recommending a CPA Firm: How to Pick a Leader*. New York: AICPA.

Porter, L., R. Steers, R. Mowday, and P. Boulian. "Organizational Commitment, Job Satisfaction, and Turnover among Psychiatric Technicians." *Journal of Applied Psychology* 59 (1974): 603–60. Cited in Mottaz, C. J. "An Analysis of the Relationship between Work Satisfaction and Organizational Commitment." *The Sociological Quarterly* 28, no. 4 (1987): 541–58.

"Washington Update." *Journal of Accountancy* (August 1986): 56, 60, 62, 64.

4

The Importance of Selecting the
Right Reviewer and How to Do It

About 10,000 to 12,000 firms will undergo quality review each year. Based on my study of AICPA Division for CPA Firms members, obtaining a helpful or value-oriented review depends largely on the person doing it. Therefore, careful attention should be given to selecting the firm's reviewer.

Many firms are unaware of the benefits associated with a peer or a quality review. A review should, of course, lead to an improved quality control system and increased compliance with professional pronouncements. As pointed out in Chapter 3, it also should improve firm morale as well as increase firm members' confidence and efficiency. Greater efficiency should result in higher profits.

Firms facing their first reviews suspect they will incur substantial costs. Firms having subsequent reviews already know the costs are significant. AICPA membership and reviewer fees are costly. There also are equally important intangible costs. All firms are apprehensive about their ability to pass their reviews no matter how often they have already done so. Yes, it does get easier, but it never gets easy. The process is always anxiety ridden.

Division members' experiences show that the benefits do exceed the associated costs. Careful selection of the reviewer will help assure this outcome.

This chapter puts the pluses and minuses of an on-site quality review into perspective. (On-site reviews are required for all firms that perform one or more audits or examine prospective financial statements. Off-site reviews are allowed for firms that provide only compilation and review services.) The chapter also will discuss ways to avoid the obstacles to a good review and offer tips on how to find the right reviewer.

Since the costs of quality review are a major concern, let's discuss that issue first.

REVIEW COSTS

Most firms find the annual dues and review fees burdensome. This is particularly true, and correctly so, for small firms. It is the old economies-of-scale predicament. While review fees are based mostly on the reviewed firms' accounting and audit hours, the relationship is not exactly linear. Fees for small and medium-sized PCPS members in 1989 ranged from a low of $1,000 to a high of $15,000. For example, in 1989, fees for firms with six to ten professionals averaged $4,566. For the calendar year 1991, however, the average cost for PCPS and quality reviews for firms with six to ten professionals was $3,507. As explained, the AICPA is not now publicizing PCPS and quality review costs separately. The reduction of the average cost by about $1,000 is probably due, in part, to lower quality review fees. The quality review program tests a smaller number of elements than does the division.

An equally important cost factor is the time firm members must devote to the many aspects of peer review. Staff hours are used in preparing for and participating in the review. Client files need to be checked for completeness, and firm and client profiles must be prepared. Key personnel must be available during the review. The estimated cost of the time spent preparing for and participating in my first review was about $8,000. Of course, this was not all out-of-pocket, but we did need to work more overtime. At these prices, it is logical to expect more than a stamp of approval. A good review, fortunately, does bring significant unforeseen benefits to the firm.

REVIEW BENEFITS

The primary purpose of review is to improve the quality of AICPA member firms' accounting and auditing practices. As discussed in Chapter 3, the author's study of 167 division members showed that peer review is perceived to improve practice quality. Table 3.1 showed that a large majority (77.7 percent) of the responding members believe their quality control systems have improved as a result of peer review. Further, an overwhelming majority (86.2 percent) thought peer review provided the impetus to maintain the highest degree of compliance with professional pronouncements. Based on the perceptions of these reviewed firms, then, the review process does improve the quality of accounting and auditing practices.

Of equal importance was the finding that a majority (60.6 percent) believed their reviewers provided suggestions that helped the firm operate more efficiently or effectively. A significant percentage (26.1 percent) thought their reviewers did not provide positive suggestions, while the remainder were not sure. Finding a good reviewer, then, is critical, but it should not be too difficult.

The quality of the reviewer can make the difference between a quality control system that is efficient and one that is not so efficient. For example, the reviewer may suggest that the firm use one of the published compilation, review, and audit practice guides. These guides contain easy-to-use preparer, reviewer, and disclosure checklists. Since publishers keep these guides reasonably current, the firm need no longer spend substantial time updating internally produced checklists. Checklists also can be important time savers on recurring engagements and can provide evidence about documentation. Properly completed preparer and disclosure checklists can and do spare reviewers the exacting, time-consuming process of reviewing the entire file, provided, however, that the reviewer relies on them. Suggestions such as these do result in greater efficiency and, therefore, greater profits. They also result in higher-quality work.

Perhaps more important, my research shows there is a relationship between the quality of the reviewer's suggestions and the peer review rewards. Table 4.1 shows the correlation coefficients between the quality of the reviewer's suggestions and the various rewards available from division membership. The higher the coefficient, the stronger the relationship. Table 4.1 also shows the significance level, with low or zero levels indicating high significance. In fact, all of the relationships are positive and statistically significant.

Item 1 indicates that there is a statistically significant positive relationship between positive reviewer suggestions and managing partner perceptions of increased compliance with professional pronouncements.

Item 2 suggests that the quality of the reviewer's suggestions is related to perceived increases in firm member confidence in the firm's practices and procedures. It is expected that a reviewer who does a meticulous review will have a greater positive effect on firm confidence than will one who performs a superficial review. A perfunctory review cannot increase firm members' faith in their work.

To limit the likelihood of cursory reviews, the AICPA quality review program requires reviewers to complete programs and checklists, including engagement checklists. "Failure to complete all relevant programs and checklists in a professional manner creates the presumption that the review has not been performed in conformity with the Standards for Performing and Reporting on Quality Reviews" [Quality Review Executive Committee, 1991: QRP, 3000.28]. Firms that receive cursory reviews are being shortchanged, and so is the profession.

Reviewers with good communication skills are more likely to inspire firm members' confidence in themselves. Most reviewers uncover quality control deficiencies. A reviewer who can explain the nature of the deficiencies and offer clear suggestions to correct them provides immediate help in improving the quality control system. An improved system will mean more confidence in firm practices.

Similarly, a reviewer who provides fitting suggestions on improvements in efficiency will influence firm confidence. Reviewer input that leads to greater efficiency makes the firm more successful. This success and the related feelings of achievement help to increase confidence.

As expected, item 3 suggests that the quality of the reviewer is positively related to perceived improvements in the firm's quality control system. And

Table 4.1
Correlation between Reviewer Suggestions and Peer Review Rewards (N = 167)

	Correlation	Significance
1/ Peer review provides the impetus to maintain the highest degree of compliance with professional pronouncements.	.28	.000
2/ Our experience with review has given us more confidence in our practices and procedures.	.32	.000
3/ Quality controls over the accounting and auditing practice have improved since becoming a division member.	.26	.000
4/ The firm's morale has improved.	.23	.001
5/ Division membership increased our standing among CPA firms in our community.	.18	.011
6/ The prestige from membership has been gratifying.	.42	.000
7/ Division membership helped us attract top-quality employees.	.27	.000
8/ We have benefited from division services, such as brochures, FASB representation, etc.	.32	.000
9/ Our ability to detect material misstatement in client financial statements has increased because of division membership.	.40	.000

morale improvement (item 4 in Table 4.1) is related to the quality of the reviewer's suggestions. The challenge of a review and its successful completion will have a positive effect on the esprit de corps. Each person in the firm will feel better about the quality of his or her own work and the work of fellow employees. These feelings often lead to greater cohesiveness among the people in the firm, which research shows can enhance productivity [Argyle, 1989: 241]. And more productivity means higher profits.

As with increased confidence, increased morale is more likely to result from successful completion of a meticulous review. It is far more satisfying to finish a task that is difficult than one that is less challenging.

A reviewer can influence firm morale in another way by demonstrating that firm success is a result of each person's efforts. For instance, a good reviewer will involve as many of the staff in the review as is practicable. As in any audit, inquiries of nonmanagement professional staff provide insights into the control system operation that cannot be acquired in other ways. Professional staff will be interviewed on the nine elements of quality control: independence, personnel assignments, consultation, supervision, hiring, professional development, advancement, acceptance and continuance of clients, and inspection. Also, the reviewer will invite all professional staff to the exit conference, when an unqualified report is to be issued. In this conference, the reviewer will discuss the findings and recommendations that will be included in the letter of comments. He or she also will make it clear that a successful review depends on each and every firm member. This affirms the importance of not only one's individual work, but also the work of fellow employees.

Item 9 in Table 4.1 is extremely important. It shows a high correlation between the quality of the reviewer's suggestions and the firm's ability to detect material misstatement in client financial statements. Reviewers are contributing to increases in firm efficiency and also are helping firms to be more effective.

Another significant finding in the study was member firms' favorable opinions of peer review. The evidence suggests that this positive overall assessment is the result of the accumulated benefits that firms experience from peer review. These benefits depend at least partially on reviewer quality. The association between a member firm's perceptions of reviewer quality and its attitude toward peer review was .28 ($p = .000$). A thorough review and thoughtful suggestions on how to improve efficiency and effectiveness lead to improved quality control, greater adherence to professional standards, more firm confidence, increased morale, and other review benefits.

However, there are obstacles to a good review. These barriers can impede the efforts of even the best of reviewers, but they can be overcome.

OVERCOMING OBSTACLES TO A GOOD REVIEW

As in any engagement, the reviewer is trying to get the job done within budget. The AICPA has developed budget guidelines based on the reviewed firms' accounting and auditing hours. Currently, it recommends that quality reviews should take significantly less than 1 percent of the firm's accounting and audit hours. Thus, if the firm spends 5,000 hours in these areas, the review should take between 25 and 40 hours to complete. Peer reviews are budgeted at 1 percent because more quality control elements are emphasized. Meeting this guideline can be difficult. For example, the firm may have a diverse clientele requiring specialized expertise. It also may operate in several locations and have several partners.

The reviewer is encouraged to consider several factors in the client engagement sample. These include the number of partners, engagements requiring specialized expertise, firm offices, and types of engagements. For example, if the firm prepares personal financial statements or financial forecasts, one or more of these engagements probably will be selected. Also, if the firm has governmental audits subject to the so-called yellow book standards or not-for-profit, financial institution, voluntary health and welfare organization, or construction contractor audits, the reviewer typically is expected to select as least one engagement from each type. In addition, the reviewer must examine a representative sample of compilation, review, and audit engagements by office and partner. Typically, the review should cover between 5 and 10 percent of engagements and total accounting and audit hours. The reviewer will not necessarily do page-by-page review of the engagement, but he or she will include all the key engagement areas.

Such special circumstances leave little, if any, time for the reviewer to make observations about firm efficiency. This time deficiency will hinder review quality.

Communication

Communication between the reviewer and the firm can help overcome these obstacles. While Chapter 6 offers details about these communication matters, a brief discussion here might be helpful. The firm should provide the reviewer with a complete firm profile one to two months before the review begins to allow time for proper engagement planning. Firm managers should discuss with the reviewer the best dates for the review to begin, the twelve-month review period to be covered, and the anticipated exit conference date. (The review must begin no later than the date set by the AICPA or the state sponsoring association.) The firm and the reviewer also must have an understanding about the scope of the review. If there are scope limitations because of litigation or the disposal of parts of the practice, the reviewer needs to know this. These limitations may, of course, result in a modified report. As important, the reviewer must be told if firm members want observations about how to practice more efficiently or effectively.

Steps to Take

Time spent planning the review will help prevent obstacles to a good review. Again, detailed suggestions will be given in Chapter 6, but a brief overview is useful here because it will help the firm overcome the obstacles to a value-oriented review. "Identify the individual—usually a partner—who will be responsible for acting as a liaison with the review team" [Quality Review Executive Committee, 1991: QRP 4100.04]. Complete the firm profile well before the review. A firm profile will include, at a minimum, the following:

1. A completed quality control policies and procedure questionnaire (One of the purposes of Chapter 5 is to convince you to prepare a quality

control document as well because, at a minimum, it makes completing the questionnaire easy.)

2. A summary of accounting and audit hours on each engagement and of hours spent by office location and partner, and so on

3. Copies of any relevant manuals and checklists

4. A listing of the firm's professional personnel, showing each person's name, position, and years of experience.

Firms should check with their reviewers about other information needed for planning purposes. Based on information the firm provides, the reviewer will make a tentative selection of engagements to be reviewed. The firm must then complete client profiles on those engagements and gather and assemble continuing professional education and personnel files in order to have them readily available on request. The reviewer probably will not provide a list of all engagements that will be selected. He or she will choose additional engagements on arrival, so client profile sheets must be prepared on these as well. The reviewer will compare the quality of the preselected engagements with that of the engagements chosen later to assure the firm has not "cleaned up" its workpapers. To avoid this problem, many reviewers select the engagements after their arrival. The firm also must collect and assemble the necessary documentation on consultations with outside parties and independence confirmations. Finally, it must make all professional staff available to the reviewer. Communication and planning, plus full firm cooperation before, during, and after the review, are the keys.

The reviewer will periodically prepare Matters for Further Consideration (MFC) forms that document quality control concerns. These MFCs typically cover issues related to noncompliance with GAAP, GAAS, and SSARS; insufficient engagement documentation; and departures from the firm's quality control policies and procedures. The reviewed firm needs to respond to matters addressed in MFCs as quickly as possible.

During the review, plan to "live" with the reviewer. By living with the reviewer throughout the day and at breakfast, lunch, and dinner, firm managers expand their opportunities to discuss engagement deficiencies. They also gain opportunities to discuss marketing strategies, personnel practices, and the like. Investing time and energy in the review will produce greater rewards.

Good reviewers do provide suggestions on how to increase firm efficiency and effectiveness. There are several obstacles to obtaining the right reviewer, but these can be overcome, too. Let's now discuss how to find the right reviewer for the firm.

FINDING THE RIGHT REVIEWER

For on-site peer (division) reviews, firms have four alternatives:

1. Reviews by committee-appointed review teams (CARTs),
2. Firm-on-firm reviews,
3. Reviews by associations of CPA firms, or
4. State society–sponsored reviews.

A CART is selected by the AICPA computer system, which matches firm and reviewer specialties. It also considers the size and location of the reviewed firm. This can be a real hit-or-miss proposition since the firm has little or no input into the reviewer selection. Here are two examples of what can happen.

When my former firm joined the PCPS, we had a CART review. The reviewer did a thorough job and provided invaluable suggestions on staffing, marketing strategies, and ways to increase productivity. The firm was very fortunate to get this reviewer. He was competent, had experience, and clearly cared about the profession. This helped us to improve our quality control system and to operate more confidently, efficiently, and profitably.

In contrast, another firm that had a CART review did not understand the nature of the quality control deficiencies uncovered in the review. Firm members did not believe the reviewer showed much interest in being helpful. As a result, firm managers did not know how to respond to the reviewer's letter of comments, and, more important, they did not know what to do to correct the deficiencies.

Fortunately, division and personal experience indicate the latter is the exception. This experience does, however, underscore the importance of playing an active role in selecting a reviewer.

Perhaps some of the other alternatives are preferable to a CART review. State society reviews, however, also offer firms little control over the choice of the reviewer. Firms should contact their state societies to inquire how selections are made. CPA association reviews do offer some choice about the reviewer, but the options may be limited.

For firms that are not members of a CPA association, the best alternative is a firm-on-firm review. The advantages are choice and cost. Having a choice "minimizes concerns about possible competition from reviewers and the danger that reviewers may use their knowledge to attempt a merger or acquisition" [Botwin, 1989: 74]. "The firm-on-firm approach has particular appeal if the reviewed firm can locate a firm that is quite similar to itself and a bit larger, so that they can provide advice or suggestions related to the reviewed firm's next level of growth" [Weinstein, 1989: 42]. The cost of firm reviews is competitive with CART rates. Selecting the firm, however, is much like finding a top-quality employee. It takes time, persistence, and good intuition. The key, of course, is to get references and conduct a thorough interview.

For on-site quality reviews, firms have three options: firm-on-firm, CPA association, and state society–sponsored reviews. There are no CART reviews under quality review.

The best way to start a reviewer search is by asking CPAs at firms that have already been reviewed. State society personnel and quality review experts are other good sources. In addition, the AICPA Division for CPA Firms has a member directory that can help locate reviewed firms. The division also publishes an annual firm-on-firm directory that lists member firms interested in performing quality or peer reviews. Some state societies publish a similar directory.

Firm management should identify a number of reviewed firms and then contact and interview each one. Who performed the review? Was it worth the costs? Are firm members more confident about their practices and procedures? Did firm morale improve? Was it a thorough review? Do firm managers recommend the reviewer? Why?

Management should contact four or more recommended reviewers. First, make sure that the reviewer is qualified. For SECPS reviews the team captain must attend a peer review course in 1992 or later. "Both the introductory AICPA training course titled 'How to Conduct a Review Under the AICPA Practice-Monitoring Programs' and the advanced AICPA course 'Current Issues in Practice Monitoring' will fulfill this requirement" [AICPA, "New Training Requirement for SECPS Peer Review Captains," 1992: 6]. For PCPS and quality reviews the team captain must have completed an approved AICPA training course conducted in 1986 or later.

The partners should provide the prospective reviewer with a firm profile. If firm and reviewer specialties match, they should go on to explain exactly what they believe the review should encompass. They should make it clear they want a thorough review. Quality review findings are confidential, so no matter how poor a firm's system might be, it is not necessary to fear an in-depth review. Quality review is not meant to be punitive. The review's thoroughness does, however, probably relate directly to the degree of quality control improvement. Management also should emphasize that it is seeking suggestions about how to improve firm efficiency and effectiveness.

Firm managers are now cast in the role of a potential client. They should listen intently and determine the following:

1. Will this person perform a meticulous review?
2. Does he or she care about the profession?
3. How much experience does this person have?
4. Are this person's communication skills adequate?
5. Is this an individual with whom firm members can establish rapport?

Individuals who perform reviews usually do so because they care about the profession. Reviews are decent off-season work, but they will not provide a reviewer with a high standard of living. To determine the reviewer's commitment to the profession, firm management should ask the reviewer's opinions of quality and peer reviews. Does he or she believe reviews are necessary? Why? The responses provide a sense of the depth and breadth of the reviewer's feelings about the profession. All in all, a person who is interested in improving the profession will offer a more satisfying review.

Experience is repeatedly the best teacher. A reviewer should not only be skilled in accounting and auditing, but also be experienced in ways to improve a firm's efficiency. A reviewer who has frequently tried and failed to improve efficiency has also probably found a few ways that work. The key to success in most endeavors is experience. Others describe the key to success as "massive failure," which is just another way of saying that experience provides lessons learned.

Good communication skills also are necessary. A reviewer who can clearly express his or her findings and recommendations serves the firm and the profession. Unfortunately, there often is no correlation between experience and the ability to communicate that experience. Do not rely, then, simply on the number of years of experience.

Rapport between the reviewer and firm members may be the most important attribute. Does the reviewer listen without interrupting and respond to firm members' concerns? Listening without interrupting shows respect, which is critical to establishing rapport. Do firm managers and the reviewer have similar interests and experiences? Managers should seek common ground. They should not give up their search until they have found the appropriate level of compatibility. Other reviewed firms' experiences suggest the chances are quite good of finding a reviewer who cares about the profession, is meticulous, is experienced, has good communication skills, and is compatible with firm managers.

Remember, meticulous reviewers do a thorough job. Is the firm's control system up to standards? It may be strongly advisable to compare the firm's system with what is described in the following chapter. Chapter 5 maintains that a firm that understands quality control and then puts this understanding in writing is well on the way to providing professional-quality service.

REFERENCES

Argyle, M. *The Social Psychology of Work*. London: Penguin Books, 1989.

Botwin, B. S. "Arranging for a Successful Review." *Journal of Accountancy* (December 1989): 72–80.

McCabe, R. K., and K. W. Lantz. "Selecting a Value-Oriented Reviewer." *The CPA Journal* (July 1991): 74–75.

"New Training Requirement for SECPS Peer Review Captains." *The CPA Letter*. New York: AICPA, November 1992, 6.

Quality Review Executive Committee, American Institute of Certified Public Accountants. *AICPA Quality Review Program Manual*. Chicago: Commerce Clearing House, 1991.

Weinstein, S. "Part 2: Your Quality Review: A Step-by-Step Approach." *The Practical Accountant* (June 1989): 37–53.

5

Understanding + A Quality Control Document + The Proper Tone at the Top = Professional-Quality Service

The purpose of this chapter is to describe and clarify SQCS 1. At the conclusion of this chapter, firms should be able to design and implement a control system that works for them. To assist firms, Appendix 5.A contains a set of policies with guidelines to consider in establishing procedures that should be considered along with SQCS 1 and its interpretations. To clarify quality control, the relationships among the nine control areas are emphasized. Then the importance of the proper tone at the top is discussed. First, let's take a look at why quality control is necessary.

IS IT NECESSARY?

Some argue that quality control may not be necessary for every firm. Pattillo [1984: 3] says it is only for firms that want to

- Retain clients
- Stay out of court
- Improve profits
- Toot their own horn
- Improve the profession
- Avoid professional sanctions

It is debatable whether a quality control system will help a firm keep clients or improve profits. Some clients simply want the lowest price, and clients that do not appreciate quality are probably not worth serving. Profits may decrease, at least in the short term, as a result of implementing a control system. In the long term, however, profits should return to normal and may, in fact, increase as the firm learns to rely on and use the system.

A quality control system may help a firm stay out of court because a well-designed and well-executed system will reduce incidences of accounting and audit failure. It is, without a doubt, an absolute necessity to survival in this litigious society. A firm that finds itself in court as a result of substandard service will have a better chance of defending its work if it also has a well-designed and well-implemented system. Allegations of gross negligence or reckless disregard of professional standards will be much more difficult to prove if the firm has a suitable control system.

Also, fewer accounting and audit failures certainly will help the profession's image. A firm that has an appropriate quality control system also will avoid professional sanctions. Whether the loss of AICPA membership is enough of a sanction still must be determined. A firm that has decided to forgo AICPA membership in order to avoid a review of its control system may have a much more difficult time defending itself in court. In particular, a firm that does not have a quality control system or subject itself to quality review is already demonstrating disregard of professional standards. The AICPA would not come to its defense except in the most unusual circumstances. It also is likely that such a firm would find it more difficult to recruit expert witnesses to support it.

The bottom line on whether a quality control system is necessary simply depends on whether the firm wants to comply with professional standards. Compliance with auditing and accounting and review standards depends totally on the effectiveness of the control system. A quality control system does limit instances of substandard service by providing the firm with reasonable assurance that its accounting and audit services comply with professional standards. It does not provide absolute assurance, nor could it, because of the inevitable mistakes in judgment and other kinds of human errors.

UNDERSTANDING SQCS 1

The authoritative guidance covering quality control is contained in SQCS 1. Some complain that the statement is so conceptual that it is difficult to understand. While many fuss about the theoretical nature of FASB standards, they do not compare in difficulty with this statement. Also, SQCS 1 deals with how to do what it is firms do. Like most professionals, CPAs do not relish being told what to do and, in particular, how to run their practices. Yet the standards do tell practitioners how to do their jobs. The combination of highly conceptual guidance that is difficult to understand and standards that tell professionals how to practice has caused resentment.

SQCS 1 identifies nine related elements that a firm should consider in establishing its quality control policies and procedures: independence, personnel assignment, consultation, supervision, hiring, professional development, advancement, acceptance and continuance of clients, and inspection.

In a very limited way, the elements resemble GAAS. For example, GAAS general standards cover the auditor's responsibilities to assign audit personnel and to be independent. The field work standards address supervision. GAAS, however, applies to the auditor's responsibility in an audit. The auditor must conduct the audit in accordance with GAAS. The quality control elements, on the other hand, deal with firm policies and procedures that provide reasonable assurance that the appropriate staff will be assigned to an engagement, that personnel will follow the independence rules, and so on. The quality control system produces the firm's compliance with GAAS or SSARS.

The quality control elements are tightly related. For example, a firm that hires recent accounting graduates must have a strong supervision policy and a well-developed professional development policy. It also should take great care in assigning personnel to engagements and have a complex advancement policy because it hires entry-level people. Conversely, a firm that hires only experienced CPAs would probably not be as concerned about personnel assignment and would probably require much less engagement supervision.

A quality control system is made up of policies and procedures, assignments of responsibilities, a communication system, and a monitoring requirement. Policies are the firm's objectives and goals under each quality control element. Procedures are the steps taken to fulfill the policies. A firm's quality control document, then, often will have multiple policies for each element and multiple procedures for each policy.

To achieve its quality control objectives, the firm must assign responsibility for carrying out its procedures. For example, one person or a group should identify situations requiring consultation so the firm can achieve its consultation objectives. Further, an individual or group should be designated to resolve independence issues.

The firm's quality control objectives can be achieved only through an effective communication system. For example, a firm must inform the professional staff of its consultation policy and situations requiring consultation. Further, professional staff must know of situations and clients to which the independence rules apply. Without communication, the control system cannot operate.

The quality control system's elements need to be checked periodically to provide assurance that the system is operating as planned. Too often, firms set procedures and find some time later that people are not using them. This check also uncovers events that call for changes in the system. For example, firm growth, employee turnover, and changes in the client mix each suggest the need for system reevaluation.

Each of the nine elements or functional areas in a firm's quality control system has one or more policies. Each policy usually has several procedures. Finally, each element involves, besides policies and procedures, assignments of responsibilities, a communication system within the firm, and periodic monitoring.

Firms can and do have quite different policies and procedures. They differ because ''the nature and extent of a firm's quality control policies and procedures depend on a number of factors such as its size, the degree of operating autonomy allowed its personnel and its practice offices, the nature of its practice, its organization, and appropriate cost-benefit considerations'' [*AICPA Professional Standards*, Volume 2, 1992: QC§ 10.06]. Firms have much latitude in designing their control systems. Generally, large, multi-office, mature firms have very complex quality control documents. These multi-office, multi-partner firms serve a diverse clientele and have a professional staff with divergent experience; thus, they need a rigorous control system to prove the work quality. At the other extreme, a small firm with experienced professionals serving a limited clientele would need a much simpler control system. In fact, the small firm's system might not even be covered in writing. Each firm is required, however, to have a quality control system that incorporates the nine elements.

Cost-benefit concerns must be addressed. The main benefit of the quality control system is, of course, that it will limit instances of substandard service. The system's cost can be substantial if it is not carefully designed. To help assure system success, the firm should assign certain responsibilities to individuals or groups. For example, rather than asking all partners to be experts on independence, it is more efficient and effective if one individual is expected to be proficient in resolving these issues. Also, firms can choose not to use easily attainable and well-developed planning, review, and disclosure checklists that document certain aspects of engagement supervision. They can, instead, rely on each engagement partner to have a perfect memory about professional standards and spend the extra time to review an engagement without the benefit of staff-prepared checklists. Either approach is probably effective, but the former is more efficient.

Communication and monitoring also are important considerations in helping to assure system success and efficiency. Perhaps the most important factor in balancing the cost-benefit equation is an understanding of all system elements. As a starting point, then, let's first review the basic elements of a quality control system.

The Nine Interrelated Functional Areas

Independence is the first functional area listed in SQCS 1. This is not surprising because of its importance to the profession's reason for being. Without independence, the justification for our services diminishes substantially. SQCS 1 requires firms to develop policies and procedures ''to provide reasonable assurance that persons at all levels maintain independence to the extent required by the rules of conduct of the AICPA'' [*AICPA Professional Standards*, Volume 2, 1992: QC§ 10.07a].

The firm should have independence policies covering adherence to the rules and interpretations of the AICPA, state society, state board of accountancy, and other applicable regulatory agencies. Responsibility for maintaining independence needs to be assigned to appropriate personnel. The firm's policies and the engagements to which the independence rules apply must be communicated to the firm's professional staff. In addition, these policies need to be incorporated into the firm's professional development area. Also, the firm needs to assure itself that it is independent on its engagements and should include a policy under supervision that requires a discussion of the importance of independence in the engagement planning process. Further, supervision should require that a check be made in the engagement review process to determine if client receivables have taken on the attributes of loans. Finally, independence needs to be incorporated into the firm's hiring policy by including an appropriate independence module in the new staff orientation program.

Engagement personnel assignment is the second element. Firm policies and procedures should "provide reasonable assurance that the work will be performed by persons having the degree of technical training and proficiency required in the circumstances" [*AICPA Professional Standards*, Volume 2, 1992: QC§ 10.07b].

Assignment of engagement personnel is connected to independence. For example, a firm that assigns experienced personnel to an engagement is providing itself with limited assurance that the firm will be independent because experienced personnel are more likely to be aware of the profession's independence requirements. The assignment element also is related to the firm's policies on supervision and professional development. For example, the planned level of engagement supervision directly affects the decision on people to be assigned to the engagement and vice versa. Since some firms emphasize on-the-job training as an integral part of their professional development programs, personnel assignment takes on a new aspect in addition to such considerations as staff availability, engagement risk, and required expertise.

Consultation is the third element. The standard requires the firm and its personnel to seek help from knowledgeable sources, who also are in positions of authority, when faced with new or uncertain situations. In addition, it requires firms to furnish the resources to do the appropriate research. A key resource is an adequate library. Another is access to technical issues specialists, both within and outside the firm.

The firm's consultation policy is associated with and dependent on its policies on hiring, professional development, supervision, and assignment of engagement personnel. For example, firms that hire entry-level people must have very strong consultation policies. This will require a complete library, identification of situations requiring consultation, and access to technical issues specialists. In addition, since documentation of a consultation is usually required, the firm's professional development and hiring policies must incorporate a provision for the necessary training. The firm also will have to distribute comprehensive and frequent summaries of new pronouncements under its professional development policy. Further, it frequently will have to update its work programs and checklists under its supervision policy. Finally, greater care will have to be given to engagement assignment.

Supervision is the fourth element. The firm must establish policies and procedures that help assure it is meeting professional standards and its standards of quality. To achieve supervision objectives, firms often require professional staff to complete extensive work programs and checklists covering planning, review, and disclosure matters. In addition, supervision encompasses such activities as instructing assistants, keeping informed of problems encountered, reviewing work, and settling differences of opinion.

Supervision is strongly associated with the firm's hiring, personnel assignment, and professional development policies. For example, firms that hire entry-level personnel need to exercise strong supervision and be much more careful in their assignment decisions. Small firms generally need to give more consideration to staff qualifications and abilities than do larger firms when making engagement assignments because they tend to have less well developed audit, review, and compilation programs. As a result, they must either be more careful about personnel assignments or rely on some of the well-designed programs from the AICPA and other publishers.

A firm's supervision policies also depend to a large degree on its professional development policies. In general, less supervision is necessary when a firm has a strong professional development policy. Well-trained personnel require less supervision.

Hiring, the fifth element, involves policies that outline minimum employment qualifications, procedures used to evaluate prospective employees, and the authority to make employment decisions. A firm's hiring policies directly affect, among other things, the amount of supervision needed, professional development, consultation, and diligence in assigning engagement personnel.

Professional development, the sixth element, is critical to rendering quality service in every profession, and especially in accounting. Keeping current with the profusion of increasingly complex FASB and ASB statements is no easy task. It is the firm's responsibility to devise policies and procedures that will provide assurance that its personnel receive required CPE and, more important, that they are competent in their assigned tasks. To do this, the firm must take steps to assure that staff receive the appropriate CPE courses. Again, a firm's hiring and supervision policies affect the amount of attention it must pay to its professional development policy.

The seventh control element is advancement. Its purpose is to encourage firms to establish criteria for promotion and to periodically evaluate employees' performance based on those standards. The evaluation process strengthens engagement supervision by connecting an individual's performance to his or her chances for advancement.

SQCS 1 requires the establishment of criteria "to provide the firm with reasonable assurance that those selected for advancement will have the qualifications necessary for fulfillment of the responsibilities they will be called on to assume" [*AICPA Professional Standards*, Volume 2, 1992: QC§ 10.07g]. It instructs firms to evaluate an employee's character, intelligence, judgment, and motivation. Few would disagree that these are desirable attributes for people as they move up the ladder in the firm. The obvious problem, of course, is, how does one define character and judgment? And, as important, how are those characteristics measured? Some characteristics are more easily measured and, perhaps, are more persuasive. Certainly a staff person's ability to get along well with clients and to beat the budget are measurable and important. But guidance on defining and measuring good judgment and character still is desperately needed. Perhaps some of the more memorable and embarrassing cases in accounting history would not have happened if it were possible to accurately evaluate these attributes.

The eighth element, acceptance and continuance of clients, is, perhaps, the most important area. It is intended to minimize the likelihood of doing business with a client that lacks integrity. It also is there to remind the firm of the need to assess whether it is competent to handle the client.

Accounting and audit failures often occur in connection with clients that lack integrity. Firms that believe careful assignment and close supervision of personnel will protect them from accounting and audit failure are in for some surprises. Intelligent, inventive clients that lack integrity, but not opportunity, have a better than even chance of deceiving the auditor. This was certainly illustrated in the recent MiniScribe case. "Indeed, the 1989 investigation by MiniScribe's outside directors concluded that Coopers (Coopers & Lybrand) had been victimized by management fraud" [Berton, 1992: A1]. It is no longer acceptable to assess simply whether the firm is capable of serving the client and whether the bill will be paid when deciding to accept or continue to do business with a client.

The responsibility to detect irregularities and illegal acts heightens the importance of this eighth control element. Great care needs to be taken in deciding who it is the firm serves.

The firm's personnel assignment, consultation, supervision, hiring, and professional development policies are affected by its acceptance and continuance policies. A firm that is willing to take on high-risk engagements must, for example, have stronger assignment, supervision, and professional development policies.

The last element is inspection. It requires firms to analyze compliance with quality control policies and procedures annually. That includes an analysis of the appropriateness of the system's design. For example, firm growth, firm mergers, and the addition or discontinuation of key personnel will require changes to the system. Inspection also includes procedures to test and evaluate system operation. These procedures involve an examination of engagement, administrative, and personnel files. Chapter 6 provides detailed suggestions on how to do an inspection.

To provide professional-quality service, firms need to understand the nine control elements and their interrelationships and to include quality service as an important firm goal. The discussion above about each control area and the appendix to this chapter provide firms with the information necessary to design a suitable system. To make the system work, however, CPA firms must have the proper tone at the top.

THE TONE AT THE TOP

A well-designed and well-implemented quality control system is imperative in order to limit substandard service. This system, however, will be only as good as the tone set at the top. Quality control depends on the proper mix of a worthwhile quality control strategy and the appropriate example at the management level.

"The National Commission on Fraudulent Financial Reporting, commonly known as the Treadway Commission, considers the tone set by top management—the corporate environment or culture—to be the most important factor contributing to the integrity of the financial reporting process" [Evers and Pearson, 1989: 97]. A similar statement can be made about CPA firms. The tone set by CPA firm management is the most important influence on the quality control system's integrity.

Firm leaders set the wrong tone when they focus on growth as their primary goal. Some firms should not be providing accounting and audit services or, for that matter, tax or MAS. These firms reward the rainmakers and shun those with technical competence. They also use audits as loss leaders and expect staff to meet unattainable time budgets. Substandard service is the result.

Firms that see profits as their primary goal should not be providing accounting and audit services either. Some of these firms expect staff to do the work, but not charge the time. They also overload partners, so that planning, supervision, and review suffer.

Growth and profitability are both worthwhile goals. They cannot, however, supersede quality service. When they do, service quality drops, and the profession bears the burden.

Some firm leaders get out of date, and this sets the wrong tone at the top too. Whether this is a function of age, an attempt to provide too many services, lack of resources, or the like is unclear. Some people are old and set in their ways at thirty-five, while others never seem to get old. Many people believe that what they learned as undergraduates, ten or fifty years ago, is enough to carry on a professional practice today. The reason is that some people are not eager to learn. Firms owned by people without a desire to keep abreast of technological developments have the wrong tone at the top. These firms use outdated procedures because they simply duplicate last year's workpapers. They overaudit cash and underaudit inventory. They are, in fact, providing low-quality services.

Another sign of the wrong tone at the top occurs in new firms. Newly established firms are often made up of partners who, because of their backgrounds, use different approaches to providing accounting and audit services. The lack of a consistent approach causes confusion among the staff and substandard service results.

Fortunately, most firms emphasize and take pride in offering high-quality accounting and audit services. As a result they have, in the main, effective quality control systems and, thus, provide professional-quality service. But not all firms specialize in accounting and auditing or, as important, take pride in providing these services.

Some firms emphasize and take pride in providing high-quality tax services. In fact, many of these firms are very good at what they do. Because they specialize in tax, they might not believe quality control is for them. Problems occur when these firms also try to provide accounting and audit services. The result is substandard service because these firms simply are not prepared to offer these services.

It is uncertain why good tax firms want to provide accounting and audit services. Maybe they believe CPA firms always provide accounting and audit services. That is, of course, the general case, but it should not be. Some firms are good at tax, others at client advisory services, and others at accounting and auditing. Very few firms are good at providing all three. Firms should concentrate on their areas of expertise. After all, that is what the client pays for, expects, and deserves.

Tax firms have a special problem because tax laws require that too many business entities and essentially all individuals have calendar year-ends. This compresses tax work into a short period of time. Because of this, these firms may feel compelled to provide accounting and audit services to keep busy during the slow season. Perhaps if congressional tax writers understood the trouble caused by requiring so many calendar year-ends, they might be persuaded to spread the workload over the year. This might convince some firms to stick to their strengths, which means in some cases providing only high-quality tax services.

A similar dilemma occurs when firms emphasize and take pride in providing MAS. It is often sporadic, so the temptation to provide continuing accounting and audit services to pay the bills may be irresistible. Without a commitment to provide high-quality accounting and audit services and a written quality control document, the management is setting the wrong tone at the top.

Firms specializing in tax or client advisory services certainly have a right to do so. They also need a quality control system in order to provide consistent quality service, regardless of the product. They, like accountants and auditors, need to be concerned about personnel assignment, consultation, supervision, hiring, professional development, advancement, acceptance and continuance of clients, and inspection. They should not, however, be providing accounting and audit services.

Understanding quality control, developing a quality control document, implementing and monitoring the quality control system, and setting the proper tone at the top are all necessary to provide professional-quality service. Once these things are done, the firm is ready for its quality or peer review. (The next chapter discusses how to plan for that review.)

APPLYING QUALITY CONTROL

The QCSC has issued a guide for applying SQCS 1 [*AICPA Professional Standards*, Volume 2, 1992: QC§ 90]. It furnishes examples of quality control document policies and procedures. The guide is a very helpful source for firms considering writing or revising their documents.

Some firms have trouble in applying the guide to their practices. Critics say the guide does a poor job of differentiating between policies and procedures. For example, the guide describes some policies using the words "provide procedures for" (see especially the supervision section of QC§ 90).

Alternative explanations or versions of an idea are sometimes helpful. What is presented in the appendix, then, is a set of policies with guidelines to consider in establishing procedures. It may be helpful to firms considering writing or revising their quality control documents. It emphasizes the relationships among the elements and, like the guide, addresses the issues of assignment of responsibilities, communication, and monitoring. It is not as comprehensive as the AICPA guide, but it does capture its essence. It is by no means meant to be definitive. Readers developing or revising their firm's documents are encouraged to compare the AICPA guide with what follows and, as important, to review other firms' documents.

REFERENCES

AICPA Professional Standards, Volume 1. "Training and Proficiency of the Independent Auditor," AU 210. New York: AICPA, June 1992.

———. "Independence," AU 220. New York: AICPA, June 1992.

———. "Planning and Supervision," AU 311. New York: AICPA, June 1992.

———. "Audit Risk and Materiality," AU 312. New York: AICPA, June 1992.

———. "Communication between Predecessor and Successor Auditors," AU 315. New York: AICPA, June 1992.

———. "The Auditor's Responsibility to Detect and Report Errors and Irregularities," AU 316. New York: AICPA, June 1992.

———. "Illegal Acts by Clients," AU 317, New York: AICPA, June 1992.

———. "Working Papers," AU 339. New York: AICPA, June 1992.

———. "Adequacy of Disclosure in Financial Statements," AU 431. New York: AICPA, June 1992.

———. "Part of Audit Performed by Other Independent Auditor," AU 543. New York: AICPA, June 1992.

AICPA Professional Standards, Volume 2. "Independence," ET §§ 101 and 191. New York: AICPA, June 1992.

———. "Statement on Quality Control Standards 1, System of Quality Control for a CPA Firm," QC§ 10. New York: AICPA, June 1992.

———. "Quality Control Policies and Procedures for CPA Firms: Establishing Quality Control Policies and Procedures," QC§ 90. New York: AICPA, June 1992.

Berton, L. "How MiniScribe Got Its Auditor's Blessing on Questionable Sales." *Wall Street Journal*, 14 May 1992, A1, A3, A5.

Committees of the SEC Practice Section. *SECPS Reference Manual*. New York: AICPA, 1992.

Evers, C. J., and D. B. Pearson. "Lessons Learned from Peer Review." *Journal of Accountancy* (April 1989): 96–102.

Loscalzo, M. "Preparing for Quality Review." *The CPA Journal* (December 1988): 24–30.

Pattillo, J. W. *Quality Control and Peer Review—A Practice Manual for CPAs*. New York: John Wiley & Sons, 1984.

Appendix 5.A
Quality Control Policies with Guidelines to Establish Procedures

This quality control document uses the same format that the QCSC used in its Guide to Establishing Quality Control Policies and Procedures [see *AICPA Professional Standards*, Volume 2, 1992: QC§ 90]. Policies are identified by number, and the guidelines to appropriate procedures are identified by letter. The first sentence after the letter describes the procedure. Following this are suggestions on how to carry out the procedure and issues that need to be considered in its formulation. The suggested quality control document contains sections that are redundant, but this cannot be avoided because of the elements' interdependence.

Independence

1. All personnel will adhere to the firm's independence rules, to the rules and interpretations of the AICPA, and to the pronouncements of the firm's state society, state board of accountancy, and other applicable regulatory agencies.
    a. Appoint an individual or group to provide guidance and resolve independence questions. Because of the importance of independence, the managing partner is often assigned this responsibility. Also, for reasons of efficiency and effectiveness, it is usually advisable to restrict this responsibility to a small number of people.
    b. Ensure that the person charged with resolving independence questions obtains periodic written confirmations from the professional staff. (A suggested confirmation requirement is provided in part 8a below.)
    c. Document all independence questions and their resolution in written memoranda and keep them in an administrative file. (An administrative file documents the firm's compliance with its independence requirements.)
2. The firm will maintain a library of professional, regulatory, and firm independence materials that is adequate to resolve independence questions.
    a. Appoint an individual to review periodically the adequacy of the library to determine if it contains AICPA, SEC, state association, and other applicable regulatory independence requirements. Encourage the reviewer to document this review and evaluation. This documentation, along with notes about the follow-up, should be kept in the administrative file. The review should occur periodically and at a minimum yearly with the firm's annual inspection.
3. The firm will review before report issuance the status of the client's accounts receivable to find out if independence has been impaired by outstanding amounts taking on the attributes of loans.
    a. Appoint an individual, usually the engagement partner, to do the investigation. This procedure should be included on the reviewer's checklist.
4. All professional personnel will be informed of the firm's independence policy and the situations and clients to which it applies.

a. Communicate the firm's independence requirements through firm manuals, training programs, memoranda, and engagement planning sessions and in firm meetings. For example, the requirements could be included in the firm's personnel, audit, or accounting manuals. Some firms may choose to advise personnel in firm meetings or engagement planning sessions. The pitfall with these approaches is the lack of documentation. To overcome this problem, prepare written agendas for firm meetings, or use checklists in engagement planning. Also, the importance of independence, particularly independence in mental attitude, should be communicated in staff training programs and in engagement planning meetings.

b. Periodically distribute a list of clients to which the independence requirements apply. This can be done by sending a list of new clients to all professional staff, announcing the names of new clients at staff meetings, posting the new client list in a conspicuous place, and so on.

5. The firm will emphasize in staff training programs and in engagement planning sessions the importance of the AICPA Code of Professional Conduct and, in particular, independence in fact, as well as in mental attitude.

a. Include requirements for professional ethics courses in the firm's professional development program.

b. Add to planning checklists a step for documentation of independence issue discussion.

6. Firms engaged to audit segments of a client must be independent.

a. Obtain an annual written confirmation from such firms. A step could be included in the audit program requiring such a confirmation.

b. Advise professional staff of engagements requiring independence confirmation. This could be accomplished by including in the client's permanent file a memorandum detailing this requirement.

7. The firm will integrate its independence requirements with its personnel assignment, hiring, and supervision policies.

a. Ensure that an appropriate independence module is included in the new staff orientation program.

b. Include in the orientation program a procedure requiring professional staff to sign an independence confirmation within thirty days after employment.

c. Verify that the firm's planning and review checklists, if applicable, contain appropriate independence questions. For example, the following two questions could be included on a reviewer's checklist:

   i. Were the professional staff advised about the need to exercise independence in mental attitude and to be independent in fact?

   ii. Was a confirmation obtained from other firms engaged to audit segments of the entity?

8. The firm will periodically review compliance with its independence policies and procedures, and evaluate whether changes to the system are necessary.

a. At least annually get from all professionals a signed confirmation of their awareness of the firm's independence requirements and the clients to which these rules apply. This confirmation should include a statement that ''they or their family members do not have investments or relationships with any client that could impair independence'' [Loscalzo, 1988: 24].

b. Assign an administrative person the responsibility to determine that all independence confirmations are signed promptly and added to the administrative file.

c. Ask the independence coordinator to periodically review and document firm compliance with the documentation requirement.

d. Periodically evaluate whether changes should be made to the firm's policies and procedures. Events that might bring about a reevaluation include firm growth, the addition of practice offices or key personnel, changes in hiring policies, employee turnover, and retirements.

Assigning Personnel to Engagements

1. The firm's objectives in engagement personnel assignments are to complete each engagement as effectively and efficiently as possible, given the size and complexity of the engagement, the risk involved, the expertise required, the planned level of supervision, the timing of the work, the need for continuity and rotation of personnel, and personnel availability.

   a. Assign responsibility for personnel assignments. Typically, small firm managing partners make all engagement personnel assignments. In large firms, administrative personnel handle the scheduling, based on engagement requirements, which include complexity, risk, planned level of supervision, and staff availability.

2. Staff assignments will integrate the guidelines and requirements of the firm's professional development program.

   a. Consider individual development needs in staff assignments. On-the-job training is one of the most important benefits of the profession and one of the main reasons the profession attracts the best people to it. This policy is perhaps most important for smaller firms because much of their training occurs on the job and because they use formal CPE courses to develop competence in other service areas, such as tax.

3. Staff assignments will integrate the firm's guidelines on engagement supervision and rotation.

   a. Consider the firm's requirements for planned level of supervision and engagement rotation in staff assignments. Firms that use detailed, comprehensible preparer and disclosure checklists; compilation, review, and audit programs; and audit and accounting manuals already provide significant engagement supervision. These firms will have much more latitude in personnel assignments. On the other hand, firms that do not use checklists and programs must show that staff have the appropriate experience and training to perform the assigned tasks.

4. The firm will advise all personnel of its engagement assignment policy.

a. Accomplish this by using firm manuals, training programs, memoranda, engagement planning sessions, and discussions in firm meetings.

5. The engagement partner will approve scheduling and staffing in writing.

a. Require the partner to consider engagement complexity and the planned level of supervision in assignments. This step can be included on the firm's engagement planning checklist.

6. The firm will periodically review compliance with its assignment policies and evaluate whether changes are necessary.

a. Periodically select an engagement, and check whether it was performed effectively and efficiently as well as its degree of conformance with the firm's personnel assignment goals. The person given overall responsibility for assigning personnel to the engagement is probably in the best position to do this. Occasionally, however, a partner other than the engagement partner should do it in the interest of objectivity.

b. Evaluate periodically the need for changes to the firm's policies and procedures. Events that might trigger a reevaluation include firm growth, the addition of practice offices or key personnel, employee turnover, retirements, and changes in the employee mix or related policies, such as hiring or supervision, changes in the types of engagements, and so on.

Consultation

1. All professional staff, including partners, will seek help from authoritative sources in complex, specialized, and other uncertain areas.

a. Appoint an individual or group to decide on areas and specialized situations requiring consultation. These might include, for example, filings with the SEC and other regulatory agencies, and engagements in specialized industries, such as financial institutions and health care. It also would include the application of new technical pronouncements and unusual accounting and auditing problems. It might involve certain complex situations, such as statistical sampling and calculation of deferred taxes and post-retirement obligations. The firm's philosophy ought to be this: When in doubt, consult. And this should be communicated to all personnel.

b. Appoint consultation service specialists.

c. Determine the specialists' authority and how disputes between specialists and engagement personnel are to be resolved. Some firms name the audit or the engagement partner as the ''authoritative source.''

2. The firm will document all situations requiring consultation.

a. Prepare memoranda in all situations requiring consultation. Describe all facts and issues, list applicable authoritative sources, report the firm's final position, and support the conclusion by citing appropriate authoritative sources.

b. Include copies of the required consultation memoranda with the engagement working papers and in the client's permanent file for future reference.

3. The firm will maintain library resources sufficient to conform with professional standards so practice problems can be researched.

a. Appoint an owner to oversee maintenance of the firm's library and individual practice office libraries. For individual offices, the partner in charge usually takes responsibility. The library would include, at a minimum, *AICPA Professional Standards*, Volumes 1 & 2; *FASB Original Pronouncements and Current Text*; *AICPA Audit and Accounting Guides* related to the firm's clients; *Codification of Original Pronouncements: Governmental Accounting and Financial Reporting Standards*; and *FASB Emerging Issues Task Force (EITF) Abstracts*. It also should include *AICPA Technical Practice Aids*, including Statements of Position and *AICPA Accounting Trends and Techniques*. The library should contain certain accounting journals, including the *Journal of Accountancy*, *The CPA Journal*, and *The Practical Accountant*. Current textbooks on financial accounting, auditing, statistical sampling, and cost accounting also should be on hand. SECPS member firms have additional needs, which include "Regulation S–X, copies of the 1933 and 1934 Securities Act, Accounting Series Releases Looseleaf Services—CCH or Prentice-Hall, Printers' services—Bowne Booklets or Pandick Press, Inc., SEC Docket or SEC News Digest, SEC Updates, SEC Accounting Report or Securities Regulation and Law Report" [Loscalzo, 1988: 26]. SECPS firms should also consider subscribing to the AICPA's Total On-Line Tax and Accounting Library (TOTAL). TOTAL provides current authoritative literature on accounting, auditing, and SEC regulations. In addition, it provides the full text of corporate annual reports for over 4,000 companies.

4. All personnel will be advised of the firm's consultation policy.

a. Address consultation requirements in firm manuals, training programs, memoranda, engagement planning sessions, and meetings. Requirements should identify areas or situations in which firm members must seek consultations. They also should include the firm's documentation requirements.

b. Periodically communicate the names of specialists and their areas of expertise. The firm also may want to advise the staff of the AICPA Technical Hotline service and its 800 number. It is probably best, though, to encourage or require that the firm research a matter thoroughly before contacting outside sources.

c. Periodically issue memoranda or discuss at staff meetings new areas requiring consultation and changes in specialists.

5. There should be a periodic review of the firm's consultation policies, including the adequacy of documentation of consultation situations, and of the reference materials, and the need to develop consultation relationships with other firms.

a. Appoint an individual to conduct regular reviews and evaluations of the firm's consultation policies and procedures, the library's adequacy, and the use of external sources. Many firms have very helpful consultation arrangements with other firms. Reevaluations may be triggered by firm growth, the addition of practice offices or key personnel, employee turnover, retirements, and changes in the employee mix or in the types of engagements and in related policies, new FASB statements, new SASs, and so on.

Supervision

1. All professional staff will be appropriately supervised. Supervision will involve "instructing assistants, keeping informed of significant engagement problems encountered, reviewing the work performed, and dealing with differences of opinion among firm personnel" [*AICPA Professional Standards*, Volume 1, 1992: AU 311.11].

    a. Appoint an individual or group to develop firm supervision guidelines and procedures. The guidelines should serve to identify supervision levels, areas requiring supervision and evidence to support supervision as well as cover identification of engagement risk.

    b. Assign responsibilities for engagement planning, overall supervision, and review. This usually is assigned to the engagement partner.

2. Engagement planning will be adequately supervised.

    a. Assign responsibility to develop firm engagement planning procedures, guidelines, and documentation requirements. These often can best be incorporated into planning checklists and audit and accounting manuals. Planning is required on all engagements, including compilations. In a compilation, planning may involve only a discussion with the client about changes in the client's business, the effect of competition, and so on. It is the "how's business" question. Planning issues in audits include:

        i. Guidelines for the nature, extent, and documentation of client background information. SAS 22, Planning and Supervision, provides important guidance [*AICPA Professional Standards*, Volume 1, 1992: AU 311].

        ii. Guidance in forming preliminary judgments about materiality levels. For example, some firms establish a certain percentage of income, such as 5 percent, as a suggested criterion in determining materiality.

        iii. Guidance for evaluating inherent and control risk. Some firms use checklists to evaluate inherent risk, and almost all use them to evaluate control risk.

        iv. Firm guidance on acceptable audit risk, tolerable errors, acceptable risk of overreliance, and so on.

3. The firm will require ongoing engagement supervision.

    a. Provide written guidance on the form and content of working papers, and the use of appropriate work programs and checklists. Comprehensive and understandable checklists, forms, and programs are available from the AICPA and several other publishers. The advantages of these packaged approaches probably outweigh the disadvantages for small and medium-sized firms.

    b. Ask the engagement partner to provide ongoing engagement supervision.

Engagement tasks should be assigned based on the planned level of supervision and the staff person's training, ability, and experience.

4. Engagement review is an important element in supervision. The firm will execute appropriate review procedures at all levels.

   a. Assign responsibility to develop review scope and procedures for each level of audit, review, and compilation engagements. On many engagements, seniors review the work of those with less experience, managers review seniors' work, and partners review managers' work. In these situations, guidance must be provided for each level of engagement review and for each kind of engagement. The individual or group given overall responsibility should consider the following:

      i. The need for concurring review on high-risk engagements and first-time audit engagements, as well as on SEC engagements.

      ii. The amounts and kinds of experience necessary to do reviews at each level for each kind of engagement.

      iii. The requirement that seniors and managers duplicate on a limited test basis the exact procedure done by someone under their supervision. This might help deter some of the undiscussable behaviors (e.g., sign-off or audit procedures that were not done) that occur on engagements. Duplication of tests was once a very common practice.

      iv. Evidence necessary to document workpaper and report review. This might include initialing workpapers, issuing a review memorandum, and completing a reviewer's checklist.

      v. Procedures to determine that the work done supports the conclusions reached. This may mean simply emphasizing the importance of a critical review at all levels.

      vi. Procedures to determine that the report complies with professional standards. A report reviewer's checklist might be useful.

      vii. Procedures to resolve differences of opinion and the related documentation. Typically, firms require staff to send the engagement partner a memorandum that outlines the issues and points of contention. The engagement partner is charged with resolving the differences and documenting its resolution.

   b. Assign responsibility to design and set up report and financial statement review procedures. These should be emphasized because of their importance in a peer or a quality review. Reviewers first review the accountant-auditor's report and the client financial statements. Consideration should be given to requiring the following in the engagement review process:

      i. A review of the client's permanent file. This file usually contains copies or excerpts of new leases, employee contracts, pension profit-sharing changes, new accounting systems, and so on, each of which affects the financial statements.

      ii. A review of proposed adjusting entries, waived adjustments, memoranda on consultation or significant accounting issues, completed checklists and programs for appropriate responses, and key financial statement workpapers, such as inventory for a manufacturing company. The reviewer also should be required to examine other key engagement areas, such as difficult areas from previous periods, events requiring the application of new SFASs and SASs, and the key areas identified in the planning memorandum.

   iii. Preparation or use of a disclosure checklist for the report and the financial statements.

   iv. A thorough review of the report and the financial statements.

  c. To document review scope, require personnel to initial workpapers, issue a review memorandum, and complete a reviewer's checklist.

  d. Assign a person or group responsibility for periodically monitoring the firm's review procedures.

5. Supervision policies will be communicated to all professional staff.

  a. Convey the firm's supervision requirements in firm manuals, training programs, memoranda, engagement planning sessions, and meetings. Manuals and planning sessions should include illustrations of workpapers, documentation requirements, checklists, and questionnaires.

6. The firm will periodically review its compliance with supervision policies and evaluate whether changes to policies and procedures are necessary.

  a. Appoint an individual to select an engagement, perhaps randomly, and evaluate its degree of conformance with the firm's supervision policies.

  b. Require the individual or group assigned responsibility for engagement supervision to evaluate periodically the necessity for changes to the firm's policies and procedures. Events that might bring about a reevaluation include firm growth, the addition of practice offices or key personnel, employee turnover, retirements, changes in employee mix and in related policies (such as assignment of engagement personnel), changes in the types of engagements, new SASs, new FASB statements, and so on.

Hiring

1. The firm will ''maintain a program designed to obtain qualified personnel by planning for personnel needs, establishing hiring objectives, and setting qualifications for those involved in the hiring function'' [*AICPA Professional Standards*, Volume 2, 1992: QC§ 90.18–1].

  a. Appoint a person or group to plan the firm's personnel needs. The plan should detail the firm's hiring objectives based on current and forecasted service levels. It also should recognize the effects of staff advancement, turnover, and retirement on the firm's hiring goals.

  b. Authorize individuals to make employment decisions.

  c. Appoint an individual or group to formulate methods of attracting qualified people to the firm and to set minimum employment qualifications. This might involve establishing good relations with colleges. Minimum qualifications might include an accounting degree, a minimum overall grade

point average, above-average interpersonal and communication skills, prior work experience, and other achievements. The firm must be aware of and follow federal and state economic opportunity laws and regulations.
2. The firm will have clear personnel objectives.
   a. Communicate personnel aims in personnel manuals or in firm meetings.
3. Firm members will be advised of personnel needs.
   a. Communicate needs in memoranda and staff meetings. One of the best sources for attracting qualified personnel to the firm is the existing staff.
4. The firm will coordinate its professional development, supervision, and advancement policies with its hiring objectives.
   a. Appoint an individual or group to coordinate the firm's personnel qualifications with its professional development, supervision, and advancement policies. A firm's hiring practices dictate to a large extent its professional development and supervision needs.
5. The firm will periodically check the efficiency and success of its hiring program and whether policy changes are needed.
   a. Appoint a person to evaluate the hiring program and to recommend possible improvements. Events that should cause a reevaluation include firm growth, employee retirements and terminations, changes in related policies (such as supervision and professional development), changes in client mix, and so on.

Professional Development

1. The firm's professional employees will follow AICPA and other applicable CPE requirements.
   a. Appoint a CPE compliance manager. This person will decide on a reporting year.
2. The firm's professional employees will keep abreast of new accounting and auditing pronouncements, be adequately trained for their assignments, and meet the firm's needs for technical expertise and industry specialization.
   a. Appoint an individual or group to integrate the firm's personnel assignment, advancement, hiring, and supervision policies into the professional development program. Critical to professional development goals is the requirement that firm personnel be adequately trained to carry out their assigned tasks. Considering its hiring and supervision practices, the firm should ascertain the nature and extent of professional development courses needed to provide assurance that its professional staff can carry out their assigned activities.
   b. Base employee evaluations in part on compliance with regulatory CPE and firm recommendations. In the periodic evaluation, advise employees about future expectations.
   c. "Distribute technical pronouncements to . . . staff and make available specialized literature and training for those involved in servicing clients in

specialized industries, for example, real estate, construction and apparel''
[Loscalzo, 1988: 28].
3. The firm will encourage employees to participate in AICPA and state association activities.
   a. Advise employees of this expectation in firm personnel manuals, staff
   meetings, and performance evaluations.
4. The firm will consider employee professional development in assigning personnel to engagements. It will expect supervisory personnel to provide on-
the-job training.
   a. For each employee or class of employees, determine necessary development stages. This might include basic tasks, such as participation in compilation engagements, as well as more intermediate and advanced tasks,
   such as attribute sampling, specific substantive tests, statistical evaluation,
   engagement planning, and report review.
   b. Require engagement supervisory personnel to discuss with staff the objectives of assigned procedures and the results of reviews of their work.
   c. Direct supervisory personnel to consider the need for on-the-job training
   when assigning engagement tasks.
5. Employees will be advised of the firm's professional development policies,
including minimum requirements, special needs, and firm reimbursement.
   a. Publicize firm policy in personnel manuals, orientation sessions, and firm
   meetings.
6. Firm in-house training programs will comply with the requirements of the
AICPA, state association, and state board of accountancy.
   a. Appoint an individual to determine the firm's professional development
   program needs and course guidelines. Each course should have a clear
   statement of objectives and provide for participant evaluation of the course
   and the instructor. A course outline must be prepared in advance and
   retained. Also, an attendance record should be kept.
7. The firm will document and periodically evaluate its professional development
program to assure compliance with minimum professional requirements and
firm needs.
   a. Ask the personnel coordinator to maintain evidence of each person's CPE,
   to evaluate each employee's conformance with the firm's requirements,
   and to advise each person and the managing partner annually about any
   deficiencies. Events that should cause an early reevaluation include firm
   growth, changes in related policies (such as supervision or hiring), new
   FASB statements, new SASs, changes in client mix, and so on.

Advancement
1. The firm will establish qualifications for the various levels of responsibility.
   a. Appoint an individual to establish minimum qualifications for each level
   in the firm. Often years of experience is important for advancement. For
   example, staff usually have two to three years of experience before they

can become seniors. Seniors must serve an additional two to three years before they can become managers. Managers will often have to serve from four years to forever (at least it seems that way) to become partners. While these partitions based on years are useful, other more direct criteria also are important. To be considered for the senior level, for instance, the person is expected to demonstrate excellent interpersonal skills, outstanding written and oral communication ability, and, perhaps, the talent to beat the budget. He or she also would have to show some capability for and enjoyment of supervision and, of course, be a CPA.

2. The firm will advise all staff of its advancement policies.
   a. Communicate through firm personnel manuals, staff meetings, and evaluation sessions the qualifications necessary for advancement.
3. Periodic evaluations will be conducted of all staff, including partners, by designated firm members. These evaluations will be documented.
   a. Appoint a person or group to determine evaluation frequency and content for each level. Communicate evaluation results and decisions to the professional staff.
   b. Establish the form of required documentation.
   c. Appoint individuals to do evaluations.
   d. Set deadlines for the completion of evaluations and periods to be covered.
4. The firm will integrate its professional development, supervision, and hiring policies into its evaluation policies.
   a. Appoint an individual or group to coordinate the firm's evaluation and advancement policies with its professional development, supervision, and hiring policies.
5. The firm will periodically assess the adequacy of its advancement policies and evaluate the need for changes.
   a. Appoint a person to monitor firm personnel files to ensure that evaluations are conducted on time and that the evidence supports the evaluation.
   b. Appoint an individual to assess the need for changes in the firm's advancement policies and procedures. Events that should cause a reevaluation include firm growth, changes in the firm's hiring policy, changes in client mix, and so on.

Acceptance and Continuance of Clients

1. The firm will do business only with clients who have an appropriately high level of integrity.
   a. Assign responsibility for development of firm procedures, guidelines, and documentation requirements for acceptance and continuance of clients. These often can best be incorporated into a checklist and audit and accounting manuals. Procedures frequently included in the acceptance and continuance decision are:
      i. Inquiries of bankers, attorneys, predecessor accountants, and others

        in the business community about the client's business philosophy and
        ethics.

    ii. Reviews of available financial information, such as annual financial
        reports and tax returns.

   iii. Evaluations of the client's reaction to engagement findings; the ex-
        istence of errors, irregularities, or illegal acts; the existence of an
        audit committee; the control environment; the reliability of manage-
        ment's estimates and representations; litigation; going-concern issues;
        and the like.

  b. Require the managing partner to make all decisions about client acceptance
     and continuance and to consider in those decisions

     i. The firm's independence.

    ii. The firm's ability to serve the client.

   iii. Unacceptable risks to the firm. These might include specified indus-
        tries (such as financial institutions or insurance companies), special-
        use financial statements, financial considerations (such as negative
        cash flow), development-stage companies, and so on.

  c. Direct engagement partners to make written recommendations to the man-
     aging partner about acceptance of new clients and continuance of existing
     clients. Evaluations should be made annually and documented.

2. For new audit clients, the firm will communicate with the predecessor auditor,
   as required by GAAS, and document this inquiry.

  a. Require the engagement partner to contact the predecessor about matters
     pertaining to the prospective client's integrity; disagreements between the
     predecessor and the prospective client about GAAP, audit procedures,
     and other matters; and the reasons for the change.

  b. Create a written checklist for the discussion, and have the engagement
     partner send a memorandum about the findings to the managing partner.

3. The firm will advise all professional staff about its policies and procedures
   on client acceptance and continuance and on conditions that should trigger a
   client continuance evaluation.

  a. Communicate policies and procedures in firm manuals, staff meetings,
     and memoranda.

  b. Prepare for each engagement a checklist of matters that should cause an
     evaluation of the firm's relations with the client, such as:

     i. Illegal acts and irregularities.

    ii. Litigation.

   iii. Changes in management, ownership, directors, the scope of the en-
        gagement, or the nature of the business.

  c. Send to the engagement partner checklists or memoranda about matters
     causing an evaluation of the firm's relationship with the client.

4. The firm will periodically assess its policy on acceptance and continuance of
   clients.

    a. Appoint a person to review and evaluate the policy. Events that should cause an assessment include threatened or actual litigation, audit or accounting failure, firm growth, changes in the economic or business environment, and so on.

Inspection

1. The firm will inspect its quality control policies and procedures annually. This inspection will encompass a review of administrative, personnel, and engagement files. The scope will be sufficient to provide reasonable assurance that the firm is complying with professional standards.
   a. Appoint an individual to coordinate the annual inspection. Use care in making the assignment. The person should spend most of his or her time on accounting and auditing activities and appreciate the importance of quality control to the firm and the profession.
   b. Direct the appointed individual to assess with management the desirability of having an outsider perform the inspection.
   c. Require the appointed individual to obtain or develop appropriate checklists to assess the firm's compliance with the internal control elements.
   d. Order the appointed individual to develop the scope of the engagement review after considering the following:
      i. The quality control document, including the appropriateness of the firm's professional development, hiring, supervision, and advancement policies.
      ii. Staff experience, the mix of accounting and audit engagements, and industry specializations.
      iii. The results of prior quality reviews and inspections.
      iv. The need to review a reasonable cross-section of both accounting and audit engagements that reflect at least 5 percent of the firm's accounting and audit hours and engagements.
      v. High-risk engagements, including those that are large or require specialized expertise.
      vi. The requirement to include, if applicable, at least one engagement under the governmental auditing standards.
2. The firm will assess its compliance with professional standards in the engagement review process.
   a. Ask the appointed individual to use appropriate checklists to assess the extent of the firm's compliance with professional standards, including GAAP, GAAS, SSARS, and OCBOA. The engagement review should assess the firm's compliance with its supervision policy and, in particular, documentation of engagement planning and review.
   b. The coordinator will develop criteria for determining the key engagement areas.
3. The firm will advise all personnel of the importance of annual inspections.
   a. Communicate to all professional staff through memoranda or firm meetings

when the annual inspection is being carried out and its importance to the firm.

b. Assign appropriate administrative and engagement review tasks. Consider the qualifications necessary to participate in the many aspects of the inspection and the efficacy of assigning engagement reviews to professional staff who worked on the engagement or who lack needed specialized expertise.

4. The firm will prepare a report that summarizes the inspection's scope, findings, and recommendations for corrective action.

a. Direct the coordinator to prepare the report and discuss it with appropriate personnel. Firm staff meetings can be useful in this regard.

5. The firm will advise professional staff of individual engagement findings.

a. Assign responsibility for advising individual professional staff of engagement findings that apply to them.

6. The firm will follow up on the implementation of the recommendations.

a. Ask the inspection coordinator to determine whether corrective actions have been implemented and decide through appropriate procedures whether they are achieving their objectives.

7. The firm will conduct special inspections when necessary.

a. Appoint a person, usually the managing partner, to identify the circumstances that would require inspections more than once a year. These usually would include threatened or actual litigation, mergers, entry into a new high-risk audit area (such as financial institutions), audit or accounting failure, and so on.

Members of the Division for CPA Firms should add to their quality control document their membership requirements. CPAs must be majority owners of PCPS and SECPS member firms. Also, each owner "residing in the United States and eligible for AICPA membership must be a member" [Committees of the SEC Practice Section, 1992: 1000.08a].

SECPS members need policies requiring partner rotation, concurring partner review, and annual reporting to client audit committees of total fees received from MAS work on SEC engagements. The partner rotation rules allow a seven-year maximum as the partner-in-charge. Concurring partner review before the report is issued is required on all SEC engagements.

SECPS member firms also must have a policy requiring communication of their firm philosophies to all professional personnel. Further, they must have a policy prohibiting certain MAS work for SEC clients. Such services as public opinion research, psychological testing, merger and acquisition assistance for a finder's fee, executive recruiting, and actuarial services to insurance companies are believed to be inconsistent with a firm's responsibilities to the public. Finally, they must have a policy requiring communication to the Office of the Chief Accountant of the SEC that a client-auditor relationship has ended.

6

The Keys to a Successful Review: Preparation and Planning

Preparation and planning are the keys to a successful review. Firms facing their first or their fourth review recognize that it is a very stressful experience. In a survey of 167 peer-reviewed firms, 59 percent expressed concern about passing their first peer review [McCabe and Brennan, 1992: 22]. Few firms ever looked forward to peer or quality review. Thorough preparation and planning will reduce stress, lower costs, and better the chances of an unqualified opinion.

Many things should be done before, during, and after the review. This chapter focuses on what a firm must do to prepare for the review by outlining ten steps necessary to a successful quality review experience.

STEPS TO A SUCCESSFUL REVIEW

These are the ten steps to a successful review, listed in approximate sequential order.

1. Review the firm's quality control document carefully.
2. Carry out an internal inspection.
3. Prepare an inspection report.
4. Get a consulting review.
5. Appoint a reviewer liaison.
6. Review and sign the engagement letter.
7. Confer with the reviewer, and determine the following:
   a. Information needed to plan the review.
   b. The twelve-month review period.
   c. Arrangements for lodging and transportation.
   d. The anticipated commencement and exit conference dates.

8. Provide the reviewer with a complete firm profile, including:

   a. The quality control document.

   b. Responses to the quality control policies and procedures questionnaire.

   c. Manuals, forms, and checklists.

   d. A list of accounting and auditing engagements in the specified format.

   e. A list of the firm's professional personnel.

   f. A copy of the last peer or quality review report, with the letter of comments, letter of response, and acceptance letter indicating any corrective or monitoring requirements.

   g. Copies of the firm's annual inspection reports since the last review.

   h. Client profiles.

9. Assemble administrative and personnel files.

10. Provide a seminar.

What follows is a discussion of each critical step.

REVIEW THE QUALITY CONTROL DOCUMENT

Before they schedule the review, the managing partner and other key personnel should examine the quality review document thoroughly. The reviewer's first step is to evaluate this document. The purpose of this evaluation is to assess whether the system design provides reasonable assurance that the firm's accounting and audit services comply with professional standards.

As explained in Chapter 5, the firm's quality control system does not have to be in writing. Lack of a document, however, adds cost to the review because it takes the reviewer extra time to determine firm policies for each element and the procedures used to achieve those goals. Also, lack of a control document is, for the most part, inexcusable. It is similar to sailing a ship without a rudder.

In an article about how to help small businesses operate better, Reeve argues that companies should prepare written quality control procedures [1992: 8]. CPAs should, too.

Sole practitioners without professional staff can get by without a document, but that is the only exception. The primary reason for this concession is that many of the quality control elements—that is, advancement, hiring, and assigning personnel to engagements—do not apply to sole practitioners without professional staff. Sole practitioners, however, do need a system of quality control that encompasses independence, consultation, acceptance and continuance of clients, professional development, and inspection. The supervision element also must be included because it encompasses engagement planning and review.

After the reviewer evaluates the quality control system, the next step is to test whether it operates as described. So often, firms prepare a commendable control document and then fail to follow it. What happens as a result? At a minimum, the firm will be embarrassed when the reviewer discovers its failure. It also is likely to cause the reviewer to be more skeptical. He or she might believe that the firm does not care enough about quality control and, thus, has the wrong tone at the top. This skepticism may cause the reviewer to expand the scope of the review or just look a little harder. This could result in a qualified or, even worse, an adverse report. Remember, the goal in review is, at a minimum, to earn an unqualified report. Many firms know that review provides the opportunity to improve the quality of their accounting and audit practices and, therefore, want much more. An unqualified report for an on-site review might say, for example:

> In our opinion, the system of quality control for the accounting and auditing practice of [Name of Firm] in effect for the year ended June 30, 19XX, met the objectives of quality control standards established by the AICPA and was being complied with during the year then ended to provide the firm with reasonable assurance of conforming with professional standards in the conduct of that practice. [Quality Review Executive Committee, 1991: QRP § 3000.77]

A thorough firm review of the quality control document is an absolute necessity. Firms with ten or fewer professionals should concentrate on the elements of independence, consultation, supervision, and professional development. "Professionals" in this context are defined as CPAs and those aspiring to become CPAs. Quality reviewers of small firms will usually restrict their study and evaluation to these broad functions. Firms with more than ten professionals need to make a thorough review of all nine interrelated elements.

Firms that are members of the AICPA Division for CPA Firms should thoroughly examine their inspection policies, regardless of their size. For peer reviews, "a reviewer must review in depth the functional areas of independence, supervision, professional development, and inspection" [PCPS and SECPS Peer Review Committees, 1991: PRM 13100.09].

Firm managers should ask questions as the document is reviewed. First, is the system appropriately comprehensive and suitably designed, given the size and nature of the practice? Usually, small firms need not be overly concerned with their policies and procedures for personnel assignment, hiring, advancement, and acceptance and continuance of clients. That is because the owners of small firms are directly involved in decisions on these issues and make them based on professional judgment, rather than previously defined criteria. Small firms that are growing rapidly, however, need to take more care. They also must adequately deal with hiring and, perhaps, assignment of personnel to engagements.

If the firm has grown substantially, the control system may not be adequate. Rapid growth should always lead to an evaluation of the firm's quality control system.

A special problem may occur when a firm takes on a large audit engagement and its control system is inadequate to handle it. If the engagement was completed during the review period, it is fairly certain to be chosen in the review because of its size. The reviewer will have to conclude that the system design is deficient, even if the audit was done in accordance with GAAS. And, depending on the other findings, the reviewer may have to issue a qualified or adverse report. The lesson here is to consider the firm's control system and its quality control document when change occurs. Other events that should trigger a reassessment of the quality control system include new SASs, and SSARSs, the opening of new offices, the acquisition of practices, and the addition or loss of key personnel.

A second question to ask in the control document review is whether it accurately describes how the firm's system operates. If some of the document's procedures are not yet in place, perhaps they should be eliminated. If some of the objectives and procedures were added after the beginning of the review period, the document should be amended accordingly. The issue here, in a sense, is whether it is better to have a design deficiency or a system that is not in agreement with the control document, a compliance deficiency. While there is no easy answer to this question, a design deficiency does not necessarily suggest the wrong tone at the top, while a compliance deficiency does. A discrepancy between the control document and the system's operation is a serious matter. It suggests that the firm knew what was right and still did not do it. While it is not the same as signing off on audit procedures that were not done (an undiscussable behavior discussed in Chapter 2), it is similar and suggests management has gone astray. Design deficiencies, of course, are serious as well. Frequently, however, they occur because the firm did not know there was a problem. Reviews are very useful in detecting and rectifying design problems.

After the firm has carefully reviewed its quality control document and made any necessary amendments, it is time to see if the policies and the procedures work as designed.

PERFORM AN INTERNAL INSPECTION

"In conjunction with your review of the quality control document, you should undertake an internal inspection" [Romig, 1982: 44]. Remember, an inspection must be done each year, and there is no better time to do it than when preparing for the review.

Inspection is the ninth element in the control system. It involves an examination of the other eight elements' policies and procedures. It includes a review of the firm's administrative and personnel files to support the firm's documentation requirements. Further, it includes an analysis of the firm's library as part of the inspection of independence and consultation elements. In addition, personnel are questioned about independence, personnel assignment, advancement, and supervision. Finally, a representative sample of the firm's engagement reports and working papers is examined.

No matter when they are done, inspections enable firms to evaluate not only engagement effectiveness, but engagement efficiency as well. They also provide the opportunity to train promising senior personnel in engagement review. Engagement review is learned, for the most part, through doing it. Hands-on review training can go a long way toward making the engagement review process both effective and efficient.

The two primary benefits of an inspection just before the review are (1) there will be no surprises in the review and (2) it will lower the review costs. Specifically, Interpretation 2 of SQCS 1 says "the scope of the peer (quality) review may be affected by the review team's evaluation of the scope and adequacy of the firm's inspection program" [*AICPA Professional Standards*, Volume 2, 1992: QC§ 10–1.09]. A thorough, well-documented inspection of the review period by management personnel will substantially reduce the review time and, thus, its cost. Reviewers will assess the adequacy of the inspection and its findings, and test some of the inspection procedures. This may result in a significant reduction in the scope of the quality or peer review.

A firm can choose to have the quality review take the place of its annual inspection requirement for the review year. This option, however, should not be seriously considered because the review may uncover troublesome surprises. It is far better for the firm to discover its shortcomings than to have the reviewers notice them first. Also, skipping the review-year inspection does not lower the firm's review costs. If anything, it would tend to increase them. Finally, firms choosing to use the quality review as a substitute for the required annual inspection must state this in the quality control document.

Assigning Responsibility for the Inspection

The responsibility for the inspection should be assigned to a partner who appreciates its importance. "The importance placed on an inspection will determine how productive it is and the benefits the firm derives" [Quality Review Executive Committee, 1991: QRP§ 9000.08]. The quality of a firm's services depends in large part on the quality of the control system. The control system can improve only through high-caliber inspections and reviews.

Expediting the Inspection

Fortunately, forms and checklists are available to expedite the inspection process. The Quality Review Executive Committee in 1989 developed a Program for Inspection of Compliance with Policies and Procedures Related to the Elements of Quality Control [1991: QRP § 9000.48]. This program is reproduced in Appendix 6.A.

The Division for CPA Firms has similar checklists that include some additional steps related to compliance with membership requirements. Also, SECPS inspection checklists include steps to ascertain compliance with SEC engagement partner rotation, concurring partner review, and other matters.

Inspection Scope

The inspection coordinator should be one of the firm's owners. The coordinator ought to define the scope of the inspection after consultation with the managing partner, partners-in-charge of practice offices, and auditing and accounting directors, as appropriate. The extent of the inspection is influenced by several factors, including the control document, firm growth, staff experience, and the mix of accounting and auditing engagements. The scope also is affected by the existence of high-risk engagements, such as those requiring specialized expertise, SEC and financial institution engagements, and those conducted under the Employee Retirement Income Security Act of 1974 (ERISA). Further, it is influenced by the appropriateness of the firm's professional development program, hiring policies and practices, acceptance and continuance policies, and industry specializations and by the results of prior inspections and quality or peer reviews.

The suggested procedures for the Program for Inspection (see Appendix 6.A) include a review and evaluation of the firm's quality control document, an examination of its administrative and engagement files, and interviews of selected professional staff. For example, the third item under "Independence" in the Program for Inspection calls for the firm to periodically notify its staff of the entities to which the independence rules apply and to make sure that they are familiar with those rules. Completing this step is easy if firms place copies of their memoranda and the professional staff independence confirmations in the administrative files. This step also calls for interviews of selected staff about their familiarity with the firm's independence rules and the situations to which they apply. Staff selected for interview should include, in addition to regular staff, a sample of new hires. Too often firms do not include an independence module in their staff orientation program, and, as a result, new hires are not familiar with its requirements.

Some of the testing called for in the Program for Inspection can be delegated to both professional and administrative staff. For example, administrative personnel could handle the program's last step under "Independence," which requires a determination of whether receivables from any client have characteristics similar to loans. Administrative personnel also might be assigned the responsibility for all the items under "Hiring." The inspection partner, of course, must resolve exceptions and questions.

The scope of the engagement portion of the inspection should be similar to the scope of a quality review. Only qualified professional staff should be involved. Staff should not, of course, review their own engagements. Sole practitioners without professional staff are the exception to this rule. Since it is difficult to review one's own work, it is probably better for a sole proprietor to arrange with another sole practitioner to inspect each other's engagements. Reciprocal inspections are not prohibited, but reciprocal peer and quality reviews are.

In selecting engagements, the goal is to review a reasonable cross-section of both audit and accounting engagements. The sample should include compilation and review engagements, as well as audits. In quantitative terms, 5 to 10 percent of the firm's accounting and auditing hours and number of engagements should be included. For firms with more than fifteen practice offices, the SECPS recommends a sample of 3 to 6 percent [Committees of the SEC Practice Section, 1991: 2000.61].

Consideration also should be given to selecting engagements that are large, high risk, and from specialized industries. Unquestionably, the sample must include an inspection of engagements with significant public interest, such as those for SEC registrants, financial institutions, and governmental entities. Thought also should be given to selecting first-time engagements and those that have not previously been included in firm inspections or quality reviews. Finally, the sample should include engagements that require special expertise, such as personal financial statements and financial forecasts. As a result, it is likely that the sample size will be nearer to 10 percent of firm engagements.

Engagement Reviews

Procedures to test the firm's compliance with its quality control policies and procedures apply to the engagement review process as well. For example, the Program for Inspection in step 2 under "Consultation" requires the inspector to determine if required consultation took place. The inspector also must determine whether consultations were documented in compliance with firm requirements.

The answers to the entire "Supervision" section of the Program for Inspection come from the engagement review. To a great extent, supervision is accomplished through the use of appropriate work programs and planning, review, and disclosure checklists. The inspector should evaluate these technical materials to make sure they reflect the professional standards in effect when the engagement was completed.

The engagement review, then, aims to gauge the firm's compliance with professional standards in addition to testing its conformance with its quality control policies and procedures. These standards include GAAP, GAAS, and SSARS, as well as the standards for forecasts and projections and the engagement auditing standards (the yellow book). The engagement review encompasses a review of the accountant-auditor's report and financial statements, including the related notes and the supporting working papers. It also usually entails a review of correspondence files and staff interviews.

It is seldom necessary to do a 100 percent workpaper review, but it is always necessary to thoroughly review the report and the financial statements. For example, the inspector should determine if the independent auditor's report

1. Is dated properly and contains the basic elements required under GAAS.
2. Covers all the periods covered by the financial statements.
3. Describes the auditor's degree of responsibility, if any, for supplemental information.

The depth of the workpaper review depends on several conditions. Weaknesses noted in the prior quality review or inspection report always should be given consideration. Areas affected by new professional pronouncements also should be given attention. Further, the workpaper review must concentrate on the key areas. A key area in every engagement is supervision, including planning and review. For example, audit planning involves the use of numerous procedures to obtain an understanding of the client and its environment so that judgments can be made about the nature, timing, and extent of the substantive procedures to be employed. The workpapers, including permanent files, should show, among other things:

1. Involvement of partners or manager-level personnel in the planning process.
2. An understanding of the client's business, including its products, personnel, and accounting practices.
3. An inherent risk assessment, including economic conditions, laws and regulations, technological factors, and so on.
4. An assessment of overall audit risk and preliminary materiality judgments.
5. The use of analytical procedures as attention-directors.
6. Evidence supporting an understanding of the control structure.
7. An audit program covering the major (key) areas that appropriately reflects the auditor's assessed inherent and control risk for each financial statement assertion.

Besides planning, the adequacy of ongoing engagement supervision must be thoroughly assessed. For example, the inspector should find information that corroborates the adequacy of the supervision, such as the following:

1. A detailed written audit program approved by the partner or manager.
2. Sign-offs on all audit procedures called for in the program.

3. The use of specialists to design and evaluate statistical samples.

4. Completion of required firm checklists, such as internal control questionnaires and disclosure checklists.

5. Documentation of the resolution of questions, audit issues, and exceptions.

In an audit review, the workpapers should show, among other things, that

1. Analytical procedures were used in the final review.

2. An evaluation was made of each passed adjustment and various combinations of those adjustments. Specifically, the workpapers should show the relationship between the adjustments not made and the tolerable misstatement amount for the particular accounts and cycles.

3. Appropriate evidence exists, such as initialing workpapers to support an assertion that the workpapers, independent auditor's report, and financial statements with accompanying disclosures were reviewed in detail.

In addition to reviewing the workpapers for planning, supervision, and review, the inspector needs to review the adequacy of the account-balance audit. Again, the key-area approach should be used. For example, the key areas in a retail business would include inventory, accounts payable, sales, and cost of sales. Fortunately, engagement review "checklists and supplements have been developed specifically for general audits, audits of governmental, not-for-profit, and banking entities" [Quality Review Executive Committee, 1991: QRP§ 9000.28]. Engagement review checklists also are available for compilations and reviews. Well-designed engagement checklists can be obtained from the AICPA, as well as from other publishers.

At the conclusion of each engagement review, the inspector must draw conclusions about the report, financial statements, and workpapers. For example, the inspector needs to assess whether the financial statements were presented in accordance with relevant accounting standards, such as GAAP or OCBOA. Also, an evaluation must be made of the firm's compliance with GAAS in its audits or SSARS in its review or compilation engagements. Further, the adequacy of the documentation supporting the firm's report must be assessed. The engagement review also must include an evaluation of whether the firm complied with its quality control policies and procedures. These conclusions or findings are then summarized in an inspection report.

PREPARE AN INSPECTION REPORT

The firm report should summarize the scope of the review, the findings, and the recommendations for corrective action. For multi-office firms, a separate report should be prepared for each office inspected. The sample inspection report from the AICPA (Figure 6.1) may be helpful.

So that corrective actions can be taken, the firm must determine each finding's implication for the quality control system. For example, a finding that a required note disclosure was missing on an engagement involving related-party transactions can be interpreted in two different ways. It may have been an oversight and, thus, a human error, or it might have happened because the firm did not use disclosure checklists. If the latter is the case, then it has a quality control implication that should be addressed.

Corrective actions usually include changes to the firm's quality control policies and procedures. They also might include amendments to staff professional development plans, changes to firm checklists and audit programs, employee reassignments, and so on. Likewise, more thorough review procedures might be required. Further, it may be necessary to expand the firm's monitoring of its compliance with quality control policies and procedures.

Without the report, the potential benefits of the inspection are lost. The report provides evidence for the reviewers that an inspection was done. In addition, it provides a basis for a decision on review scope that may save time and money during the review. Further, the findings help identify potential problem areas and provide the firm with the opportunity to amend its checklists, work programs, and quality control document. It also affords the opportunity to instruct staff about tasks that were overlooked or that should be done differently and to evaluate engagement efficiency. Overall, it provides the opportunity for the firm to improve its practice quality and efficiency.

The completed inspection report should be filed with the checklists, programs, and notes made during the inspection for the reviewer's analysis. After his or her analysis, the firm should consider disposing of the checklists, programs, and notes because they could be the subject of legal inquiry. In this litigious environment, one cannot be too cautious. Only the inspection report should be retained. Of course, the inspection checklists, programs, and notes for inspections done in the years between reviews also should be discarded.

After the report has been completed, the inspection coordinator should check to see if all corrective actions have been implemented. This might also involve procedures to determine if the corrective actions are achieving their objectives. For example, if the firm decided to use disclosure checklists, the inspection coordinator should follow up to make sure they are being used appropriately.

Consider an External Inspection

Occasionally, all firms should elect to have an outside professional carry out the inspection. Outsiders often bring a higher level of objectivity to the inspection. They also have different views on what constitutes adequate planning, appropriate supervision, personnel assignment documentation, and so on. Further, they may be able to offer ideas about how to increase engagement efficiency and effec-

Figure 6.1
Sample Inspection Report

Inspection period from _____ to _____

Name of inspectors _____

_____

Timing of Inspection _____

Briefly describe the inspection program (including major considerations in selecting engagements and offices to be reviewed). _____

_____

_____

_____

_____

Scope of engagements reviewed:

	Firm Totals*		Engs. Reviewed*	
	Hrs.	No. of Engs.	Hrs.	No. of Engs.
Audits				
Reviews				
Compilations				
Other Accounting Services	_____	_____	_____	_____
Total	=======	=======	=======	=======
Percentage of A&A Practice Reviewed			=======	=======

Did the inspection disclose any situations that would require the firm to take action to prevent future reliance on a report issued by the firm or require the firm to perform additional auditing or review procedures to provide a basis for the report issued? If yes, describe the situation and the action taken by the firm. _____

_____

_____

_____

_____

The inspection findings and the recommendations regarding actions taken for improvements in the firm are attached.

Inspection Coordinator Signature _____ Date_____

Approved _____ Date_____

*Approximate totals may be used.

Source: From Quality Review and Program Manual, Copyright © 1991 by American Institute of
Certified Public Accountants, Inc. Reprinted with permission.

tiveness. For instance, some firms have very well developed planning, review, and disclosure checklists that may be well suited to the reviewed firm.

GET A CONSULTING REVIEW

Firms about to undergo their first review definitely should get a consulting review from the AICPA Division for CPA Firms. For firms with up to twenty professionals, the cost is $700 plus expenses, half of which is refunded if the firm has its initial review under the PCPS. For firms with over twenty professionals, the fee is $1,400 plus out-of-pocket expenses, and $350 is refunded. For firms with up to twenty professionals, the consulting review is a one-day, confidential, high-spot review. The consulting reviewer will not retain any checklists or workpapers and is prohibited from disclosing the results to anyone outside the firm.

The consulting reviewer examines the quality control document, firm checklists, and audit and other work programs. Staff is questioned, and a few representative engagements are reviewed. The reviewer will identify system weaknesses and offer suggestions to correct them. In addition, the reviewer will spot engagement deficiencies the firm should address. As a result, the firm will be better prepared and receive fewer comments in its actual review.

Some state societies offer a brief on-site review at a low cost. They will usually answer any specific firm questions at no charge. Consulting reviews also can be obtained from other firms.

Some firms choose to expand the consulting review into the annual inspection. Reviewers who provide consulting reviews or inspections also can provide quality reviews. It makes economic sense for first-time firms to get their quality reviews from consulting reviewers. There also are possible savings for firms facing subsequent reviews. These arrangements, however, open up the question of independence in appearance. Will the consulting reviewers be as rigorous as required in the regular review? Will the consulting reviewers overlook some findings in the regular review that should have been discovered in the consulting review? Using the same reviewers for the regular review and the consulting review subjects the profession to unnecessary criticism. This practice ought to be discouraged.

APPOINT A REVIEWER LIAISON

One of the partner-shareholders should be assigned to act as a coordinator between the firm and the reviewer. Care should be taken in making this choice. Like the inspection coordinator, the liaison should have primary responsibility in accounting and audit, believe strongly in the importance of reviews for the profession and the firm, and have excellent interpersonal skills. In most cases, the firm should assign reviewer liaison responsibility to the same person who acted as the inspection coordinator.

The liaison's job is to be both the engagement partner and the staff on the review. He or she must make the arrangements for arrival and departure, hotel accommodations, and work space, and be the firm's spokesperson. The reviewer should be treated as a guest. Hotel accommodations should not be extravagant, but they should be comfortable. The reviewer also should be assigned the firm's best conference room.

The coordinator should plan to work closely with the reviewer. It is not uncommon, particularly on out-of-town assignments, for the reviewer to work from 8:00 A.M. to 9:00 P.M. In the little time that remains, the coordinator should try to have the other partners join the reviewer for breakfast, lunch, and dinner. These social sessions are a great opportunity to share ideas and experiences about ways to increase firm efficiency, marketing strategies, staff training, and the other myriad problems and opportunities that face an accounting business. They also provide the firm the chance to show that it does have the proper tone at the top.

The reviewer needs a lot of information to plan the review. The liaison must make sure he or she receives it promptly. The reviewer usually needs the firm's quality control document, its responses to the quality control policies and procedures questionnaire, and, if appropriate, copies of manuals and checklists. He or she also needs a list of accounting and auditing engagements in a specified format, a list of the firm's professional personnel, copies of inspection reports since the last review, and copies of the last quality review report, letter of comments, letter of response, and acceptance letter. The coordinator and the reviewer also should choose the twelve-month period to be covered by the review and the anticipated exit conference date. Once the review period is decided, it should remain so for all subsequent inspections and reviews.

The reviewer may provide the firm with a tentative list of engagements to be reviewed. The coordinator should make sure client profiles are completed on these engagements before the review begins. Some reviewers prefer to select the engagements when they arrive.

The liaison also should schedule and conduct a staff seminar about a week before the review starts. Items to be emphasized in this seminar are covered in the last part of this chapter.

REVIEW AND SIGN THE ENGAGEMENT LETTER

If the firm has followed the recommendations outlined in Chapter 4, this preliminary step is somewhat automatic. A few things, however, have not been discussed and deserve comment. They entail some explicit and implicit promises that the reviewer and the profession are making in the contract to provide review services. A sample engagement letter is provided in Figure 6.2.

For example, the engagement letter explicitly specifies that the review, either quality or peer review, will be conducted in conformance with the confidentiality requirements of the AICPA Code of Professional Conduct. As stated previously,

Figure 6.2
Sample Engagement Letter

[Letterhead of Administering Entity for CART Reviews]

(Date)

(Firm Contact)

(Firm Name)

Re: Review Number_____

Dear (*Mr. or Ms. Firm Contact*):

You have requested that a review team be appointed to perform a quality review of your firm's accounting and auditing practice. We are willing to arrange for such an engagement, subject to the terms and conditions set forth in this letter.

The attachment to this letter contains information on the review team. If any changes need to be made in the review team, we will notify you immediately and ask you to authorize those changes.

Scope of the Review

The review will be performed in accordance with the *Standards for Performing and Reporting on Quality Reviews*, issued by the AICPA Quality Review Executive Committee. These standards require, among other things, that the review be conducted in compliance with the confidentiality requirements set forth in the AICPA Code of Professional Conduct. Information concerning the review firm or any of its clients or personnel, including the findings of the review, that is obtained as a consequence of the review is confidential. Such information shall not be disclosed by review team members to anyone not involved in carrying out the review or administering the program or used in any way not related to meeting the objectives of the quality review program unless authorized by your firm. Also, no review team member will have contact with clients of your firm.

If it is necessary to obtain the consent of your clients for review of files and records pertaining to them, you will assume the responsibility for obtaining such consent.

Liability and Subpoena

You agree not to take, or assist in, any action seeking to hold liable, jointly or singly, us or the review team—including any staff, assistants, committees or the review team's firms—for damages on account of any good faith act or omission or on account of any deficiency in the files overall, unless those damages arise from malice, gross negligence, or recklessness. Also, you agree not to subpoena any of those persons or organizations, or otherwise call them to testify, in any action to which they are not a party, with respect to any of the work performed, reports made, or information acquired or developed in connection with this review. However, this provision shall not apply if some other person has done that successfully and you conclude you must do so in response.

Timing of Review and Fees

We anticipate that the review will begin on (*date of commencement*) and take between _____ and _____ hours to complete. However, this is only an estimate and reviewer time will be billed at actual.

The billing rates are set forth in the attachment. Your firm will also be expected to pay for all reviewer out-of-pocket expenses and the administrative fees established by the American Institute of Certified Public Accountants for the scheduling of the review and the evaluation of the review results. The administrative fee structure is also set forth in an attachment to this letter.[1]

Invoices are due upon presentation. Normally, fees will be billed after the report is issued on the review. However, under certain circumstances, progress billings may be rendered.[2]

• • • • •

If you accept these terms and conditions, please sign and return the enclosed copy of this letter. This letter, including the attachments, will then become a contract between you and us.

Sincerely,

_____

_____

_____

We consent to the terms and conditions described in this letter.

| _____ | _____ |
| Firm To Be Reviewed | Date |

| _____ | _____ |
| By | Position |

[1]The AICPA or state society may insert the information needed in this sentence, delete it entirely, or revise it, depending on the fee structure adopted.

[2]State societies may wish to revise this paragraph.

Source: From Quality Review and Program Manual, Copyright © 1991 by American Institute of Certified Public Accountants, Inc. Reprinted with permission.

this rule prohibits disclosure of any information obtained from the review. The firm, then, need not be concerned that the reviewer might share his or her opinion of its quality with anyone not involved in carrying out or administering the review.

Firms, too, need to consider the confidentiality issue, but from a different perspective. Some state statutes or ethics rules of state boards of accountancy do not clearly allow an exemption from the client confidentiality requirement for quality or peer reviews. Contact the AICPA for a list of states that do not and for advice on what to do. Affected state societies also will offer guidance.

There are, in addition, implicit promises made between the reviewer and the reviewed firm. While these promises are not apparent in the engagement letter, they are part of the understanding between the reviewed firm and the profession. The reviewer represents the profession and, as a result, is expected to be independent and competent. He or she also is expected to exercise due professional care and to avoid conflicts of interest.

Reciprocal reviews are prohibited under the independence rules. Also, a reviewer cannot review an engagement of a company in which the reviewer owns securities. Office-sharing arrangements and similar relationships between the reviewer and the reviewed firm are considered to impair independence. The reviewer also needs to assess family and other relationships that might hamper independence.

Reviewer competence is critical to the entire quality review program. The reviewer must be competent in the type of practice being reviewed. In terms of minimum requirements, "on-site reviewers for the AICPA quality review program and the AICPA Division for CPA Firms must be active at the manager level or above in the accounting and auditing function of the CPA firm" [McCabe, 1991: 111]. The reviewer must be a licensed CPA and an AICPA member with current knowledge of professional standards and have at least five years' experience in accounting and auditing.

The quality review program recognizes that many CPAs also do tax and client advisory work and that, as a result, they find it difficult to comply with this standard. The Quality Review Executive Committee says that "the standard is not intended to require that reviewers be individuals who spend all their time on accounting and auditing engagements. However, CPAs who wish to serve as reviewers should carefully consider whether their day-to-day involvement in accounting and auditing is sufficiently comprehensive to enable them to perform a quality review with professional expertise" [Quality Review Executive Committee, 1991: footnote to QRP§ 3000.18].

The review team captain (the in-charge) must come from a firm that is a member of the AICPA quality review program or the Division for CPA Firms. On division reviews, the team captain must be from another division firm. Also, the team captain's firm must have received an unqualified opinion on its review in the past three years. Finally, "team captains on quality reviews must be proprietors, partners or shareholders of enrolled firms and must have completed an approved reviewer training course" [McCabe, 1991: 111].

Like accountants and auditors, the reviewer is expected to exercise due professional care. "This imposes an obligation on all those involved in carrying out the review to fulfill assigned responsibilities in a professional manner similar to that of an independent auditor examining financial statements" [Quality Review Executive Committee, 1991: QRP§ 3000.13]. The due care requirement directs the reviewer to adequately plan the review. The keys to a successful review, from the standpoint of both the reviewer and the reviewed firm, are adequate planning and preparation. The due care requirement also means the reviewer must carry out the review to the best of his or her ability.

In conducting the review, the reviewer must consider the best interests of the firm and the public, and balance them against each other. It certainly is in the public interest to demand and receive high-quality accounting and audit services. Because of this, it is in the profession's and the firm's long-range best interest to design and implement a high-quality control system backed by periodic review. While cutting corners may appear prudent in the short run, the missing variable in this equation is the cost of providing substandard service. The profession bears the burden of a member's substandard service through lost reputation and increased governmental scrutiny accompanied by cries for more regulation. If firm members are going to hold themselves out as CPAs, they must uphold the profession's standards.

In carrying out this obligation of due professional care, then, the reviewer must convince the firm to raise its standards. To do this, the reviewer must first earn the firm management's trust.

Earning trust is not an easy task. A reviewer who cares about the profession, has experience, has good interpersonal skills, and is meticulous in his or her work has a better chance of earning management's confidence. Also, once the reviewed firm realizes that quality review's real purpose is to educate and not to punish, then the process of improving professional practice quality can begin. Many have overlooked the role of education as the predominant purpose of quality review. According to the Quality Review Executive Committee, "the program is based on the principle that a systematic monitoring and educational process is the most effective way to attain high-quality performance throughout the profession" [Quality Review Executive Committee, 1991: QRC§ 3000.06]. A firm that has confidence in its reviewer and that also understands the review's educational purpose will be persuaded to correct any significant design or compliance deficiencies. The reviewer who exercises due professional care, and maybe at times extraordinary professional care, uses his or her persuasive skills to improve the quality of professional accounting service.

Another implicit promise between the reviewer and the reviewed firm is that the reviewer will not have a conflict of interest. This obligation deals in a sense with the issue of independence in appearance. The reviewer is obligated to "avoid contacts with clients or personnel of the reviewed firm that could be asserted to be evidence of a conflict of interest" [Quality Review Executive Committee, 1991: QRP§ 3000.11].

At this writing CART-sponsored PCPS peer reviews use the following rates [Committees of the Private Companies Practice Section, 1992: 5000.51]:

	Number of Professional Staff	
	1 - 10	11+
Team captain	$85	$95
Team members who are partners	75	85
Team members who are not partners	65	75

CART-sponsored SECPS peer reviews use the following rates [Committees of the SEC Practice Section, 1992: 5000.47]:

	Number of Professional Staff		
	1 - 10	11 - 49	50+
Team captain	$85	$100	$120
Team members who are partners	75	90	105
Team members who are not partners	65	80	90

In addition, the AICPA charges certain administrative fees for scheduling and evaluation for all peer reviews.

For quality reviews the CART rates are similar and are currently $95 an hour for the team captain, $85 for member partners and $75 for others on reviews of firms with over ten professionals. Firm-on-firm rates vary substantially, with some being higher and others lower than the above rates.

The engagement letter, then, contains both explicit and implicit promises. After both sides agree on the financial terms, the firm managers should review the letter, sign it, and return it to the reviewer or coordinating administrative organization at least a month before the review begins.

CONFER WITH THE REVIEWER

The better the communication between the firm and the reviewer, the more successful the review. After the firm has selected its reviewer, it must keep in frequent contact. Information needed for planning should be discussed well before the review. For example, as mentioned above, both sides must agree on a twelve-month review period. Also, the anticipated commencement and exit conference dates must be scheduled. The reviewer will request certain material, such as a completed quality control questionnaire. The reviewer will supplement this request by asking for other data to create an adequate firm profile. Part of the reviewer's obligation is to answer questions prior to the actual review. Do not hesitate to contact the review team captain as questions arise.

PROVIDE A FIRM PROFILE

The firm profile is a picture of the firm—including its policies and procedures, its clients and personnel—and it provides insight into the tone at the top. It includes the firm's quality control document, its responses to the quality control procedures questionnaire, and its manuals, checklists, and forms. For SECPS members, it also includes the firm's statement of philosophy.

The firm must complete a quality control policies and procedures questionnaire. Because of its importance, the questionnaire that the quality review program uses for firms with two or more professionals is reproduced in Appendix 6.B.

The questionnaire is very easy to complete if the firm has a quality control document. The firm is asked to respond to each question with "Yes," "No," or "N/A." These responses should be supplemented with a brief description of the firm's policy and procedures.

With a quality control document, it is necessary to refer only to a document paragraph or page number. Without a quality control document, the completion of the questionnaire can be a difficult and, perhaps for a few, a humiliating task. Some firms have not given enough thought to their quality control systems and find that they have serious weaknesses when firm managers attempt to complete the questionnaire.

A review of the questionnaire serves as a useful reminder that planning and preparation are the keys to a successful review. Firms should finish their quality control document.

For the firm profile, the firm needs to provide a list of its accounting and audit engagements. In addition, it needs to summarize these engagements in three different formats. Also, a list of its professional personnel is required.

Reviewers use the list of accounting and audit engagements to make engagement selections. A suggested format is shown in Table 6.1. Firms may already have time and billing systems that provide this information. The reports from these systems are acceptable if they supply the necessary information.

Client codes are assigned for the review. Some firms use the first digit to indicate the type of engagement, so that the number 1 denotes an audit, 2 a review, and 3 a compilation. Firms can use their regular client numbers for the client codes, but this is not recommended because of confidentiality concerns. The period covered is the date of the financial statements. Reviewers will supply the industry codes.

The column for approximate total hours shows the actual or estimated accounting or audit hours on each engagement and the firm totals. A firm's time

Table 6.1
List of All Clients Serviced during Review Period

Client Code	Period Covered	Service Code	Initial Eng.	Industry	Partner Name	Approx. Total Hours
1001	12/31/93	A3	N	220	Adams	600
*	*	*	*	*	*	*
*	*	*	*	*	*	*
*	*	*	*	*	*	*
3002	9/30/93	C	Y	270	Costin	100
*	*	*	*	*	*	*
*	*	*	*	*	*	*
*	*	*	*	*	*	*
*	*	*	*	*	*	*
				Total		6,100

Service Codes:

A1   *Audit of SEC registrants.*

A2   *Audit performed under the government auditing standards issued by the U.S. General Accounting Office.*

A3   *Other regular audits of historical financial information.*

A4   *Examination of prospective financial information.*

A5   *Other special audits - identify on the list.*

R   *Review of historical financial statements.*

C   *Compilation of historical financial statements with disclosures.*

CO   *Compilation of historical financial statements omitting substantially all disclosures.*

CP   *Compilation of prospective financial statements.*

system usually captures total engagement time, which includes the time for accounting and audit services as well as other time. Total engagement time, then, often includes time spent rendering tax and client advisory services. This nonaccounting time must be excluded in preparing this form.

Besides the list of accounting and audit clients, three summaries of the firm's accounting and audit engagements are very helpful to the reviewer in developing the firm profile. First, a summary of engagement types gives the reviewer a

Table 6.2
Summary of Engagement Types

Engagement Type	No.	Client Hours
Audits	11	2,200
Reviews	20	1,000
Compilations	75	2,500
Other	5	400
Totals	111	6,100

Table 6.3
Industry Concentration Summary

Type of Industry	No.	Client Hours
Manufacturing	85	3,565
Restaurants	20	1,700
Construction	5	650
Governmental	1	185
Totals	111	6,100

picture of the engagement mix. The format shown in Table 6.2 would be helpful to the reviewer. The totals in this summary, like all summaries, should agree with the list of accounting and audit engagements.

Next, an industry concentration summary is helpful. An example is given in Table 6.3.

Finally, a summary by partner also is very helpful. It should show for each partner the number of audit, review, and compilation clients separately and the related number of accounting and audit hours. An example is provided in Table 6.4.

Multi-office firms should prepare a list of accounting and audit engagements for each office. Separate summaries for each office also are needed.

The firm must prepare a list of professional personnel, including partners. It should include each person's name, position, years of experience with the firm, and total years in public accounting.

Table 6.4
Partner Summary

Engagement Type	Adams No.	Hours	Brock No.	Hours	Costin No.	Hours	Firm No.	Total Hours
Audit	8	1,600	-	-	3	600	11	2,200
Reviews	11	500	2	150	7	350	20	1,000
Compil.	25	1,000	30	800	20	700	75	2,500
Other	1	50	4	350	-	-	5	400
Totals	45	3,150	36	1,300	30	1,650	111	6,100

Finally, the firm should provide the reviewer with a copy of the last peer or quality review report, including the letter of comments, letter of response, and letter of acceptance indicating any corrective or monitoring requirements. In addition, the reviewer should be given copies of the firm's annual inspection reports since the last review. Once the reviewer has these firm profile documents, he or she can tentatively select the engagements to be reviewed. Based on that selection, the firm can prepare client profile forms.

The client profile forms (also called engagement profiles) are supplied by the reviewer. They are generally easy to complete. There are two items, though, that deserve comment. The forms ask for a list of the engagement's "complex or troublesome areas." The engagement partner probably will have to review parts of the client file to complete this section. Also, for audit engagements, information is required about time spent on planning, field work, and review. Specifically, an analysis should be made of the time spent by the engagement partner, managers, seniors, and concurring reviewer, if applicable, on the three time categories of planning, field work, and review.

ASSEMBLE ADMINISTRATIVE AND PERSONNEL FILES

Shortly after the review begins, the reviewer will want to examine the firm's independence, personnel, and CPE files. The independence files should contain the periodic independence confirmations of all professional staff, including partners. As noted in Appendix 5.A, the firm should have a procedure requiring at least an annual signed confirmation from its professional staff. This confirmation should indicate that the staff person is aware of the firm's independence requirements and the clients to which these rules apply. It also should include a statement that "they or their family members do not have investments or relationships with any client that would impair independence" [Loscalzo, 1988: 24].

The independence files also should include copies of any memoranda notifying the professional personnel of new clients to which the independence rules apply. In addition, these files should contain "documentation of correspondents' independence and documentation supporting the resolution of independence questions" [Botwin, 1989: 79].

If applicable, memoranda documenting the periodic monitoring of the firm's independence library, memoranda addressing independence in mental attitude, and meeting agendas showing discussion of independence should be available, too. The independence files also might include copies of reviewers' checklists showing inquiry into the status of client receivables, planning checklists, and staff orientation material. Finally, the firm should make available firm manuals that discuss its independence policy.

The firm's personnel files, including the personnel manual, should be assembled so the reviewer can assess the adequacy of the support for the firm's hiring and advancement policies. These files should include resumes of professional staff, periodic evaluations, and evidence supporting payment of professional dues, such as AICPA and state association fees. They also should include memoranda documenting the firm's communication of its hiring and advancement policies.

The professional development files should contain the state association and board of accountancy CPE requirements, if different from those of the AICPA. Copies of memoranda transmitting technical pronouncements to professional staff should be placed here, too, as should material supporting the firm's assessment of employee conformance with firm CPE requirements. These files also should contain attendance sheets, course materials, and the like.

If the firm uses administrative files, rather than engagement files, to document its client acceptance and discontinuance decisions and its consultation procedures, these should be ready as well.

PROVIDE A SEMINAR

The firm should schedule a one- to two-hour seminar for all accounting and auditing partners and staff about a week before the review. At this seminar, the liaison partner should explain the objectives of the review. He or she may want to use the following quote from the Quality Review Executive Committee: "quality in the performance of accounting and auditing engagements by AICPA members is the goal of the quality review program. The program seeks to achieve its goal through education and remedial, corrective actions. This goal serves the public interest and, at the same time, enhances the significance of AICPA membership" [1991: QRP§ 3000.01]. The seminar also should stress the firm's commitment to the goals of review and the importance of earning an unqualified report. The meaning and implications of the three types of reports—unqualified, modified, and adverse—should be explained.

It must be made clear that everyone's total cooperation with the reviewer is needed and expected. Among other things, staff should be asked to respond to

Figure 6.3
Matters for Further Consideration

REVIEWER'S DESCRIPTION OF THE MATTER   CONTROL NO. _____

REVIEWED FIRM AGREES WITH THE DESCRIPTION OF THE MATTER?   YES ___ NO ___
REVIEWED FIRM'S COMMENTS ON CIRCUMSTANCES, SIGNIFICANCE OF MATTER, ETC.

REVIEWER'S ADDITIONAL COMMENTS   Type of Matter: Performance   _____
                                                          Compliance   _____
                                                          Documentation   _____
                                                          Design   _____

TEAM CAPTAIN'S COMMENTS, IF ANY

FIRM _____   CONTROL NO. _____
OFFICE CODE NO. _____

Signatures   *Dates*

Engagement Partner _____ _____
Reviewer _____ _____
Team Captain _____ _____

Program Questionnaire   *Engagement*

Section _____   No. _____
Element _____   Checklist Page _____
Program Step _____   Question _____

Source: From Quality Review and Program Manual, Copyright © 1991 by American Institute of
         Certified Public Accountants, Inc. Reprinted with permission.

reviewer questions quickly, directly, and honestly. Partners and managers should know that the reviewer will be preparing MFC forms, which are used to detail system design and compliance deficiencies as well as engagement deficiencies. "The natural instinct of any partner is to argue (fight back) if his or her work is questioned" [Weinstein, 1989: 43]. The liaison must acknowledge this tendency and try to convince the other partners that a different strategy may yield better results. The deficiency noted on the MFC form does not always exist. Partners should review them thoroughly and, if they think the reviewer is wrong, state their case as simply as possible. Often, however, the matter noted by the reviewer does exist, and the best response is simply to agree. Agreeing on an issue usually does not affect the reviewer's report. Denying an obvious problem or being uncooperative, however, will lead to trouble.

Figure 6.3 shows what an MFC form looks like. Firms reviewed for the first time may be shocked at how many of these they receive. They should not be disturbed though because it is simply part of the process.

Because staff are curious, it also may be helpful to give some background on the reviewer. Information about his or her firm, specialties, partnership status, years in the profession, and such is interesting to staff. Also, it should be emphasized that the firm has carefully chosen its reviewer and that while the reviewer does have a reputation for being meticulous, he or she also is known for being able to improve professional practice quality.

The seminar should concentrate on what the reviewer will be doing. If it has not been done before, this is a perfect opportunity to discuss the quality control document and the firm's responses to the quality control questionnaire. The staff should be told that the reviewer will be asking them questions about the quality control system. For example, some staff will be asked such questions as "How does the firm inform you of its policies and of those entities to which the firm's independence policies apply?" and "Has the firm identified any specialized situations requiring consultation?" [Quality Review Executive Committee, 1991: QRP§ 4600.04]. Again, staff should be urged to respond directly and honestly.

Finally, everyone should be told that a review provides them with the opportunity to be in the position of the client and that they can learn from that experience. Firm members should be aware that the firm fully expects to earn an unqualified report because it has planned and it is prepared.

Chapter 7 describes what happens in a review and what to do afterward. In addition, it details the questions that might be asked during the review. A thorough reading of that chapter may be beneficial for all firm members facing an upcoming review.

REFERENCES

AICPA Professional Standards, Volume 2. "Interpretations of Quality Control Standards," QC§§ 10–1.00 through 10–1.21. New York: AICPA, June 1992.

Botwin, B. S. "Arranging for a Successful Review." *Journal of Accountancy* (December 1989): 72–80.

Committees of the Private Companies Practice Section. *Private Companies Practice Section Reference Manual.* New York: AICPA, 1992.

Committees of the SEC Practice Section. *SECPS Reference Manual.* New York: AICPA, 1992.

Loscalzo, M. "Preparing for Quality Review." *The CPA Journal* (December 1988): 24–30.

McCabe, R. K. "Wanted: A Few Good Reviewers." *Journal of Accountancy* (August 1991): 109–14.

———. "A Quality Review Checklist." *Journal of Accountancy* (September 1990): 69–74.

McCabe, R. K., and T. Brennan. "Self-Regulation: Can It Be Preserved?" Paper presented at the Western Regional Conference of the American Accounting Association, San Jose, Calif., 1 May, 1992.

PCPS and SECPS Peer Review Committees. *Division for CPA Firms Peer Review Manual.* New York: AICPA, 1991.

Quality Review Executive Committee, American Institute of Certified Public Accountants. *AICPA Quality Review Program Manual.* Chicago: Commerce Clearing House, 1991.

Reeve, J. T. "Prescription for a Small Business Internal Audit." *The Practicing CPA* (February 1992): 1, 2, 8.

Romig, C. J. "8 Steps in Preparing for a Peer Review." *The Practical Accountant* (September 1982): 43–49.

Weinstein, S. "Part 2: Your Quality Review: A Step-by-Step Approach." *The Practical Accountant* (June 1989): 37–53.

Appendix 6.A
Program for Inspection of Compliance with Policies and Procedures Related to the Elements of Quality Control

Period Covered _____

	Findings, Including Extent of Testing	Done By

Independence

1. Identify a sample of situations in which independence questions arose during the period being inspected and consider whether the resolution of such questions appears appropriate.

2. Review the written independence confirmations obtained by the firm for a sample of professional personnel, if required by firm policy.

3. Determine by review of appropriate documentation and by discussions with selected staff that the firm has advised all professional personnel on a timely basis of entities to which the independence rules apply and that professional personnel are familiar with the firm's independence policies and procedures.

4. Determine by a review of selected engagements whether fees were paid for the prior year's services prior to the issuance of the current year's report.

Consultation

1. Inspect the firm's library for its audit and accounting practice and determine whether it is sufficiently comprehensive and current. Specifically determine that the library includes recent pronouncements and literature appropriate for the firm's specialties and that loose-leaf services are filed on a timely basis.

2. On the engagements reviewed, determine whether consultation took place and was documented in accordance with the firm's policies.

3. If sufficient testing of consultation policies and procedures was not performed in 2 above, determine through inquiry or review of subject files whether consultations took place and were correctly applied.

Supervision

1. On the engagements reviewed:

   a. Determine whether the technical materials (audit manuals, standardized forms, checklists, and questionnaires) that are required by firm policy were used.

   b. Evaluate whether the technical materials are sufficiently comprehensive and up-to-date.

   c. Determine whether the firm complied with its policies and procedures for the review of engagement working papers, reports and financial statements.

   d. Determine whether the firm's procedures for resolving differences of opinions among members of the engagement team were followed and are appropriate.

Appendix 6.A (continued)

	Findings, Including Extent of Testing	Done By

Professional Development

1. Review the firm's CPE records on a test basis and consider whether:

   a. They appear adequate to demonstrate compliance with AICPA, state board, and state society requirements and whether they indicate that the firm's plans for CPE were carried out.

   b. Professional personnel have complied with the CPE requirements set forth in *Government Audit Standards* (if applicable).

   c. Professional personnel have complied with the Section's requirements (if the firm is a member of either the PCPS or the SECPS).

Assigning Personnel to Engagements

1. Determine whether staffing and scheduling requirements were identified on a timely basis and approved by appropriate personnel.

2. Determine by interviews with selected staff whether they believe the assignments they have received are appropriate.

Hiring

1. Determine by reviewing personnel files of recently hired employees whether:

   a. The background information and other documentation required by firm policy were obtained.

   b. The individuals possessed the desired attributes, achievements, and experience and, if not, why an exception was made.

Advancement

1. Determine by reviewing personnel files whether personnel have been evaluated and promoted in accordance with the firm's policies and procedures.

Acceptance and Continuance of Clients

1. Review the documentation maintained for selected acceptance and continuance decisions and evaluate whether the firm is complying with its policies and procedures and with professional standards.

Inspection

1. Determine whether appropriate corrective actions were taken, including effective follow-up, with respect to the prior period's inspection findings.

Source: From Quality Review and Program Manual, Copyright © 1991 by American Institute of Certified Public Accountants, Inc. Reprinted with permission.

Appendix 6.B

Quality Control Policies and Procedures Questionnaire for Firms with Two or More Professionals

This questionnaire provides the reviewer with basic information. It is not necessarily a checklist of all the policies and procedures that might be applicable to a firm's practice. Firms about to be reviewed should respond directly with "yes," "no," or "N/A" answers and briefly describe, where appropriate, the policies and procedures they have in effect that relate to the questions asked. Where appropriate, firms should make reference to any firm documents that describe those policies and procedures in more detail. Examples of such documents might be personnel manuals, audit and accounting manuals, a quality control document or manual, and firm forms and checklists.

Response, Including Reference to Firm Documents

A. Independence

1. Does the firm, including all its professional personnel, adhere to the independence rules, regulations, interpretations, and rulings of the—

   a. AICPA?

   b. State CPA society?

   c. State board of accountancy?

   d. State accountancy laws?

   e. SEC and other regulatory agencies?

2. Describe how the firm informs its professional personnel of the applicable independence requirements (for example, through its personnel manual, audit and accounting manual, training meetings, memoranda).

3. How does the firm inform its professional personnel of the new clients to which independence requirements apply? For example, does the firm—

   a. Circulate new client lists to all personnel?

   b. Post new clients on a staff bulletin board?

   c. Report new clients at staff meetings?

   d. Use other (describe) means?

4. Does the firm obtain at least annually written representations from all professional personnel concerning their compliance with applicable independence requirements? If not, how does the firm monitor compliance with its independence policies? If yes, do these representations affirm that:

Appendix 6.B (continued)

Response, Including Reference to Firm Documents

    a.   The individual is familiar with the firm's independence policies and procedures?

    b.   Prohibited investments are not held and were not held during the period?

    c.   Prohibited relationships do not exist and that transactions prohibited by firm policy have not occurred?

5.   Who is responsible for resolving independence questions:

    a.   The engagement partner?

    b.   The managing partner?

    c.   Someone else (identify individual)?

6.   In connection with the resolution of independence questions—

    a.   In what circumstances must the question and its resolution be documented?

    b.   Where is the documentation maintained (for example, the working paper files or other specific firm or client files)?

    c.   What sources are or would be consulted?

    d.   Has the firm found it necessary within the last year to consult with individuals outside the firm on independence matters?

7.   Does the firm have any engagements where it acts as principal auditor or accountant and another firm of CPAs is engaged to perform segments of the engagement?

8.   If the answer to (7) above is "yes"—

    a.   Does the firm confirm the independence of such other firm(s)?

    b.   Does it do so in writing?

    c.   Does it do so annually?

9.   Does the firm review accounts receivable from clients to ascertain whether any outstanding amounts have taken on some of the characteristics of loans and, therefore, may impair the firm's independence?

    a.   Who does this?

Appendix 6.B (continued)

    b.   How often is it done?

    c.   Have there been any such situations during the year under review?

B. Assigning Personnel to Engagements

1. Describe the method the firm uses to assign professional personnel to engagements. In that description, include—

    a.   The basis on which assignments are made. For example, some firms make assignments on an engagement by engagement basis; others assign personnel to specific clients and hold them accountable for all services to those clients.

    b.   How staff are advised of their assignments. For example, some firms do this orally; others issue memoranda or copies of scheduling forms; others post assignments to a staff bulletin board.

    c.   Who is responsible for making staff assignments on a day-to-day basis.

    d.   How that person is informed of estimated time requirements and of any special skills or experience that a given assignment might demand.

    e.   How far in advance assignments are typically made.

C. Consultation

1. During the year under review, has the firm sought advice from outside parties to resolve questions involving professional standards or specialized industry practices?

2. How does the firm determine when to consult with outside parties and with whom to consult?

3. Describe the extent to which the firm expects consultations with outside parties to be documented. Where is such documentation maintained?

4. Does the firm's library include current editions of—

    a.   AICPA *Professional Standards*?

    b.   AICPA industry audit guides relevant to the firm's practice?

    c.   FASB pronouncements?

    d.   GASB pronouncements, *Government Auditing Standards* (the "yellow book") and other government audit guides relevant to the firm's practice?

Appendix 6.B (continued)

D. Supervision

1. Does the firm follow documented procedures for planning audit and accounting engagements and, if so, where are those procedures found (e.g., in an audit and accounting manual)?

2. If the answer to (1) is "no," briefly describe the procedures the firm performs in planning audit and accounting engagements in practice, including the information obtained and considered and the nature, timing and extent of partner involvement in the planning process. Also describe any variations in those procedures based on factors such as the nature and size of the engagement and prior experience on the engagement.

3. Is a written audit program used on all audit engagements? If yes, who is required to review and approve the audit program, and how is this approval documented?

4. Indicate whether the firm has written guidance materials regarding the following matters. If so, indicate where the material is found and whether it was developed internally or was obtained from an outside source, and name the source.

    a. Evaluation and documentation of internal controls, including computer controls?

    b. Consideration of internal controls in planning the audit?

    c. Audit risk and materiality considerations?

    d. Audit sampling techniques?

    e. Degree of reliance to be placed on analytical procedures?

    f. Form and content of working papers?

    g. Other audit and accounting matters, in the form of an audit and accounting manual?

5. Does the firm use any standardized forms, checklists, or questionnaires? If so, attach a list and indicate whether the use of each is required or discretionary. (Note that the reviewer will want to inspect these forms during the review.)

6. Has the firm established procedures to be followed when differences of opinion exist among firm personnel on an audit (see AICPA *Professional Standards*, AU section 311.14)?

Appendix 6.B (continued)

    a.   Are those procedures documented? Where?

    b.   Do those procedures allow an assistant to document his or her disagreement with the conclusion reached?

7.   Does the firm use other offices or correspondents for audit or accounting engagements? If "yes," describe the form in which instructions are given to other offices or correspondents and the extent to which their work is reviewed, or indicate where the firm's procedures for the supervision and control of that work are found.

8.   Does the firm have documented procedures for review by supervisors and partners of the reports, financial statements, and working papers for —

    a.   Audits?

    b.   Reviews?

    c.   Compilations?

9.   If the answer to (8) is "yes," indicate where those procedures are found. If the answer is "no," briefly describe the procedures that are followed, including how the review process is documented.

10.   Does the firm require that an individual having no other significant responsibility for the engagement perform a preissuance review of some or all engagements? If "yes," indicate who performs such preissuance reviews and briefly describe the extent of the review and how the review is documented, indicating the types of engagements to which the procedures are applicable. Alternatively, indicate where these procedures are found.

11.   Has the firm merged with any other firm since the date of its last quality review or in the last three years? If "yes"—

    a.   How did the firm evaluate the quality of a potential merger candidate?

    b.   Did the firm acquire any professional personnel in the merger?

    c.   Did the firm acquire and retain any new office or offices in the merger (indicate the locations of any such offices)?

    d.   Have the personnel of the merged firm adopted the firm's quality control policies and procedures?

Appendix 6.B (continued)

E. Hiring

1. Briefly describe how the firm identifies its professional personnel needs, how it goes about recruiting such personnel, and who makes the decision to hire an applicant.

2. Briefly describe the personal, educational, and experience attributes sought in entry-level personnel and in experienced personnel and indicate whether they are objectives or requirements.

3. Identify the types of background information the firm requires for new hires, such as resumes, transcripts, and personal or employment references.

4. Briefly describe how new professional personnel are informed about the policies and procedures that are applicable to them. Also, attach a list of the manuals, professional publications, and other documents relevant to their professional assignments that are provided to them individually.

F. Professional Development

1. Are all professional personnel in compliance with state and AICPA Continuing Professional Education requirements? If not, attach a list of those personnel who are not in compliance and indicate the firm's plan for correcting the situation.

2. Briefly describe how the firm plans the allocation of CPE hours among accounting and auditing, tax, and other topics and indicate when that is done.

3. Provide an approximation of the nature of the CPE taken by professional personnel assigned to audit and accounting engagements:

   a. Self-study courses . . . . _____%

   b. In-house training programs—
      (i) Developed by the firm . . . . _____%
      (ii) Obtained from outside vendors . . . . _____%

   c. State society or AICPA programs . . . . _____%

   d. Other programs . . . . _____%

4. Who maintains CPE records and course materials?

Appendix 6.B (continued)

5. How are professional personnel made aware of changes in accounting and auditing standards and in the firm's technical policies and procedures (for example, by distributing technical pronouncements and holding training courses on recent changes and areas noted by the firm as needing improvement)?

G. Advancement

1. What levels of responsibility exist within the firm (e.g., partner, manager, senior)?

2. Are personnel at all levels aware of the responsibilities of each of these positions? How is this accomplished? Are those responsibilities documented in, for example, a personnel manual?

3. Does the firm periodically evaluate the performance of professional personnel and advise them of their progress in the firm?

   a. When are these evaluations performed?

   b. Are they documented?

   c. Are standard evaluation forms used?

4. Are partners periodically evaluated, and by what means (e.g., peer evaluation, self-appraisal, counseling)?

5. Briefly describe how advancement decisions are made (a) within the professional staff and (b) to the partnership.

H. Acceptance and Continuance of Clients

1. Briefly describe the procedures followed by the firm, including any documents generally obtained and reviewed and any inquiries generally made of third parties, before accepting a client for whom the firm will provide audit or accounting services in order to provide the firm with reasonable assurance that the client has integrity, to identify any unusual risks that might be associated with the client, and to evaluate the firm's ability to serve the client in a competent and independent manner. Also indicate any variances in those procedures, depending on, for example, the services to be provided.

2. Indicate when or under what circumstances current audit and accounting clients are evaluated to determine whether the relationship should be continued, and briefly describe the procedures that are followed.

3. Were any audit or accounting client relationships terminated by the firm during the year under review?

Appendix 6.B (continued)

I. Inspection

1. Has the firm performed a timely, formal, documented inspection of its quality control policies and procedures for each year since its last peer or quality review (or for the year preceding the review year if the firm has not previously had a review)? If "yes," briefly describe—

    a. The scope of the program, including who carries it out.

    b. The materials used, such as questionnaires, programs, and checklists.

    c. The documentation of the work performed and conclusions reached and the period of time such documentation and conclusions are retained.

2. Has the firm taken appropriate corrective action in response to the findings on its most recent quality review or peer review?

Source: From Quality Review and Program Manual, Copyright © 1991 by American Institute of Certified Public Accountants, Inc. Reprinted with permission.

7

The Review: What Happens and What to Do Afterward

The purpose of this chapter is to describe the entire review process, including the actions the firm must take after the review. It is particularly helpful to firm members facing their first review. It also will help some of the old timers who have undergone several reviews. Reviewers will benefit from reading this chapter closely because it ties the review process into a cohesive whole and provides suggestions about how to perform a better review. Review team captains also may gain something from this section since it provides suggestions about additional questions to ask and procedures to implement in order to better assess firm quality control.

The review's first few hours are possibly the most important for the reviewer and the firm. There are always a few things that could have been done better, no matter how ready the firm intended to be. Maybe the reviewer did not receive the firm profile early enough to make an appropriate analysis. Maybe there was an emergency at the reviewer's end or at the reviewed firm. As we all know too well, things happen. As a result, the reviewer usually arrives with several unanswered questions.

The big question, of course, is whether the firm provides professional quality service. If the firm has followed the ten steps to a successful review, it shows. A reviewer is well on the way to being persuaded of the firm's high quality if he or she knows it has developed a quality control document, performed an internal inspection, prepared an inspection report, and had a consulting review. Initial impressions are hard to change, so firm members should make sure the first few hours go well. Here are some tips on what to do and what to avoid.

WHAT TO DO

Treat the Reviewers as Guests

On out-of-town engagements, the reviewer usually arrives the prior evening. If the reviewer is coming by air or train, the liaison partner should greet him or her at the gate. The coordinator also should confirm the hotel reservations and arrange for local transportation. The partner should determine the reviewer's wishes. The reviewer may be tired and prefer to be alone. Others are rested and sociable and would enjoy having dinner that evening and, perhaps, breakfast in the morning with the liaison and other key personnel.

On larger reviews, the team captain usually starts one day before the other reviewers to give him or her time to make engagement selections and modify the review checklists to fit the firm's control system.

Have All Key Personnel Greet the Reviewers

On the morning of the review, the liaison should join the team captain and the other reviewers for an early breakfast. On arrival at the office, all the partners and other key personnel should be present to greet the reviewers. The reviewers should receive an office tour that highlights the things the partners are proud of, such as a new computer network system. Also, the reviewers should see the firm's library, which should be well organized and look like people use it.

Arrange for a Private Work Environment

Because of the nature of the review process, the office space assigned to the reviewers must be private. It is unwise to allow staff to overhear conversations among reviewers or between a reviewer and one of the professional personnel. Reviewers share their findings and concerns with each other, and these conversations should not be spread through the office.

The team captain should already have the firm's quality control document, quality control questionnaire responses, inspection compliance reports since the last review, and manuals, forms, and checklists. The captain also should receive the list of the firm's accounting and audit engagements in the format specified in Chapter 6. In addition, the firm summaries covering client and engagement types and partner summaries should be ready, as should a list of the firm's professional personnel and a copy of the most recent peer or quality review with the letters of comments, response, and acceptance. SECPS firms must provide reviewers with a copy of their statements of philosophy.

If the team captain has made tentative engagement selections, the engagement profiles and the client files should be brought to the reviewers' office. These should include engagement workpapers, correspondence, and permanent files. The in-charge also needs the administrative and personnel files, which should contain the firm's documents on independence, hiring, advancement, and professional development. The independence materials should contain the most recent professional staff and correspondent independence confirmations. They should include memoranda about clients to which the independence rules apply, staff orientation materials that discuss independence, and the firm's independence policy and procedures.

The hiring and advancement files should contain staff resumes, copies of periodic evaluations, and evidence supporting payment of professional dues. The professional development files should include firm member professional development course attendance sheets and the firm's assessment of its compliance with AICPA and other professional development requirements.

Answer All Questions Candidly

To keep the work flowing, instruct all personnel to answer reviewer questions quickly, directly, and honestly. Talkative personnel should be reminded that the reviewers have a lot of work to do in the allotted time. "There is a tendency for certain partners (or staff), particularly those that tend to be worriers or talkers to engage reviewers in lengthy superfluous conversations" [Weinstein, 1989: 43]. Worriers' fears need to be allayed. Perhaps the review coordinator should take these people aside and explain that the firm is fully ready for its review. In addition, the coordinator should explain that the review's purpose is to improve the firm's quality, so deficiencies probably will be uncovered and the firm will, as a result, become a better firm.

WHAT TO AVOID

Do Not Tell the Reviewer That Review Is a Waste of Time and Money

Be positive. For the most part, reviewers care a lot about improving the profession. They are committed to the idea that the road to a healthier profession is through quality control and review. While some CPAs believe review is unnecessary, I doubt any of them will read this book. If you are one of them and you have read the first six chapters, then I have failed. Keep reading though.

Do Not Be Uncooperative

Help the reviewers. Cooperation assures the firm of receiving the many significant benefits of review. These include perceptions of improved quality control and better compliance with professional pronouncements, which result in a higher-quality product. They also include improvements in firm member morale and confidence. Finally, a major consequence of review is the sharing of ideas between the reviewer and the reviewed firm on ways to practice more efficiently and, therefore, more profitably.

Anything less than total cooperation is not in the firm's or the profession's best interests. Uncooperativeness can be momentarily gratifying, but the reviewers are not the firm's adversary, so there is no reason to make it hard on them. The reviewers are there to help the firm improve its quality control and, as a result, the firm's and the profession's practice quality. Being uncooperative just causes inconvenience for everyone.

Quality review results are confidential so the firm does not risk public embarrassment. Plainly, any firm that receives a modified report will be embarrassed even though the result is known only by firm members. Rejecting the review results by failing to take corrective actions, for example, only exacerbates the firm's problems. Failing to take corrective actions can and will result in loss of AICPA membership.

While peer reviews are publicly available, failure to cooperate during a peer review also is counterproductive. Division firms that are facing modified or even adverse reports should take them as an opportunity to improve the quality of their practices. One firm managing partner had his firm join the PCPS knowing that the firm would fail because he believed that it was the only way to convince his partners that they were not complying with professional standards. The firm, of course, requested an accelerated review, which it passed easily. That firm is now providing quality service.

The truest form of failure to cooperate occurs when a firm decides to drop its AICPA membership to avoid review. Firm members should thoughtfully consider the implications of such a decision. First, a quality control system supplemented by review helps protect the firm against accounting and audit failures. Second, review is an opportunity to measure the firm against its peers. Third, the courts, in litigation, are likely to be less critical of firms that have submitted their practices to review. Finally, practice monitoring of some kind is destined to become a condition of licensing. In fact, the AICPA and the National Association of State Boards of Accountancy (NASBA) recently issued a model Uniform Accountancy Act for consideration by the fifty-four licensing jurisdictions that would require quality review [Uniform Accountancy Act, 1992: 25]. Those who have dropped their membership to avoid review may find it more difficult to reenter the profession. Moreover, firms can and do successfully complete reviews and thus improve their practice quality and the profession's image.

Following these do's and don'ts should make the first few hours go well. This, along with planning and preparation, will help convince the reviewers of the firm's high quality and inspire the in-charge to share ideas about how to practice more efficiently and effectively.

ENGAGEMENT REVIEW

Assignment and Selection

The team captain supervises all aspects of the field work. He or she selects the engagements to be reviewed, assigns some to the other reviewers, and does most of the administrative work.

Many engagements are selected for review. As mentioned above, about 5 to 10 percent of the firm's engagements and accounting and auditing hours are included. Large engagements and those with high risk are usually selected, as is at least one engagement performed under the GAO's government auditing standards. The review will cover a cross-section by partner, client, and engagement type, and it almost invariably will spot the firm's worst engagement, or so it seems.

Reviewer assignments are designed to match reviewers' specialties with engagement requirements. The team captain also will consider each reviewer's experience and preferences.

Reviewing the Engagement

The assigned reviewer handles all engagement aspects. This includes examining the client profile, the accountant-auditor's report, the financial statements, and the key area workpapers. Usually, the reviewer will request a ten- to fifteen-minute preliminary conference with the engagement partner in order to discuss the engagement's key areas and "any unique or complex accounting, reporting or auditing issues . . . as well as the nature of the client's business and records" [Weinstein, 1989: 46]. After the reviewer obtains this information, the engagement review begins.

Engagement checklists are used on both quality and peer reviews. The Quality Review Executive Committee has developed three general checklists that cover general audits, reviews, and compilations and three specialized checklists that cover governmental, not-for-profit, and prospective financial statements. It also has supplemental audit checklists for banks, voluntary health and welfare organizations, construction contractors, employee benefit plans, and common interest realty associations. These can be used on reviews and compilations as well. Similar checklists are used on peer reviews.

The engagement checklists are very detailed. They contain questions on the accountant's report and the related financial statements and notes. A firm that uses comprehensive reporting and disclosure checklists on engagements saves the reviewer time and the firm dollars. The reviewer can skip completing the disclosure portion of the peer or quality review engagement checklist each time if three conditions are met. First, the reviewer must be satisfied with the appropriateness and comprehensiveness of the firm's checklist. Second, the checklist must have been used on the engagement. Third, the reviewer's evaluation of the engagement must indicate that the appropriate disclosures have been made.

A firm that has acquired its programs and checklists from a publisher of such materials should give the reviewer a copy of the most recent review report on those materials and, if applicable, the letter of comments and letter of response. Publishers' materials, just like firms, must be evaluated by the AICPA Division for CPA Firms or the quality review program once every three years.

The reviewer's engagement checklist also covers general audit and engagement issues, such as planning, assessment of inherent and control risk, statistical sampling, and other matters. These issues often show up in letters of comments. Appendix 7.A contains the checklist used on general audits; Appendices 7.B and 7.C contain the checklists used on review and compilation engagements.

Engagement Problems

In a 1989 analysis of SECPS peer reviews, "thirteen percent of the supervision deficiencies concerned the improper application of or inadequate documentation of compliance with SAS 39, Audit Sampling" [Evers and Pearson, 1989: 101]. These letter-of-comments deficiencies might have been prevented had the firms used programs or checklists similar to those used by reviewers. For example, questions A239 through A247 in Appendix 7.A relate to audit sampling issues.

In the same study, 12 percent of the supervision deficiencies involved SAS 47, Audit Risk and Materiality in Conducting an Audit [Evers and Pearson, 1989: 101]. Again, these weaknesses could have been avoided by using comprehensive audit programs. For example, questions A213, 214, 227, 229 through 231, 233, and 236 in Appendix 7.A deal with audit risk and materiality. Firms should compare their programs with the checklist in Appendix 7.A.

In a similar study, Wallace and Wallace reported that 5 percent of letter-of-comments items dealt with lack of an engagement letter [1990: 48]. An engagement letter is not required under GAAS or SSARS. On compilations and reviews the accountant must have an understanding, preferably in writing. A written understanding could take the form of an engagement letter or a memorandum to the file. Why an engagement letter is not required in this litigious society is puzzling. The first question in Appendices 7.B and 7.C—R201 and C201, respectively—covers engagement letters on reviews and compilations.

Many firms now require a signed engagement letter before they furnish accounting or audit services. Most claims, however, seem to involve tax services. For example, CPA Mutual reports that 39 percent of its claims involved tax services and 8.5 percent, 25.0 percent, 8.0 percent, and 4.0 percent involved accounting, audit, compilation, and review services, respectively [1991: 3]. The lesson, of course, is this: Always get an engagement letter, regardless of the service.

Wallace and Wallace frequently found that firms "failed to document the client industry, accounting system, and other general information as required under SSARS 1" [1990: 52]. SSARS, interestingly, does not require documentation of the client's industry and accounting practices. It does, however, require the accountant to understand the industry. How one can demonstrate understanding without documentation again is puzzling. Questions R202 and C202 in Appendices 7.B and 7.C, respectively, deal with that issue.

The appendices to this chapter cover important aspects of engagement supervision and other matters. Firms are strongly encouraged to compare these checklists with what they are using and to consider appropriate changes.

Lack of documentation often is a difficult and contentious review area. For example, Wallace and Wallace said that "many findings relate purely to documentation without giving question as to whether the actual underlying audit step had in fact been performed. These findings appeared in over a third of the files" [1990: 52]. Bremser [1983] cites many findings of deficient documentation, as do Evers and Pearson [1989]. My experience as a reviewer and as a Colorado Society of CPAs Quality Review Board member supports these results, at least partially. Yes, there are many documentation deficiency findings. The reviewer, however, is required to determine whether the underlying work was done. Lack of documentation makes it difficult for the reviewer to know whether the engagement was performed in accordance with professional standards. For example, the workpapers may not document whether a critical inquiry was made, but the engagement partner says it was. Here is where the controversy begins. Why weren't the inquiry and the response documented? Maybe the problem is simply lack of documentation. It is impossible for the reviewer to know with certainty. If lack of documentation is unusual, the firm will earn a clean opinion. The reviewer, however, leaves the firm wondering whether the engagement partner did make the inquiry and, if he or she did not, whether an audit or review was not done in accordance with GAAS or SSARS—and, even worse, whether statements were prepared that are not in accordance with GAAP.

Faced with lack of documentation, the reviewer can draw different inferences, most of them not good. The quality of the documentation often relates directly to the caliber of the firm's supervision. Poor documentation suggests that professional staff, including partners, need additional professional education. Lack of documentation also suggests that the firm is being mismanaged, or perhaps not managed at all. The reviewer also will wonder whether the lack of documentation on audit, review, and compilation engagements is caused by underbidding, which sometimes results in time budgets that do not allow for proper documentation. This could make the reviewer question whether the firm emphasizes growth and profitability at the expense of quality. While the reviewer may not be able to resolve these concerns directly, he or she may look a little harder and, as a result, issue a modified report. For peer and quality review to succeed at improving professional practice, successive reviews must become stricter about work documentation.

Key Areas

The audit engagement checklist in Appendix 7.A includes a detailed section on specific audit areas. The reviewer generally does not complete every section, preferring instead to emphasize key audit areas. He or she will consider several factors in choosing the important sections, including:

1. Critical areas in the client's industry, such as inventory for a manufacturing or retail company and revenue recognition for a construction contractor.

2. Issues identified by the engagement partner.

3. Planning memorandum concerns.

4. The effect of new SASs or SFASs.

5. Weaknesses in prior inspections, quality or peer reviews, or engagement reviews.

The reviewer's audit engagement checklist (not included in this volume) asks the usual questions on bank account confirmations and confirmations of accounts receivable, notes receivable and payable, and bonds payable. It also covers lawyer letters. Because it is comprehensive, the checklist includes some unusual questions. For example, for a client using last-in, first-out (LIFO), the checklist asks whether the LIFO technique was generally consistent with the guidance contained in the AICPA issues paper.

Each section—cash, receivables, inventory, and so on—contains a final question about whether the substantive tests were adequate based on the firm's assessment of control risk. Control-risk documentation for each major cycle and financial statement assertion is, therefore, crucial.

The reviewer's engagement checklist contains questions on each of the functional (quality control) areas, except inspection. The team captain tailors the reviewer's engagement checklist to reflect the firm's quality control system. On audit engagements, the questionnaire asks whether an independence confirmation was obtained from firms engaged to audit segments of the entity. It also asks whether fees from the prior period were paid before the current report was issued. Further, it includes questions on personnel assignment, consultation, and supervision. The supervision questions cover the use of checklists and audit programs. The other quality control areas are covered, too. Checklists for reviews and compilations include similar questions.

"Most reviewers find it effective to perform the review—that is, read the financial statements, and the related report, review the 'top files,' applicable sections of the audit program, correspondence files, consolidating working papers and other 'key audit area' working papers—and then complete the engagement checklist" [Quality Review Executive Committee, 1991: QRP § 5100.09]. The reviewer might ask questions during the engagement review or wait until it is completed. Some reviewers use the MFC forms as notepads and as a means of raising questions; others use them only for significant matters. To reduce tension, it is probably best to ask the reviewer about his or her style.

MFCs—Matters for Further Consideration

Deficiencies indicated on the MFC forms are classified into four categories: (1) performance, (2) compliance, (3) documentation, and (4) design. Performance deficiencies cover situations in which the reviewer believes the reviewed firm did not follow professional standards (i.e., GAAS, SSARS, GAAP, and government auditing standards). Matters categorized as performance deficiencies are very serious and will, if material, result in an adverse report and require the firm to take specified actions. For example, for noncompliance with GAAP, the firm may be required to recall, revise, and reissue the financial statements. For failure to follow GAAS, the firm could be required to let foreseeable users know they should not rely on the report.

Compliance deficiencies are not as serious as performance deficiencies. They occur when the firm has not followed one of its policies or procedures, but did comply with professional standards. For example, the firm may require completion of a reviewer checklist on all engagements. Professional standards do require financial statement, report, and working paper review, but do not mandate completion of a review checklist. If the engagement partner can show that a review was made, the finding probably will be included in the letter of comments, but it will probably not influence the type of report.

Documentation issues arise when the reviewer believes the work was performed, but not properly documented. This is the most frequent deficiency. Documentation inadequacies also often occur on engagements in which the engagement partner does much of the work. While staff are not likely to believe this, partners occasionally do find themselves serving as engagement partner, manager, and staff. As a result, the partner may fail or refuse to recognize the engagement planning and review must be documented even when he or she is doing the work. Sole practitioners without professional staff must watch for this as well.

A design deficiency is as serious as a performance deficiency. It means that the firm's quality control system is not likely to provide reasonable assurance of compliance with professional standards.

The Quality Review Executive Committee does not take a very convincing position on the gravity of design deficiencies. The committee says, ''in the absence of deficiencies in the engagements reviewed, the reviewer would ordinarily conclude that the matter should be dealt with in the letter of comments'' [Quality Review Executive Committee, 1991: QRP § 3000.75]. In the AICPA Division for CPA Firms, a design deficiency is the kiss of death and usually will result in a modified report. The Quality Review Executive Committee may very well do this, too, once firms have had a few reviews and practice monitoring becomes a condition of licensing.

QUALITY CONTROL ASSESSMENT THROUGH STAFF INQUIRIES

The review team captain does most of the nonengagement work. This includes an evaluation of the firm's quality control document and its responses to the quality control questionnaire. It also covers interviews of professional staff and partners to assess the adequacy of the firm's quality control policies and procedures. Further, it involves observation of the firm's operation and inspection of documents that support the firm's adherence to its policies and procedures.

The goal of the staff interviews is to corroborate the information in the firm's quality control document and its responses to the quality control questionnaire. They also are designed to ensure that the firm's policies and procedures have been communicated effectively throughout the organization.

The team captain selects the staff to be interviewed. As in engagement selection, he or she will try to pick a good cross-section. At least one person at each level will be selected. The team captain also considers years of experience and specialties. His or her evaluation of the responses must take experience, specialty, and rank into account. For example, junior staff should be familiar with the firm's independence requirements and the clients to which they apply. However, they probably cannot fairly assess the appropriateness of the engagement assignments they receive.

Staff selected for an interview should be advised that their responses are confidential. Confidentiality is critical to assuring unrestricted responses. The Quality Review Executive Committee says that "the interviewee should be advised that no record is kept of his or her name" [Quality Review Executive Committee, 1991: QRP § 4600.04]. Not keeping a record of the person's name is, in my opinion, far different from promising confidentiality.

The staff interviews cover the nine quality control areas. Questions that the reviewer may ask are listed below under each functional area. The firm should be making similar inquiries during its inspection, so it may be advisable to add these items to the firm's inspection program.

The list below includes those questions usually asked on reviews plus additional queries that have proved to be particularly helpful in making the quality control assessment. These items may be helpful to reviewers in better assessing the firm's quality control.

1. *Independence*

   a. Questions for staff:

      How were you informed of the firm's independence policies? How are you kept informed of the entities to which the firm's independence rules apply?

      Describe situations that might raise independence questions. Whom would you consult about those questions?

      Have you worked on engagements during which other auditors were engaged to audit a segment of the engagement? Did the other firms confirm their independence?

      Describe any discussions of the importance of independence in mental attitude that have taken place in staff or planning meetings.

Briefly explain the firm's independence policies and how periodic confirmations are obtained.

b. Questions for partners and managers:

Do you know of instances in which reports were issued while there were unpaid fees outstanding? If so, what were the circumstances?

2. *Assignment of Personnel to Engagements*

a. Questions for staff:

Describe the types of assignments you have received. Do you believe they were appropriate?

How were you advised of the firm's assignment policies? How do these policies work?

b. Questions for partners and managers:

In deciding on engagement staffing, do you take into account required expertise, audit risk, and business risk? Describe a recent example.

What role do professional development needs play in determining staff assignments? Are these needs considered in assigning engagement tasks? How?

3. *Consultation*

a. Questions for staff:

In which situations does the firm require consultation?

Who are the firm's technical or industry specialists? What is their authority in decision making?

What are the firm's documentation requirements? Describe an instance in which you have documented a consultation.

How are you informed of new additions to the firm's library? Do you find the library holdings adequate for necessary research and education?

b. Questions for partners and managers:

The questions above are suitable for partners and managers as well.

Does the firm reevaluate its consultation policy when economic conditions change? Describe such changes.

Does the firm distribute AICPA risk alerts?

Does the firm's policy on resolving disputes between engagement personnel and technical specialists work satisfactorily?

4. *Supervision*

   a. Questions for staff:

      Describe the firm's documentation requirements on sample selections and evaluations.

      What are the firm's requirements for documenting electronic data processing controls?

      What are the firm's requirements for documenting reportable conditions?

      How are the firm's supervision policies and procedures communicated and implemented? Can you give a recent example?

   b. Questions for senior staff:

      Which forms and procedures are required to plan an engagement?

      In the planning process, what steps do you take to assess the effect of economic conditions and changes in the client's management or products? How do you document these considerations?

      Describe the preliminary analytical procedures you use in engagement planning. How do the results affect audit planning?

      How do you assess and document inherent and control risk? How are these assessments related to the nature, timing, and extent of audit tests to be performed?

      Describe how you go about developing audit or work programs and determining the need for specialized knowledge.

      How would you rate the adequacy of the training you have received to supervise others on an engagement?

      How are differences in judgment resolved on an engagement?

   c. Questions for partners and managers:

      How do you make materiality judgments and determine sample sizes, tolerable error rates and amounts, and so on? (The decision to ask this question usually depends on engagement review results.)

      Describe the firm's engagement review process. How is it documented?

      How do you review the accountant-auditor's report on supplementary information? (This has been a troublesome area for some firms on audits, reviews, and compilations. Too often, the accountant's responsibility, if any, for supplementary information is not indicated.)

5. *Hiring*

a. Questions for staff:

How are you informed of the hiring quality control policies and procedures?

Has the firm amended its hiring policies and procedures? If so, what is your opinion of these changes?

b. Questions for partners and managers:

What characteristics and experience does the firm seek in new hires (if not indicated in the quality control document)? Has the firm succeeded in meeting these goals?

Is the firm's hiring program effective in obtaining suitable personnel?

Has the staff turnover rate been high? If so, what are its causes? What have you done, or what do you plan to do to reduce it?

6. *Professional Development*

a. Questions for staff:

Which professional development courses have you taken this past year? Have these courses contributed to your competence in accounting and auditing? If so, how? How would you describe the quality of the firm's on-the-job training?

Describe the AICPA's continuing professional education requirements.

Does professional development contribute to performance evaluation ratings? If so, how?

Which technical pronouncements does the firm distribute? How frequently do you receive updates? Are they timely?

b. Questions for partners and managers:

Describe the firm's philosophy toward professional development.

Are staff encouraged to take their continuing professional education courses in accounting and auditing? Are other areas advocated as well?

Does the firm stress in-house CPE to the exclusion of AICPA and state society courses?

Are the firm's professional development policies appropriate for the needs of its personnel?

7. *Advancement*

   a. Questions for staff:

   Describe your responsibilities. What qualifications will you need to advance to the next level?

   Describe the employee evaluation process. What is your opinion of the process?

   b. Questions for partners and managers:

   Describe the criteria used in evaluating manager and partner performance. How frequently are managers and partners evaluated? What is the relationship between the criteria and the firm's goals?

   Profits, growth, and quality are each worthwhile firm goals. Based on your observation, what is the relative importance to the firm of each of these goals?

8. *Client Acceptance and Continuance*

   a. Questions for staff:

   Describe events and circumstances—such as irregularities, illegal acts, changes in management, and the like—that you would report to your superiors in keeping with your professional responsibility.

   How are you advised about the firm's client continuance decisions?

   b. Questions for partners and managers:

   What steps do you take in investigating a potential client?

   Describe the circumstances that would persuade you to refuse to take on or continue servicing a client. Have you ever done so? Explain.

   Have you taken on clients that required specialized expertise? If so, what did you do to obtain the required knowledge? Similarly, does the firm have high-risk engagements? If so, what additional steps does the firm take to obtain satisfaction on these engagements?

9. *Inspection*

   a. Questions for staff:

   Did the firm's recent inspection cover an engagement you worked on? If so, were you advised of its findings?

   What were the overall results of the firm's most recent inspection?

   b. Questions for the inspection coordinator:

   Depending on the completeness of the inspection report, additional questions may be appropriate. These might include inquiries on whether the inspection's scope included new or high-risk engagements, those not covered in previous inspections or reviews, and a cross-section by partner and engagement type.

By making the inquiries suggested above, the reviewer gains important corroborative information about the nature and extent of the firm's quality control policies. The answers also provide the reviewer with meaningful insight into possible weaknesses in the engagement review.

A few other general questions should also be asked because the issuance of professional standards should always cause a reevaluation of the firm's control system. In addition, practice acquisitions, turnover in key staff, significant growth, and the like should cause the firm to reevaluate its system's adequacy. The following questions may be useful in evaluating whether the firm does amend its system as things change:

a. Questions for staff:

Have the firm's quality control policies and procedures been changed in the past year or so? If changes were made, describe them. How were these changes communicated to you?

Did the issuance of SAS (mention one) prompt changes in the firm's policies or procedures on supervision, consultation, and so on? (Fill in as appropriate). Similarly, did the issuance of SFAS (mention one) cause a change to the firm's disclosure checklists? Were you given adequate and timely explanations of these new pronouncements?

b. Questions for partners and managers:

Has the firm amended its control system in the past year or so? If it did, please describe the changes. Why were they made? Did you consider them appropriate?

Has the firm grown significantly in the past year or so? (Depending on the circumstances, this may lead to other questions. For instance, a practice acquisition, high turnover, or new engagements requiring specialized expertise should trigger a reevaluation of the control system.)

OTHER QUALITY CONTROL ASSESSMENT PROCEDURES

Besides staff interviews, the review team captain takes several other steps to determine if the firm's quality control system provides reasonable assurance of complying with professional standards. Firms designing their inspection programs should consider similar procedures. Team captains also may find this section particularly helpful, as will reviewers about to take on their first team captain assignments.

The assessment procedures include review and evaluation of the firm's quality control document and its responses to the quality control questionnaire. To clarify this information, the in-charge will hold discussions with the area coordinators, other partners and managers, and the managing partner, as appropriate. For each functional area, the in-charge will determine whether the firm has assigned responsibility for the area to a person or group and evaluate the adequacy of the firm's communication policy and the sufficiency of its monitoring policy. In addition, the team captain will take other steps, including inspection of the firm's library and examination of the firm's administrative and personnel files. Further, the in-charge will study the relationships between a particular functional area and related areas. Weaknesses in one area frequently are offset by strengths in others. Finally, the team captain will assess whether amendments should have been made to firm policies and procedures because of changed circumstances. For example, as mentioned above, a practice acquisition usually requires a reevaluation of the entire control system. Each of these issues is discussed in the context of the functional area in the sections that follow.

Independence

The primary objective of the firm's independence policy is to require firm member compliance with the AICPA independence requirements (rules, regulations, interpretations, and rulings). The SEC and some state societies and boards also have independence requirements that firms must follow. Some firms have developed more stringent requirements. The team captain, then, needs to assess whether the quality control system adequately addresses these requirements.

The team captain will discuss with the managing partner or the independence coordinator financial and other relationships prohibited by the profession's independence rules. This discussion will focus on the firm and its employees, and explore whether the firm has business relationships with clients in which the firm or its personnel might be considered investors or recipients of investment funds. There will be questions about loans from financial entities and unpaid client fees as well as discussion of situations in which the firm has identified itself as not independent. To the extent not accomplished in the engagement review, the firm's report will be examined to see if the report was modified appropriately in these situations. This discussion will also include questions about staff and partners who have family members in managerial or director positions with clients.

The team captain will ask about the nature of the firm's MAS assignments for accounting and audit clients to see if the firm took on the role of management in performing the client advisory service. SECPS members will be asked about prohibited engagements, such as actuarial services for insurance companies.

Assigning responsibility for each functional area is an important quality control goal, so this will be evaluated as well. For example, a quality control system that does not assign accountability to someone (preferably an owner) for the independence objective would have a design weakness. Assigned responsibilities include resolving independence questions and maintaining a comprehensive, up-to-date independence library. The independence coordinator will be asked how he or she keeps up with new independence requirements. The team captain will inspect the coordinator's independence library and the firm's independence files. The independence library must include current requirements of applicable organizations.

The independence file inspection will cover documentation of independence questions. If it was not accomplished in the engagement reviews, the team captain will inspect the evidence that the engagement partner checked the status of client receivables before the report was issued. The independence rules require a firm to confirm the independence of others auditing a client segment, so the team captain should examine related confirmations not covered in the engagement reviews.

The firm must have policies on communication and monitoring. The team captain will review the firm's independence policies to ensure that professional personnel are periodically advised of these policies and the clients to which they apply. In addition, the firm's communication of its independence rules will be evaluated by examining firm manuals, training program material, and memoranda for evidence that the independence policies are communicated on a timely basis. These policies also must require periodic monitoring by mandating staff independence confirmations. The absence of communication or monitoring policies would be a design weakness.

In evaluating the firm's independence policies and procedures, the team captain will study the relationships between them and the firm's hiring and supervision policies. For example, firms that include an independence module in their new staff orientation are strengthening their independence. Also, firms that include independence questions in engagement planning or review checklists as part of their supervision policies are fortifying this area.

The team captain will ask the independence coordinator or managing partner about situations that caused or should have caused a reevaluation of the firm's independence policies. For example, a practice acquisition and the addition of new professional personnel may require independence policy revisions. At a minimum, they would require special steps to assure that independence is maintained, such as getting signed independence confirmations from all professional staff, including partners, based on a review of the combined client list. There also should be a program to educate new professional staff about the firm's requirements.

Assigning Personnel

Quality review teams must perform additional procedures on large firms in relation to personnel assignment, hiring, and advancement, as well as acceptance and continuance of clients and inspection. These procedures also are required in small firms when significant engagement deficiencies exist. (The distinction between large and small firms is based on the number of professionals. "Professionals" in this context refers to CPAs and those aspiring to be CPAs. Large firms are those with more than ten professionals.)

For all firms, the evaluation of personnel assignment is based on professional staff interviews, engagement reviews, and an analysis of the firm's quality control document and questionnaire responses. Again, the focus is on the degree to which the policies encompass assignment of responsibility, communication, and monitoring. The reviewer will check that these are integrated with the policies on hiring, supervision, and professional development. For example, a firm that does not use audit, review, and compilation programs must have strong assignment policies. A firm that requires only the minimum CPE hours under its professional development policies must be more careful in personnel assignment. In addition, a firm that allows its professional staff to take their CPE in areas other than accounting and audit will be scrutinized more closely in the assignment area.

Another supplementary procedure for large firms and for small firms with engagement problems is partner interviews focusing on the relative importance of assignment decision variables. In making these decisions, a firm wants to staff an engagement to maximize efficiency and effectiveness. To be effective, the firm must consider the engagement's size, complexity, and risk, plus the expertise required and the planned supervision level. Further, it must consider the timing of the work, need for continuity and rotation, and staff availability. Finally, the firm decision model sometimes considers staff professional development opportunities through on-the-job training.

Engagement partners, the area coordinator, and the managing partner each will be interviewed about the relative importance of the factors affecting personnel assignment. A firm that assigns higher importance to such variables as engagement complexity and planned supervision level would have stronger assignment policies.

The team captain will inspect the firm's documentation of priority systems for assigning personnel to engagements. For example, some firms use a scoring system that attempts to match engagement needs and personnel skills. An engagement that is highly complex and could be most efficiently completed with low supervision would be assigned a high score. Such an engagement would call for personnel with specialized expertise and extensive experience. In other firms, the engagement partner completes a planning checklist showing that he or she considered each engagement variable in the assignment decision. Firms should be aware of the need for a priority system. Staff assignments can no longer be made based on availability.

A firm that uses comprehensive, understandable checklists and work programs can defend its assignments. Programs and checklists lower engagement complexity and risk, and are an effective means of exercising engagement supervision. Strong supervision policies and procedures compensate, to some extent, for weaker assignment and hiring policies.

The team captain performing the additional procedures will discuss with the personnel assignment coordinator any assignment policy and procedure amendments or revisions. The assignment coordinator must be prepared to explain the rationale behind policy changes. On initial reviews, the period of concern is the review year. Subsequent reviews cover the term since the last review.

A firm that experiences significant growth or employee turnover probably should have strengthened its assignment policies. The assignment coordinator must be prepared to discuss the rationale behind policy changes or the lack of them.

Consultation

The firm's quality control document and questionnaire responses are the basis for evaluating its consultation policies. Critical to this evaluation is the expectation that these policies will mandate appointment of an owner or group to target situations requiring consultation. A firm also must appoint technical and industry specialists, and detail its library specifications. Further, it should establish consultation documentation requirements. Finally, the policies must include appropriate communication goals and a monitoring provision.

The team captain will check whether the library holdings are appropriately comprehensive and up-to-date. (See the listing of suggested minimum library holdings in Appendix 5.A.) The reviewer will assess how the library is used. It is not uncommon for it to appear as if the library holdings have never been touched. He or she also will check to see if loose-leaf services are current.

If it is not accomplished in the engagement reviews, the team captain will inspect the consultation files to see if the firm has followed its consultation policies. Also, the reviewer will assess whether consultation has been documented as required. The team captain may ask questions of the technical and industry specialists to determine if the firm's policy is working as designed.

The team captain will also assess whether changes should have been made to the consultation policies and procedures. A firm that takes on high-risk engagements or those requiring specialized expertise should have strengthened its procedures. One that is experiencing disagreements between technical specialists and engagement partners must specify who has the authority. Changes in economic conditions also should cause a reassessment of consultation policies, as should findings from the last inspection or review.

Supervision

The supervision assessment depends for the most part on the results of the engagement reviews and the responses to the staff interview questions, which were previously discussed. In addition, it involves review and evaluation of the firm's programs, checklists, and manuals. For example, audit, review, and compilation programs are assessed for comprehensiveness and clarity. Ordinarily, an audit program, perhaps in combination with an audit manual, covers audit risk, materiality, sampling, analytical procedures, assessment of inherent and control risk, and specific substantive tests for accounts and cycles.

The firm's planning and review checklists will be analyzed. The planning checklists should incorporate guidance on documentation of client background, materiality judgments, evaluation of inherent and control risk, acceptable audit risk, tolerable errors, and so on. The review checklists should include firm requirements on what must be reviewed and the extent of the review. For example, many review checklists require an examination of permanent files, passed adjustments, memoranda on consultations, and significant accounting issues. Well-designed programs and checklists save engagement review time.

The reviewer will assess the firm's procedures for resolving differences of opinion on an engagement. In addition, the team captain will take special care to evaluate the firm's supervision documentation requirements. This analysis includes an evaluation at each review level, such as seniors, managers, and partners. It also covers, if applicable, an analysis of instances requiring a concurrent or preissuance review on SEC and high-risk engagements.

The supervision coordinator and engagement partners will be interviewed about the nature, timing, and extent of changes to the firm's programs and checklists. The issuance of SASs and SFASs and the addition of clients in specialized industries should prompt amendments to these materials. The in-charge will evaluate how well these changes were communicated to the professional staff.

Hiring

As with assignment of personnel, the team captain will evaluate hiring based on an analysis of the firm's quality control document, the engagement review findings, and inquiries of selected personnel. Additional procedures are required for large firms and small firms with engagement problems.

The starting point, as always, is to evaluate the appropriateness of the firm's policies and procedures. They must require the appointment of a person to set up and monitor the firm's hiring goals. In addition, they should authorize people to make hiring decisions and delineate desired employee characteristics.

Reviewers inspect personnel files in large firms. Specifically, they examine employee resumes to determine the degree of correspondence between the desired characteristics and the attributes of those hired. The personnel files also are examined for required documentation, such as reference checks, college transcripts, and the like. The team captain also may ask to see the firm's memoranda to staff about hiring objectives and needs.

The firm's hiring policies strongly influence its policies on advancement, professional development, and supervision, and vice versa, so they should be coordinated. The reviewer will evaluate how well this has been accomplished.

If necessary, the reviewer also may interview the person charged with monitoring the firm's hiring policies. Close monitoring is called for in instances of high employee turnover, changes in client mix and engagements, and firm growth. When, for example, a firm starts to do more audits than compilations, it should reassess its hiring program.

Professional Development

Professional development, like supervision, is a deciding quality control element. The team captain will analyze this area closely. The firm's policies must include a provision requiring the firm to properly train personnel for their assignments. The professional development coordinator or managing partner, as appropriate, will be asked how the firm plans its CPE program. In particular, the coordinator will be asked the basis for selecting employee training. For example, staff with primary responsibility in accounting and auditing should fulfill their CPE requirement by taking appropriate courses in these areas. Those who wish to take courses in tax or other topics should do so, but not as a substitute for courses in accounting and auditing.

The team captain will examine firm memoranda distributed with professional pronouncements, as well as the literature or training provided to those servicing specialized industries. For example, firms with governmental audits must provide specialized training under government auditing standards. Further, the team captain will inspect, perhaps on a test basis, the professional development files to determine if firm personnel are following AICPA, state board, state society, and other regulatory requirements.

Firms that do in-house training should have files showing that the courses follow AICPA, state board, state society, and other regulatory guidelines and recommendations. At a minimum, these files should include a statement of objectives for each course. They also should contain course outlines, attendance sheets, and course and instructor evaluations, as well as documentation supporting an analysis of the evaluations. Finally, the team captain will seek to review the notes made about actions taken as a result of the evaluation analysis.

The quality control questionnaire asks the firm to summarize the CPE courses taken, specifying the percentage of hours using self-study, in-house, state society and AICPA, and other courses. The team captain may doubt the firm's commitment to professional development if it focuses on self-study and in-house training to the exclusion of state society and AICPA programs.

The professional development policies should be coordinated with staff evaluations, and the integration of these two elements should be documented. Some firms include professional development as a criterion in employee evaluations. Also, firms that have professional development policies encouraging participation in AICPA and state association activities should document the policies' success.

The professional development coordinator should be prepared to show the team captain that firm policies are reevaluated when appropriate. For example, obtaining clients in specialized industries requires revision of the professional development program and personnel assignment policies. The CPE coordinator also should be prepared to show that firm members receive timely education when new pronouncements are issued.

Advancement

To evaluate this area, the team captain will rely on staff interviews, engagement reviews, and an evaluation of the firm's quality control document and questionnaire responses. This includes assessment of the appropriateness of the minimum qualifications for each level in the firm. He or she also will consider the firm's employee evaluation criteria, the content and frequency of employee reviews, and required documentation.

Expanded procedures for large firms involve discussion of "the firm's underlying philosophy with respect to advancement, termination, and partner responsibilities" [Quality Review Executive Committee, 1991: QRP § 4500.04G1b]. Also, if applicable, the team captain will evaluate the reasonableness of job descriptions and criteria for advancement.

The expanded procedures include personnel file inspection supporting the nature and timeliness of employee evaluations. Partner evaluations also are an important quality control component. To assess them, the team captain will examine the supporting documentation and the appropriateness of the criteria. For example, criteria focusing on rainmaking ability may raise questions about firm quality.

The in-charge also will study the relationships between the firm's policies on advancement and those on hiring, supervision, and professional development. A firm that has strong supervision materials such as programs and checklists can promote its personnel more quickly. On the other hand, a firm that hires only entry-level personnel will probably need more conservative advancement policies.

Client Acceptance and Continuance

This evaluation is based on engagement reviews and responses to the staff inquiries. It also depends on an analysis of the quality control document, questionnaire responses, and partner interviews. Firm policies should state that it will take on engagements only when it is independent, can serve the client properly, and believes in the client's integrity level. In addition, some firm policies include a requirement to assess firm risk when making acceptance and continuance decisions. The firm should detail as well the procedures necessary to make these decisions. For example, some firms use acceptance checklists that require a partner to contact bankers and attorneys about the potential client. They often require a review of the potential client's financial information, its audit committee, and its viability as a going concern.

The acceptance policies must require communication with predecessor auditors. The continuance policies must specify conditions that should cause a reevaluation of the client relationship. Some firms make a continuance decision on every client annually and include the evaluation steps in a continuance checklist. Both continuance and acceptance decisions involve evaluations of client integrity and of the firm's ability to serve the client properly. Continuation decisions should include an assessment of the client's reaction to the existence of errors, firm suggestions for improvement, the reliability of management estimates, and so on.

The reviewer also will examine firm policies on special situations, such as the discovery of illegal acts and irregularities, litigation, changes in management, changes in engagement scope, and the like. These situations should always cause the firm to evaluate whether it should continue servicing the client.

The team captain will perform additional procedures for large firms and small firms with engagement deficiencies. He or she might, for example, request information about the circumstances of client terminations. Also, the team captain will review documentation of acceptance and continuance decisions not accomplished in the engagement reviews and inspect documentation of communication with predecessor accountants.

The team captain will discuss with the managing partner situations that caused or should have caused a reevaluation of acceptance and continuance decisions. Certainly a downturn in the economy or in a particular industry should spur a review of firm acceptance and continuance policies. Threatened or actual litigation and alleged accounting or audit failure are other important reasons for a reassessment.

Inspection

On all reviews, the team captain will evaluate the firm's inspection policies and procedures. Inspection is a strategic component of a quality control system.

Additional procedures for large firms and small firms with engagement deficiencies include an assessment of the inspection's scope and the assignment of inspectors. Checklists are examined for comprehensiveness, and the findings and recommendations are assessed. On all peer reviews, the firm's most recent inspection is analyzed.

The team captain knows that the inspection's scope is affected by the appropriateness of the firm's hiring, professional development, and supervision policies. Staff experience, industry specialization, types of engagements, and the results of prior quality reviews and inspections also have an impact. Firms that hire only experienced CPAs and that have strong professional development programs and supervision policies can probably limit the inspection scope. On the other hand, firms that service clients in multiple industries and that hire entry-level personnel must expand the scope of their inspections.

The team captain also will assess the degree of care taken in assigning tasks and engagements to inspectors. For example, an engagement requiring special-ized industry knowledge should be assigned to an inspector with the correct skills.

The reviewer will determine whether comprehensive engagement checklists were used. These checklists should encompass a review of the independent accountant-auditor's report, financial statements, and key workpaper areas. They should cover general audit, review, and compilation considerations and planning and review procedures, as well as analyzing quality control system functional areas. They should include detailed audit, review, and compilation procedures.

The in-charge will assess the adequacy and timeliness of the communication of the inspection's findings to the professional staff. Staff members should be advised about the findings on the engagements they worked on.

To verify these procedures, the team captain will review the firm's memoranda used to advise the professional staff of the findings. Inspectors will be interviewed and asked which engagements they reviewed, what the scope of those reviews was, and what forms and checklists they used. The reviewer also will request access to inspection notes and review the firm's plans for corrective actions and their implementation. The reviewer will request to see engagements where cor-rective actions were taken.

If the team captain is satisfied that the tests suggest that all procedures were followed, then the scope of the quality review can be reduced. Unfortunately, the quality review steps require an inspection evaluation only for large firms and small firms with problems. Small firms, then, may not be able to reduce their review costs, even though they have done a thorough inspection.

DRAWING CONCLUSIONS

Perhaps the most difficult area in the entire review is the process of synthesizing the review findings and deciding on the type of report to be issued. It involves classifying the deficiencies into two types, design and compliance, and assessing the materiality of those deficiencies.

The review team prepares an evaluation of the quality control document, the quality control questionnaire responses, and staff interviews. Supplementing this evaluation with system tests and the engagement reviews, the team captain can draw conclusions in two areas: the appropriateness of the quality control system and the extent of the firm's compliance with it. To help the reviewer in this assessment, the Quality Review Executive Committee has developed a ques-tionnaire listing objectives for each element. For example, the reviewer must answer "yes," "no," or "N/A" to these five independence goals:

1. Requires all professional personnel to adhere to applicable independence rules, regulations, interpretations, and rulings?

2. Communicates its policies and procedures relating to independence to all professional personnel?

3. Requires, when acting as principal auditor, confirmation of the independence of another firm engaged to perform segments of an engagement?

4. Adequately monitors compliance with its policies and procedures relating to independence on a timely basis?

5. Complied with its independence policies and procedures during the period and adequately documented its compliance to the extent required by firm policy? [Quality Review Executive Committee, 1991: QRP § 4700.05A].

For each "No" answer, the team captain must decide if the firm has a design or a compliance deficiency. For example, a firm has a design deficiency if it lacks a monitoring policy requiring periodic independence confirmations. If it has such a policy, but did not get the periodic confirmations, it has a compliance deficiency.

Compliance Deficiencies—Two Types

Compliance deficiencies are further separated into performance or documentation deficiencies. A compliance performance deficiency means the firm failed to comply with an existing policy. For example, a firm that does not follow its policy to obtain periodic independence confirmations as part of its monitoring goal would have a compliance performance deficiency. A compliance documentation deficiency means the firm complied with its policy, but did not document it.

Of the different deficiencies, design and performance are the most serious. Documentation deficiencies might end up in the letter of comments, but they probably will not affect the type of report.

Reports—Which Type?

The decision on whether to issue an unqualified, modified, or adverse report is a matter of professional judgment. It is based on the review team's perceptions of a deficiency's materiality. Material design deficiencies often lead to a modified or adverse report and are always in the letter of comments. Also, a firm with design deficiencies must amend its quality control policies and procedures. Significant design deficiencies coupled with engagement deficiencies could well result in an adverse report.

Modified reports often arise from scope limitations. A modified report would be issued when a reviewed firm excludes, for justifiable reasons, certain significant engagements from the review. If the reviewers cannot satisfy themselves about the firm's compliance with professional standards on those engagements, they will issue a modified report. For example, a firm that disposes of a significant portion of its practice before the review would probably receive a modified report due to the scope limitation. Every effort, however, is made to avoid these modifications.

A modified or adverse report may be appropriate when compliance deficiencies are coupled with engagement deficiencies. Compliance deviations occur for several reasons. Sometimes a firm fails to communicate its policies as well as it should. Some firm policies are poorly written and are, thus, incomprehensible. Perhaps the most common reason is lack of commitment to make the system work.

A firm with a well-designed, but ignored, quality control system and significant engagement deficiencies could receive either a modified or an adverse report. The decision will depend on the extent of noncompliance and the nature and significance of the engagement deficiencies. If the firm has one or more significant engagement deficiencies traceable either to a poorly designed system or to noncompliance with a good system, then some report modification will be considered.

A modified review report, like an audit qualification, involves a statement before the opinion; for example:

> As discussed in our letter of comments under this date, our review disclosed that the firm's quality control policies and procedures for supervision regarding audit planning were not appropriately designed to provide the firm with reasonable assurance of conforming with professional standards.
>
> In our opinion, except for the deficiency described in the preceding paragraph, the system of quality control. . . . [Quality Review Executive Committee, 1991: QRP § 3000.78]

An adverse report, like a modified report, includes a statement before the opinion and changes the opinion to adverse. This paragraph and opinion might read as follows:

> As discussed in our letter of comments under this date, our review disclosed several failures to adhere to professional standards in reporting material departures from generally accepted accounting principles, . . . , and in complying with the standards for accounting and review services. In that connection, our review disclosed that the firm's quality control policies and procedures were not appropriately designed because they do not require the preparation of a written audit program, which is required by generally accepted auditing standards. In addition, our review disclosed failures to complete financial statement reporting and disclosure checklists required by firm policy and failures to review engagement working papers in the manner required by firm policy.
>
> In our opinion, because of the significance of the matters discussed in the preceding paragraph, the system of quality control for the accounting

and auditing practice of [Name of Firm] in effect for the year ended June 30, 19XX, did not meet the objectives of quality control standards established by the AICPA, was not being complied with during the year ended and did not provide the firm with reasonable assurance of conforming with professional standards in the conduct of that practice. [Quality Review Executive Committee, 1991: QRP § 3000.78]

The chances, however, of receiving an unqualified opinion are very good. Among AICPA Division for CPA Firms members, 86 percent "of the firms received 'clean' opinions on the initial review and 92% did so on subsequent reviews" [Evers and Pearson, 1989: 96]. For 1991, the division reported again that 86 percent received unqualified opinions on initial reviews and 97 percent did so on subsequent reviews [Based on author's correspondence with AICPA]. The early statistics on initial quality reviews are not as good. This is not surprising, however, since division membership review results are publicly available, so a division firm takes greater risk and should, therefore, be better prepared.

A primary purpose of review is to educate and thereby improve the quality of the firm's practice. The success of this effort will be revealed on subsequent reviews. The pass-fail rates on initial reviews are only important because they demonstrate the need for mandatory quality review.

Firms that receive unqualified reports should not rest on their laurels. "Sixteen (5%) of the firms reviewed during the past two years learned this important lesson the hard way. They apparently had become complacent and, as a consequence, received modified reports after receiving previous clean opinions" [Evers and Pearson, 1989: 96].

Regardless of the type of report the firm receives, it is almost certain to get a letter of comments. In the PCPS and the quality reviews, the unqualified report will not refer to the letter of comments, while modified reports will. On SECPS reviews, the letter of comments is referred to in the report.

LETTERS OF COMMENTS

In 1991, the AICPA Division for CPA Firms reported that 85 percent of reviewed firms received letters of comments on their initial reviews. The Quality Review Executive Committee says, "such letters are expected to be issued on most on-site reviews" [1991: QRP § 3000.79]. The early statistics suggest they meant the word "most."

The letter of comments details the review findings and provides reasonably precise recommendations for corrective action. The findings are divided between those that resulted in a report modification and those that did not.

Remote-Possibility Criterion

In deciding if an item ought to be included in the comments letter, the reviewer uses a remote-possibility criterion. An item is included if it suggests that a firm may not conform with professional standards on accounting and audit engagements. This low limit will, in the main, result in several comments for most firms.

> Deficiencies in the design of the reviewed firm's quality control system should be included in the letter of comments if the design of the system resulted in one or more quality control objectives not being accomplished, and, as a result, a condition was created in which there was more than a remote possibility that the firm would not conform with professional standards on accounting and auditing engagements, even though there was a reasonable assurance of conforming with professional standards. [Quality Review Executive Committee, 1991: QRP § 3600.09]

The Quality Review Executive Committee suggests that compliance performance and compliance documentation deficiencies also should be included in the letter.

Presentation

The letter of comments will not list each engagement deficiency. Findings will be grouped. For example, documentation deficiencies, while quite common, often are combined into a single comment. Findings also are grouped into individual causes traceable to the quality control system. For example, disclosure deficiencies often result when firms do not require completion of comprehensive disclosure checklists as part of their supervision policies. The letter of comments will not list individual disclosure deficiencies but, rather, might state the following:

Finding—

The firm's supervision policies do not require completion of comprehensive reporting and disclosure engagement checklists as an aid in the review of client financial statements. On several reviewed engagements, the financial statements did not include all the disclosures required by generally accepted accounting principles, including, in particular, related-party and lease obligations. The missed disclosures were not significant; therefore, the statements were not misleading.

Recommendation—

While professional standards do not require the use of disclosure checklists, the firm should acquire or develop such checklists to assure compliance with professional standards. The firm should then amend its quality control policies and procedures to require their completion on all compi-

lation, review, and audit engagements. The checklists should be retained
in the client files.

The Quality Review Executive Committee and the Division for CPA Firms
recognize that not all quality control objectives were created equal. For example,
a reviewer would be more tolerant of failure to comply with an advancement
policy covering employee evaluations than of failure to follow a supervision
policy that requires completion of certain planning procedures.

Isolated deficiencies, such as human error, usually are not included in the
letter of comments, but they are covered in the exit conference. The firm,
however, is responsible for showing that the error was isolated.

EXIT CONFERENCE

If the firm receives an unqualified report, the team captain will suggest that
all professional staff be allowed to attend the exit conference. Successfully
completing a review builds morale and confidence. The reviewers will emphasize
that a successful review depends on the efforts of each firm member. The team
captain will stress that the recommended report is tentative and can be made
public only after the AICPA or state administering society has approved it.

The team captain will discuss the purpose of review and the review scope and
findings, including the items to be covered in the comments letter. He or she
will cover items that will not appear in the letter, such as isolated oversights
and insignificant design and compliance deficiencies. Because of the strong
interdependence among the control elements, some areas compensate for others.
A significant design weakness may not be included in the comments letter because
other elements offset it. For example, a firm hiring only experienced CPAs can
probably offset failure to comply with some supervision policies. The reviewer
also may mention excessive procedures that are inefficient.

In the case of a report modification, only the key personnel should attend the
exit conference. The team captain will discuss the reasons for a modified report
and matters that did not contribute to modification, but will be included in the
comments letter.

AFTER THE REVIEW

Within thirty days of the exit conference, the team captain will provide the
firm with a written report and, if applicable, a comments letter. The nature of
the report and the comments letter items should be detailed in the exit conference.

Review the Letter of Comments

Firm leaders should thoroughly review the comments letter. If it includes items
not discussed in the exit conference, which sometimes happens, the review

coordinator should contact the team captain. The reviewer may be amenable to changing some of its wording. Further, reviewers are sometimes wrong. "Reviewers are occasionally surprised to find that some generally accepted professional standards are, in reality, only a preferred treatment by their firm" [Quality Review Executive Committee, 1991: QRP § 3600.06].

The reviewed firm must draft a response to each point in the letter of comments, so it is very important that the firm understand the nature and significance of each finding and its related recommendation.

Draft the Firm's Response

The firm is required to respond to the letter of comments within thirty days of its receipt. It must send the administering organization the review team's comments letter and report and the firm's response.

The response is critical to the administering organization's evaluation and ultimate acceptance of the review report. It should describe the remedial, corrective actions the firm has taken or will take in response to each letter of comments finding. It should detail actions that will prevent the deficiencies from occurring again. Figure 7.1 illustrates such a response.

In a few instances, the firm may disagree with an item in the letter. The firm and the reviewer should do everything possible to resolve the matter. If they cannot, the firm should carefully prepare its reasons for disagreeing. When a disagreement persists on a significant matter, and especially when it causes a report modification, the administering organization will appoint an individual to investigate it.

Appoint Someone to Implement and Monitor the Remedial Actions

The firm should appoint an owner to implement the corrective actions covered in the firm's response and the other items discussed at the exit conference. Implementation procedures might include designing and holding a training session for professional staff to review the letter of comments and the firm's response to it. This session might include a review, if applicable, of the firm's amended quality control document, the adoption of planning and review checklists, work programs, and so on. It should stress the importance of complying with the quality control system.

The appointed person also should develop procedures to check firm compliance with the new policies and procedures. In addition, the next inspection should include procedures designed to test the firm's compliance with noted quality control weaknesses.

Figure 7.1

Illustration of Response by a Reviewed Firm to a Letter of Comments on an On-Site Quality Review

The purpose of a letter of response is to describe the remedial, corrective actions that the firm has taken or will take to prevent a recurrence of each matter discussed in the letter of comments. If the reviewed firm disagrees with one or more of the findings or recommendations in the letter of comments, its response should describe the reasons for such disagreement. The letter of response should be carefully prepared because of the important bearing it may have on the decisions reached in connection with acceptance of the report on the review (see the section of these Standards on "Acceptance of Reviews").

• • • •

September 15, 19XX

[Addressed to the Entity Administering the Review, which may be the AICPA Quality Review Division or a participating State Society of CPAs]

Ladies and Gentlemen:

This letter represents our response to the letter of comments issued in connection with our firm's on-site quality review for the year ended June 30, 19XX. The matters discussed herein were brought to the attention of all professional personnel at a training session held on September 10, 19XX.

Matters That Resulted in a Modified Report

Partner Involvement in Audit Planning—The firm modified its quality control policies and procedures to require partner involvement in the planning stage of all audit engagements. In addition, we identified review engagements that are sufficiently large or complex to warrant partner involvement in the planning stage. The revised policies and procedures require the engagement partner to document his or her timely involvement in the planning process in the planning section of the written work program. The importance of proper planning, including timely partner involvement, to quality work was emphasized in the training session referred to above.

Matters That Did Not Result in a Modified Report

Financial Reporting and Disclosure Checklists—All professional personnel were reminded of the importance of complying with the firm's policy requiring completion of its financial reporting and disclosure checklist at the training session held on September 10, 19XX. In addition, the firm's engagement review questionnaire is being revised to require the engagement partner to document his or her review of the completed checklist. (The engagement review questionnaire is a brief form completed by the engagement partner and manager at the conclusion of an audit to document their completion of their assigned responsibilities.)

Responsibility for Reference Library—The responsibility for keeping the firm's reference library comprehensive and up-to-date and for advising professional personnel of additions to the library has been assigned to an experienced audit manager. Current editions of industry audit and accounting guides have been ordered.

• • • •

We believe these actions are responsive to the findings of the review.

Sincerely,

[Name of Firm]

Source: From Quality Review and Program Manual, Copyright © 1991 by American Institute of Certified Public Accountants, Inc. Reprinted with permission.

SURVIVAL

The firm has survived its review. Few do it unscathed. When the dust clears, firm members will realize they are now able to provide a better quality product than ever before. They also will know that they have helped preserve the CPA designation. Finally, they will realize that it was not nearly as bad as they feared.

REFERENCES

Bremser, W. G. "Peer Review: Enhancing Quality Control." *Journal of Accountancy* (October 1983): 78–88.

CPA Mutual. *Of Mutual Interest*, December 1991.

Evers, C. J., and D. B. Pearson. "Lessons Learned from Peer Review." *Journal of Accountancy* (April 1989): 96–105.

Quality Review Executive Committee. *AICPA Quality Review Program Manual*. New York: AICPA, 1991.

Uniform Accountancy Act. AICPA and the NASBA. New York: AICPA, 1992.

Wallace, W. A., and J. J. Wallace. "Learning from Peer Review Comments." *The CPA Journal* (May 1990): 48–53.

Weinstein, S. "Part 2: Your Quality Review: A Step-by-Step Approach." *The Practical Accountant* (June 1989): 37–53.

Appendix 7.A
General Audit Procedures

	QUES.	N/A*	YES	NO	REF.**

In planning the audit engagement, did the auditor properly consider:

Matters affecting the industry in which the entity operates, such as accounting practices, economic conditions, laws and government regulations, and technological changes? (AU Secs. 311.03 and 801.11) — A204

Matters affecting the entity's business, such as organization and types of products and services and contractual obligations? (AU Sec. 311.03-.04) — A205

Preliminary judgment about materiality levels? (AU Secs. 311.03 and 312.08) — A206

Did the auditor:

Make an assessment of the risk of material misstatements of the financial statements, including those resulting from violations of laws and regulations that have a direct and material effect on the determination of financial statement amounts? (AU Secs. 312.12 and 316.05) — A207

Assess the risk of management misrepresentation by reviewing information obtained about risk factors and the internal control structure? (AU Sec. 316.12) — A208

Design the audit to provide reasonable assurance of detecting errors and irregularities that are material to the financial statements? (AU Sec. 316.05) — A209

Did the auditor use analytical procedures in planning the nature, timing and extent of other audit procedures? (AU Sec. 329.01 and .06) — A210

If the auditor succeeded a predecessor auditor, did the auditor:

Communicate with the predecessor auditor to ascertain whether there were disagreements between the predecessor auditor and the entity's management on accounting or auditing matters and consider the implications of such matters in accepting the client? (AU Sec. 315.03 and .06) — A211

Make other inquiries of the predecessor auditor on significant matters? (AU Sec. 315.08) — A212

Reach satisfaction on the fair presentation of opening balances, such as by reviewing the predecessor auditor's working papers? (AU Sec. 315.08) — A213

If consideration was given to the work of internal auditors in determining the scope of the examination, was it done in accordance with professional standards? (AU Sec. 322) — A214

Appendix 7.A (continued)

	QUES.	N/A	YES	NO	REF.
Did the auditor:					
Obtain a sufficient understanding of the entity's internal control structure to plan the audit? (AU Secs. 319.16 and 324.07-.10)	A215				
Document the understanding of the internal control structure? (AU Sec. 319.26)	A216				
Document the conclusion that control risks are at the maximum level for those financial statement assertions where control risk is assessed at the maximum level? (AU Sec. 319.39)	A217				
Document the basis for the conclusion (i.e., tests of controls) that the effectiveness of the design and operation of internal control structure policies and procedures supports the assessed level of control risk when that assessed level is below the maximum level? (AU Sec. 319.39)	A218				
If the methods used by the client to process significant accounting information include the use of a service organization, was consideration given to the internal controls of the accounting applications, if any, at the service organization? (AU Sec. 311.03)	A219				
If the auditor relied on the internal accounting controls at a service organization, was a service auditor's report obtained and appropriately considered, or test performed by the auditor at the service organization? (AU Secs. 319 and 324.14-.16)	A220				
If the engagement included the use of the work (domestic or international) of another office, correspondent or affiliate:					
Do the instructions to the other office or firm appear adequate? (AU Sec. 311)	A221				
Does it appear that the control exercised over the work of others through supervision and review was adequate? (AU Sec. 311)	A222				
Was there appropriate follow-up of open matters? (AU Sec. 311)	A223				
In those cases where another firm is used, were appropriate inquiries made as to its independence and professional reputation? (AU Sec. 543.10)	A224				
Was an appropriately tailored, written audit program prepared? (AU Sec. 311.05 and applicable AICPA Industry Audit Guide)	A225				
Was the audit program responsive to the needs of the engagement and the understanding of the internal control structure obtained during the planning process? (AU Sec. 319.02 and .05)	A226				
Was consideration given to applicable assertions in developing audit objectives and in designing substantive tests? (AU Sec. 326.09-.13)	A227				
If conditions changed during the course of the audit, was the audit program modified as appropriate in the circumstances? (AU Sec. 311.05)	A228				
Have all procedures called for in the audit program been signed? (AU Sec. 339)	A229				

Appendix 7.A (continued)

	QUES.	N/A	YES	NO	REF.

If statistical or nonstatistical sampling was used in tests of controls (AU Secs. 319 and 350):

In your consideration of the adequacy of the sample size, does it appear the firm gave appropriate consideration to the specific objective of the test of controls, tolerable rate, allowable risk of overreliance, and likely rate of deviations? (AU Sec. 350.31) — A230

Was the sample selected in such a way that it could be expected to be representative of the population? (AU Sec. 350.39) — A231

Were the results of the sample evaluated as to their effect on the nature, timing and extent of planned substantive procedures? (AU Sec. 350.40-.43) — A232

In evaluating the sample, was appropriate consideration given to items for which the planned test of controls or appropriate alternative procedure could not be performed, for example, because the documentation was missing? (AU Sec. 350.40) — A233

Was the documentation of the foregoing considerations in accordance with firm policy? — A234

If statistical or nonstatistical sampling was used for substantive tests of details:

In your consideration of the adequacy of the sample size, does it appear the firm gave appropriate consideration to the specific audit objective, tolerable misstatements, acceptable level of risk of incorrect acceptance, and characteristics of the population? (AU Sec. 350.16) — A235

Was the sample selected in such a way that it could be expected to be representative of the population? (AU Sec. 350.24) — A236

Were the misstatement results of the sample projected to the items from which the sample was selected? (AU Sec. 350.26) — A237

In evaluating the sample, was appropriate consideration given to items for which the planned substantive tests or appropriate alternate procedure could not be performed? (AU Sec. 350.25) — A238

In the evaluation of whether the financial statements taken as a whole may be materially misstated, was appropriate consideration given, in the aggregate, to projected misstatement results from all audit sampling applications and to all known misstatements from non-sampling applications? (AU Sec. 350.30) — A239

Was the documentation of the foregoing considerations in accordance with firm policy? — A240

During the performance of the engagement, did the auditor:

Consider the guidelines in professional standards in developing, performing, and evaluating the results of analytical procedures used as substantive tests? (AU Sec. 329) — A241

Use analytical procedures in the overall review stage of the audit? (AU Sec. 329.01) — A242

Appendix 7.A (continued)

	QUES.	N/A	YES	NO	REF.
Has the auditor evaluated the reasonableness of accounting estimates made by management? [1] (AU Sec. 342)	A243	___	___	___	___
Did the auditor obtain a timely and appropriate letter of representation from management? (AU Secs. 333.01 and 801.16)	A244	___	___	___	___
Did the auditor obtain timely and appropriate responses from the client's attorney concerning litigation, claims, and assessments? (AU Sec. 337.06)	A245	___	___	___	___
Have all questions, exceptions, or notes posed during the audit been followed up and resolved?	A246	___	___	___	___
Does it appear that appropriate consideration was given to all passed adjustments and to the risk that the current period's financial statements are materially misstated when prior-period likely misstatements are considered with likely misstatements arising in the current period? (AU Sec. 312.27 and .30)	A247	___	___	___	___

During the performance of the engagement, did the auditor:

	QUES.	N/A	YES	NO	REF.
Follow up on errors and irregularities in accordance with professional standards? (AU Sec. 316.24-.29)	A248	___	___	___	___
Consider the implications of an irregularity in relation to other aspects of the audit, including the reliability of the client's representations? (AU Sec. 316.25)	A249	___	___	___	___
Obtain assurance that the audit committee or others with equivalent authority and responsibility had been adequately informed of all but clearly inconsequential irregularities identified during the engagement? (AU Sec. 316.28)	A250	___	___	___	___

When the auditor's procedures disclosed instances or indications of illegal acts, did the auditor:

	QUES.	N/A	YES	NO	REF.
Follow up on illegal acts having a direct and material effect on the financial statements and on all other illegal acts in accordance with professional standards? (AU Secs. 316.24-.28 and 317.10)	A251	___	___	___	___
Consider the implications of a detected illegal act in relation to other aspects of the audit, including the reliability of the client's representations? (AU Sec. 317.16)	A252	___	___	___	___
Communicate directly with the audit committee if the illegal act involved senior management, document that communication and obtain assurance that all illegal acts which come to the auditor's attention are adequately communicated? (AU Sec. 317.17)	A253	___	___	___	___
Did the auditor consider if there was substantial doubt about the entity's ability to continue as a going concern for a reasonable period of time? (AU Sec. 341.02)	A254	___	___	___	___

---

[1] The auditor has this responsibility under SAS No. 31, but has been given more specific guidance in SAS No. 57.

Appendix 7.A (continued)

	QUES.	N/A	YES	NO	REF.

If the auditor believed that there was substantial doubt about the entity's ability to continue as a going concern for a reasonable period of time, did the auditor obtain information about management's plans and evaluate the likelihood that such plans could be effectively implemented? (AU Sec. 341) — A255

If the auditor's substantial doubt was alleviated, did the notes to the financial statements adequately disclose the principal conditions and events, the possible effects, and any mitigating factors, including management's plans? (AU Sec. 341) — A256

If the auditor's substantial doubt was not eliminated, did the auditor's report include an explanatory paragraph which adequately communicates the auditor's substantial doubt (e.g., includes the terms "substantial doubt" and "going concern")? (AU Sec. 341) — A257

During the performance of the audit:

If there were reportable conditions identified were they communicated to the audit committee, management and others within the organization on a timely basis (If the communication was oral was it documented in the working papers)? (AU Sec. 325.09) — A258

Does the auditor's conclusions in the working papers regarding whether internal control matters noted during the audit were (or were not) reportable conditions appear appropriate? (AU Sec. 325) — A259

If a report was issued on reportable conditions did it: indicate the purpose of the audit, include the definition of reportable conditions and include the restriction on distribution? (AU Sec. 325.11) — A260

If a letter was issued that did not include reportable conditions did it omit an opinion that there were no reportable conditions? (AU Sec. 325.17) — A261

If the auditor was engaged to prepare or perform procedures on interim financial information filed with a specified regulatory agency and the auditor became aware of matters that caused the auditor to believe such information is probably materially misstated as a result of a departure from the application of generally accepted accounting principles did the auditor:

Discuss the matter with the appropriate level of management? (AU Sec. 722.20) — A262

Timely inform the audit committee or others with equivalent authority and responsibility, if management did not respond appropriately or timely? (AU Sec. 722.21) — A263

Evaluate whether to resign or remain as the client's auditor, if the audit committee did not respond appropriately or timely? (AU Sec. 722.22) — A264

If the auditor, subsequent to the date of the report, became aware of facts that may have existed at that date which might have affected the report, had the auditor then been aware of such facts, did the auditor consider the guidance in professional standards, in determining an appropriate course of action, and does the matter appear to be properly resolved? (AU Sec. 561) — A265

Appendix 7.A (continued)

	QUES.	N/A	YES	NO	REF.
If there is an indication that the auditor, subsequent to the date of the report, concluded that one or more auditing procedures considered necessary at the time of the audit of the financial statements in the then existing circumstances were omitted from the audit, did the auditor consider the guidance in professional standards in determining an appropriate course of action, and does the matter appear to be properly resolved? (AU Sec. 390)	A266				

Where there is a formal oversight committee, did the auditor:

	QUES.	N/A	YES	NO	REF.
Ensure that appropriate matters were communicated to those with responsibility for oversight of the financial reporting process? (AU Sec. 380.01-.02)	A267				
If the communication was in writing, prepare a written report that included a statement that the communication was intended solely for the use of the audit committee or the board of directors and, if appropriate, management? (AU Sec. 380.03)	A268				
If the communication was oral, document the information communicated by appropriate memorandum or notations in the working papers? (AU Sec. 380.03)	A269				

*The N/A column should be used when the item either does not exist or is not material.

**All "no" answers should be handled in either of the following ways: (1) discussed on an MFC with the MFC form number noted in the REF column, or (2) discussed on the pages provided at the end of this checklist if no MFC was generated.

Source: From Quality Review and Program Manual, Copyright © 1991 by American Institute of Certified Public Accountants, Inc. Reprinted with permission.

Appendix 7.B
General Review Procedures

	QUES.	N/A *	YES	NO	REF. **

Was an engagement letter issued or a written memorandum of an oral understanding prepared to provide a record of the understanding with the client as to the services to be provided? (Professional standards require the accountant to establish an understanding with the entity, preferably, though not required to be, in writing.) (AR Sec. 100.08)

	R201	___	___	___	___

Was information obtained about the accounting principles and practices of the industry in which the entity operates and about the entity's business or, if information was obtained from prior engagements, was it updated for changed circumstances, and given appropriate consideration preferably, though not required to be, in writing (e.g., proposed work program, manpower requirements, etc.)? (AR Sec. 100.24-.26)

	R202	___	___	___	___

If the engagement was originally intended to be an audit, rather than a review of financial statements, did the accountant consider (AR Sec. 100.44-.49):

The reason given for the client's request, particularly the implications of a restriction on the scope of the audit, whether imposed by the client or by circumstances?

	R203	___	___	___	___

The additional audit effort required to complete the audit?

	R204	___	___	___	___

The estimated additional cost to complete the audit?

	R205	___	___	___	___

Did the accountant's inquiries and analytical procedures consist of the following (AR Sec. 100.27):

Inquiries concerning the entity's accounting principles and practices and the methods followed in applying them?

	R206	___	___	___	___

Inquiries concerning the entity's procedures for recording, classifying, and summarizing transactions, and accumulating information for disclosure in the financial statements?

	R207	___	___	___	___

Analytical procedures designed to identify relationships and individual items that appear to be unusual?

	R208	___	___	___	___

Inquiries concerning actions taken at meetings of stockholders, board of directors, committees of the board of directors, or comparable meetings that may affect the financial statements?

	R209	___	___	___	___

Reading the financial statements to consider, on the basis of information coming to the accountant's attention, whether the financial statements appear to conform with generally accepted accounting principles?

	R210	___	___	___	___

Obtaining reports from other accountants, if any, who have been engaged to audit or review the financial statements of significant components of the reporting entity, its subsidiaries, and other investees?

	R211	___	___	___	___

Appendix 7.B (continued)

	QUES.	N/A	YES	NO	REF.
Inquiries of persons having responsibility for financial and accounting matters concerning (1) whether the financial statements have been prepared in conformity with generally accepted accounting principles consistently applied, (2) changes in the entity's business activities or accounting principles and practices, (3) matters as to which questions have arisen in the course of applying the foregoing procedures, and (4) events subsequent to the date of the financial statements that would have a material effect on the financial statements?	R212				
If the accountant became aware that information that came to the accountant's attention was incorrect, incomplete, or otherwise unsatisfactory, did the accountant perform additional procedures as deemed necessary to achieve limited assurance that there were no material modifications that should be made to the financial statements in order for the statements to be in conformity with generally accepted accounting principles? (AR Sec. 100.29)	R213				
Do the accountant's working papers adequately reflect (AR Sec. 100.30):					
The matters covered in inquiry and analytical procedures?	R214				
Unusual matters that were considered during the performance of the review, including their disposition?	R215				
If the accountant decided to obtain a representation letter from the owner, manager, or chief executive officer, does it appear to be appropriate in the circumstances? (Note: Under the early application of the Omnibus Statement on Standards for Accounting and Review Services, the accountant is required to obtain a representation letter.) (AR Sec. 100.31)	R216				
If any circumstances were encountered by the accountant that precluded the accountant from performing inquiries and analytical procedures as deemed necessary (AR Sec. 100.36):					
Did the accountant consider whether these circumstances would have resulted in an incomplete review and therefore afford the accountant an inadequate basis for issuing a review report?	R217				
Did the accountant consider whether these same circumstances would also preclude the accountant from issuing a compilation report on the entity's financial statements?	R218				
Do such determinations by the accountant appear to be proper?	R219				
Have all questions, exceptions or notes, posed during the work been followed up and resolved?	R220				
If there is an indication that the accountant had become aware that information supplied by the entity was incorrect, incomplete or otherwise unsatisfactory subsequent to the date of the report, did the accountant consider the guidance in professional standards, in determining an appropriate course of action, and does the matter appear to be properly resolved? (AU Sec. 561)	R221				

Source: From Quality Review and Program Manual, Copyright © 1991 by American Institute of Certified Public Accountants, Inc. Reprinted with permission.

Appendix 7.C
General Compilation Procedures

	QUES.	N/A*	YES	NO	REF.**

Was an engagement letter issued or a written memorandum of an oral understanding prepared to provide a record of the understanding with the client as to the services to be provided? (professional standards require the accountant to establish an understanding with the entity, preferably, though not required to be, in writing) (AR Sec. 100.08)   C201   ____ ____ ____ ____

Was information obtained about the accounting principles and practices of the industry in which the entity operates and about the entity's business transactions, the form of its accounting records, the stated qualifications of its accounting personnel, the accounting basis on which the financial statements are to be presented, and the form and content of the financial statements or, if information was obtained from prior engagements, was it updated for changed circumstances, and given appropriate consideration preferably, though not required to be, in writing (e.g., proposed work program, manpower requirements, etc.)? (AR Sec. 100.10-.12)   C202   ____ ____ ____ ____

If the engagement was originally intended to be an audit or review, rather than a compilation, did the accountant consider (AR Sec. 100.45):

The reason given for the client's request, particularly the implications of a restriction on the scope of the audit or review, whether imposed by the client or by circumstances?   C203   ____ ____ ____ ____

The additional effort required to complete the audit or review?   C204   ____ ____ ____ ____

The estimated additional cost to complete the audit or review?   C205   ____ ____ ____ ____

Is there an indication, in accordance with firm policy, that the accountant read the compiled financial statements and considered whether such financial statements appeared to be appropriate in form and free from obvious material errors? (AR Sec. 100.13)   C206   ____ ____ ____ ____

If the accountant became aware that information supplied by the entity was incorrect, incomplete, or otherwise unsatisfactory for the purpose of compiling financial statements, did the accountant obtain additional or revised information? (AR Sec. 100.12)   C207   ____ ____ ____ ____

Have all questions, exceptions or notes, posed during the work been followed up and resolved?   C208   ____ ____ ____ ____

If the accountant became aware that information supplied by the entity was incorrect, incomplete or otherwise unsatisfactory subsequent to the date of the report, did the accountant consider the guidance in professional standards in determining an appropriate course of action, and does the matter appear to be properly resolved? (AU Sec. 561)   C209   ____ ____ ____ ____

*The N/A column should be used when the item does not exist or is not material.

**All "no" answers should be handled in either of the following ways: (1) discussed on an MFC with the MFC form number noted in the REF column, or (2) discussed on the pages provided at the end of this checklist if no MFC was generated.

Source: From Quality Review and Program Manual, Copyright © 1991 by American Institute of Certified Public Accountants, Inc. Reprinted with permission.

8

Problems to Avoid

Earning an unqualified report is an enormously satisfying experience. However, the letter of comments diminishes the enjoyment for many firms. It should not though because the vast majority of firms do receive a comments letter. Reviewers use a "remote possibility" criterion in deciding whether to include an issue in the letter. The letter of comments should, for most, be viewed simply as suggestions for improvement. For a few, it says much more.

For those wishing to limit the number of comments that accompany their review reports, this chapter is a must. It details the common problems found on reviews. It also provides suggestions on how to prevent them from happening. All firm managers should read this section thoroughly. It may also be helpful to reviewers.

Many deficiencies occur on compilations and reviews. The chapter begins, then, with a discussion of the importance of better compliance with the SSARS requirements. The available guides to compilation and review can be particularly helpful here. This chapter also contends that additional professional guidance is necessary to improve compilation and review services.

Disclosure deficiencies also are quite common. Including disclosure requirements in the firm's review checklists could lower instances of omitted disclosures. Another common deficiency occurs because firm reviewers do not thoroughly examine engagement workpapers for completeness.

The chapter also includes a brief discussion of the more common functional area deficiencies. It concludes with the assertion that the underlying cause of all deficiencies uncovered in peer and quality reviews is CPA firm management that does not understand and, in some cases, does not care about the importance of professional-quality service.

COMPLY WITH SSARS ... AND THEN SOME

SSARS 1, Compilation and Review of Financial Statements, provides the authoritative engagement guidance [*AICPA Professional Standards*, Volume 2, 1992: AR 100]. Some of the more frequent engagement deficiencies on compilations and reviews include the following.

1. *Some firms neglect to get an engagement letter.* As discussed in Chapter 7, SSARS requires an understanding, preferably in writing. A written understanding could take the form of a signed engagement letter or a memorandum to the file. A signed engagement letter is much more persuasive than a person's recollections. It also is better than a memorandum because it shows the client agreed with the engagement scope.

The *1136 Tenants Corporation* case made it clear that an engagement letter is an absolute necessity. A signed engagement letter does provide limited protection against litigation losses. To avoid misunderstanding, the engagement letter on a review or compilation should include an example of what the report will say. It also should include this statement: "our engagement cannot be relied upon to disclose errors, irregularities, or illegal acts, including fraud or defalcations, that may exist" [*AICPA Professional Standards*, Volume 2, 1992: AR 100.53]. While CPAs are responsible for designing audits to detect material errors and irregularities, we disclaim any such responsibility on compilations and reviews. Including the quoted statement in the engagement letter should make clear our understanding of the engagement's limitations.

Some may disagree, but I believe compilations and reviews are high-risk engagements because of their limited scope. There is, therefore, a higher chance of material misstatement. The courts, however, do not always agree with our claim that limited-scope engagements correspondingly limit our responsibility. Certainly the *Ryan v. Kanne* decision, involving a compilation, discussed in Chapter 1, ignored the profession's claim that limiting the scope limits our responsibility. The "court was unwilling to accept the accounting profession's concept of unaudited services, a rejection which was probably attributable to the court's perception of the public expectation of accountant's responsibility" [Ostling, 1986: 15]. Recommendations contained in Chapter 9 cover society's expectations and the necessity of an engagement letter. They include a proposal that would require the accountant's report to be more truthful. One of the difficulties in the *1136 Tenants* case was that the accountant did perform a limited audit test, which is quite common on compilations and reviews. This is discussed in more detail later in this chapter in the section titled "Then Some."

2. *Some practitioners do not realize that compilations and reviews, just like audits, require the accountant to have a reasonable understanding of the client's industry and operations.* This should include documenting an understanding of the accounting principles and practices used in the client's industry. Many firms do not require that this understanding be documented. This is unfortunate, par-

ticularly when the client is in a specialized industry. Failure to show evidence of such an understanding may be cited in the letter of comments.

Similarly, some firms neglect to document their perceptions of the form of the client's accounting records and the qualifications of its accounting personnel. Further, the accountant must take care to show an understanding of the nature of the client's transactions. Completing compilation and review checklists would limit the number of documentation deficiencies.

3. *Some firms fail to document the engagement partner's review of the compilation or review report.* This oversight can cause embarrassment. For example, one firm had issued a compilation report that did not say the financial statements were prepared on a basis other than GAAP when that was the case. While an OCBOA such as the cash or tax basis of accounting is permissible, the report has to disclose the basis used. Also, compilations can, in the interest of economy, omit substantially all disclosures required under GAAP. This departure, however, must be stated in the report. If firms had controls requiring partners to complete review checklists, there would be fewer failures to conform with professional standards. At a minimum, engagement partners ought to be required to initial a report route sheet as evidence of their review.

4. *Certain firms do not document the reviewer's conclusions.* Before the report is released, the engagement partner must conclude the financial statements are appropriate in form and free of obvious material error. Similarly, documentation of the engagement partner's satisfaction with the integrity of client-provided information often is inadequate. Specifically, the engagement partner must assess whether the information is incorrect, incomplete, or otherwise unsatisfactory. Again, a reviewer's checklist would be helpful in documenting these considerations and conclusions.

5. *Exceptions, notes, and questions are left unresolved.* For some inexplicable reason, many firms do not follow their workpaper requirements on compilations and reviews. Perhaps they believe that since no assurance or only limited assurance is provided, less care is necessary. Due professional care is required on every engagement and is particularly important on high-risk engagements such as compilations and reviews. Adequate documentation is an integral part of that requirement. Also, failure to show that all exceptions and questions have been resolved shows insufficient supervision.

Compilation and review checklists are an effective and efficient means of documenting the engagement partner's review and conclusions. They also are useful in instructing staff about specific steps that must be completed on each engagement. Finally, they should contain reminders that the firm's workpaper requirements apply to all engagements.

6. *Failure to keep abreast of professional standards.* There is a continuing problem on peer and quality reviews. For example, in November 1992 SSARS 7, Omnibus Statement on Standards for Accounting and Review Services—1992, was issued. It revises the wording of compilation and review reports, makes

obtaining a representation letter a requirement on review engagements, and clarifies existing standards. This statement is effective for fiscal periods ending after December 15, 1993.

While firms sometimes fail to comply with SSARS in some material aspects, many do much more than the professional standards require for fear of being associated with materially misstated financial statements. Many CPAs, like numerous physicians, practice defensively. Both do more testing than the circumstances require or suggest. Physicians order tests for unlikely conditions just to protect themselves from malpractice claims. CPAs know that mere compliance with SSARS is not enough to prevent materially misstated financial statements. To avoid malpractice claims and other consequences, they, too, perform more tests. The section that follows discusses this practice of doing more than what is required.

Then Some

The profession claims that since compilations provide no assurance about financial statement integrity, then the accountant has no responsibility for misstatements. But if we are not providing assurance, why have us? Some might respond, because the client needs his or her books done. This is true, but in most cases clients can hire more inexpensive non-CPAs to provide that service. If clients truly believed we were not providing assurance, they would not need our services. As a result, CPAs do quietly perform certain added tests, such as checking the mechanical accuracy of client-prepared receivable and payable schedules and reconciling the bank accounts. They also inquire about unusual transactions and events, and perform analytical procedures. Further, they calculate and record depreciation, interest and tax accruals, and compensated absence liabilities.

Compilation reports most often are prepared in conjunction with providing bookkeeping services. The report and financial statements are, in a sense, the finished product. Doing the bookkeeping and preparing the statements and report obviously make the CPA more responsible than the compilation report indicates.

In addition, CPAs know the courts have rejected their claims that they bear no responsibility for misstatements. A CPA firm can suffer severe losses for compilations or reviews in which the financial statements are materially misstated. These losses include, at a minimum, the thousands of staff hours taken up in the firm's defense, as well as the loss of reputation and, perhaps, confidence in its procedures and practices—and in the firm itself. It is not unheard of for a firm to go out of business because of this kind of litigation. To meet client expectations and protect their practices, most intelligent CPAs do more than what is required.

The profession should change its compilation standards to reflect what it is that accountants actually do and clients expect. Chapter 9 provides a recommendation to do just that. The profession also needs to reevaluate its review standards. Again, Chapter 9 provides alternatives.

Review Engagements

Review engagements are the subject of many comments letter findings. The common deficiencies include the following.

1. *Neglecting to note the analytical procedures performed on the engagement.* On reviews, analytical procedures are intended to identify unusual relationships and items and, thus, potential errors or irregularities. As with any engagement, due professional care and supervision require a record of the analytical procedures completed.

Similarly, some reviews document several analytics, but do not explain why they were used. Some procedures are simply exploratory, and others are designed to test the reasonableness of account balances. For example, a comparison of current-period data with prior-period amounts is, for the most part, aimed at discovering unusual fluctuations. A comparison of current-period amounts with auditor-determined amounts, such as what commission expense ought to be, is done to test the reasonableness of a balance.

2. *Failing to perform sufficient analytical procedures.* Reviews disclose instances when analytical procedures were inadequate to provide even limited assurance. The procedures used depend on the engagement's unique circumstances and demand professional judgment, which requires extensive industry and accounting experience. The choice of analytical procedures should be made only by a manager or a partner.

Often the analytical procedures performed involve simply a comparison of aggregate current-period data with prior-period data. This approach seldom provides a sufficient basis for a review report. Accountants need to expand these procedures to include comparisons of client data with industry data and with accountant-determined expected results and to document these comparisons on their workpapers. For example, a comparison of inventory turnover information and gross margin percentages with industry data can raise questions on pricing changes, obsolete inventory, unusual costs, improper cutoff, and the like. The availability of industry databases on computer makes these comparisons efficient and effective. A recommendation in Chapter 9, if followed, would make industry data more affordable to small and medium-sized firms.

Comparison of accountant-determined expected results with client data is a powerful analytical tool. For example, expected interest expense is readily calculated by multiplying the weighted average interest rate times the average loan balance. Similar procedures are used in verifying commissions, payroll taxes, and other variable expenses. Also, calculating expected revenue is relatively uncomplicated with cable television companies, hotels, and similar businesses. Further, manufacturing payroll can be estimated based on hours worked times the average wage rate. Sometimes cost of goods can be estimated based on units times average cost.

Accountant-determined expected results are only as good as the underlying nonfinancial data, so procedures must be employed to verify their reliability. For example, evidence about hours worked can be checked by taking a sample of weekly time cards and extrapolating the sample results to the year.

Analytical procedure effectiveness could be improved significantly, but it will not happen soon. Low-cost microcomputers enable us to perform complex calculations that were not previously practicable. The impediment, however, is that too few accountants know how to use these analytical approaches because they lack the appropriate training. Education, and accounting education in particular, has not fully prepared graduates to use better analytical approaches. CPE courses are not doing the job either. The section that follows examines why analytical procedure effectiveness will not be improved soon. It is critical, however, that we begin the process.

The typical college freshman has a rather dismal understanding of the sciences, arts, and mathematics. Many do not have basic skills, such as the ability to write a complete paragraph, multiply 11 times 12, or use a typewriter or computer keyboard. By the time they graduate, they claim spreadsheet proficiency. While there is some truth in that claim, they still hunt and peck the keyboard. Some firms have complained that using computers on audits has not improved their efficiency. This is partially due to accounting graduates' inability to type.

Accounting education needs to better prepare its students for the profession. A major effort to do just that is under way. The Accounting Education Change Commission hopes to bring about innovation and excellence in accounting curricula.

These curriculum changes are going to have to provide accounting students with additional training in mathematics and statistics. This is necessary so they can confidently employ such analytical techniques as multiple regression analysis, an absolutely necessary tool on reviews. Without it, many relationships cannot be analyzed. Unfortunately, the mention of the words "multiple regression" in my auditing class strikes terror in students' hearts. This terror results from inadequate mathematics training beginning in primary school. If taught correctly, however, regression can be understood and used without much mathematical background.

Accounting education also must spend more time on case analysis, rather than focusing on just those subjects tested on the CPA examination. Most students have a fairly good entry-level understanding of GAAP and GAAS, but they have not had experience in applying these standards in any real sense. They have had almost no experience dealing with uncertainty, and that is what analytics are all about.

Education, and specifically accounting education, is not likely to change significantly in the short term. Adoption of the AICPA's recommended 150-hour program will require a significant reallocation of state university educational resources. For this reason and others, state legislators are resisting approving this program. As evidence, less than thirty states had approved it as of June 1993, and the list does not include many large states. While nearly all politicians voice support for education, they find it difficult to vote for funds to finance it. They do not hesitate, however, to vote themselves middle-of-the-night pay raises and play bounce the check. Chapter 9 develops a proposal that could result in better education that could then lead to better analytics.

Neglecting to note the analytical procedures used on an engagement and failing to perform sufficient procedures are just two of the common review engagement problems. There are more.

3. *Certain firms do not document the questions they asked as a result of their analytics*. When a particular analytical procedure points to unusual relationships or items, the accountant must investigate the potential error. This investigation consists for the most part of questions that must be addressed, along with management's responses. This is, in many cases, yet another example of failure to document work. For example, a gross profit deviation should raise many questions, including inquiries about cutoff procedures on both sales and costs and about sales mix information. It also should include questions about pricing changes, design changes, and so on. These issues point to the need to collect and analyze disaggregated data. Gross profit changes result from shifts in both cost of goods sold and sales, so the analysis must focus on individual components. Further, these individual account changes usually are made up of separate products, product lines, and the like. Analytical procedures must incorporate a study of disaggregated data as well.

Peer and quality reviews show that accountants do much more than make inquiries and perform analytical procedures on review engagement. The section that follows discusses why audit procedures are frequently used in conjunction with or in lieu of analytical procedures.

And Then Some More

Many reviewed firms carry out audit procedures on reviews in the belief that standard audit procedures fulfill the analytical review requirement. This again may be defensive accounting. Perhaps it is also attributable to a belief that documentary evidence about account balance details is more persuasive. Others are convinced that using audit procedures is about as efficient as doing analytical procedures and then making inquiries. The pitfall is that, because the firm performed audit procedures, the firm may be held responsible for doing an audit when a full audit has not been performed.

In some respects, audit procedures are easier than analytics. Analytical procedures, as explained, often require seasoned judgment, industry databases, computer proficiency, and some, if not considerable, mathematical skill. If the firm does not have these resources, then audit procedures offer an alternative.

In addition, engagement partners know that many analytical procedures do not reveal underlying relationships. As a result, it is reasonable to use limited audit procedures.

Audit procedures sometimes are simply more efficient than analytics. Small businesses requiring reviews often have inadequate books of account. Errors are expected in many accounts, so it is simply easier and more efficient to apply such procedures as documentation, confirmation, inquiry, and mechanical accuracy checks while correcting the client's financial statements and doing the review.

Audit procedures are used routinely on reviews, and professional standards should provide guidance on their use. At times it seems the standard writers are unaware of what goes on in practice. For example, as discussed in connection with compilations, keeping an entity's books should certainly allow a more courageous stance than no assurance. Could we not at least list the procedures performed and then let the readers make their own assessment of the financial statement's integrity? Also, limited audit procedures should be exchangeable for some analytics.

The AICPA needs to address the reality of practice on compilations and reviews, and consider revising its standards. Returning to unaudited statements on compilations and reviews is certainly an alternative worth considering. The unaudited accountant's report would explicitly state, as a compilation report does now, that no assurance is provided. It would, however, list the services rendered and the procedures performed. A recommendation in Chapter 9 explains this more fully.

The AICPA also needs to provide partners and managers with better training on performing analytics. Finally, it needs to alert the professional community to support its 150-hour educational proposal.

USE THE GUIDES TO COMPILATION, REVIEW, AND AUDIT

Many of the cited problems can be diminished by acquiring or developing a guide to compilations and reviews. The AICPA and other publishers provide excellent guides that contain work programs and planning, review, and disclosure checklists. Some include direction on documenting functional area concerns. Many firms adopt one of the available guides after their reviews. Why wait? These checklists and work programs will, in most instances, have to be modified to fit the firm's control system, but they do provide excellent starting points.

Although many firms develop very adequate guides internally, it is frequently difficult and expensive to keep them current. For many firms, they are sadly out of date much of the time.

Using a guide to compilation and review provides limited assurance of complying with professional standards. To provide reasonable assurance, due care is required. The Quality Review Executive Committee says, "be careful not to overemphasize the use of standardized forms and checklists as a recommendation for improving the firm's quality control system'' [Quality Review Executive Committee, 1991: QRP § 3600.24p]. The reason for this cautious position, I believe, is that standardized forms and checklists provide a false sense of security. No program or checklist is sufficient to meet every engagement's requirements. Each must be modified, so due care is required in engagement planning. Perhaps this cautious advice is also due to a perception that some firm personnel may not understand what these standardized forms and checklists call for. Too many in the profession take their CPE courses in nonaccounting and audit areas. They have not kept up, so the guidance provided in these packages will not be very helpful.

Preparers have a tendency to complete work programs and checklists blindly. Sometimes checklists cause people, this writer included, to go brain dead. Firms need to emphasize the importance of completing these documents with due care. The firm's reputation and, consequently, its success and longevity depend on it.

When a firm obtains, develops, or modifies programs, checklists, and manuals, it must do so with great care. In addition, staff, including partners, should be trained on their use. Packaged programs, checklists, and manuals must be evaluated for their clarity and comprehensiveness. This task should be assigned to a group, rather than to an individual, to ensure that they are comprehensible. The same is true for program modifications. While one person could develop changes, others should review them before they are carried out.

Often firms introduce programs and checklists without offering proper training under the assumption that they are self-explanatory. Experience tells us that even veteran managers and partners need detailed instruction. Also, what is self-explanatory to a partner is often nothing more than a maze to a young staff member. Detailed instruction on what each step calls for is necessary.

The guidance contained in elegant manuals, programs, and checklists will not be helpful if the firm puts profit ahead of quality. Partners and managers who pressure staff to meet unattainable time budgets are risking accounting and audit failure. They also risk the financial well-being of the firm and their fellow partners. Well-designed programs and checklists will not alleviate this problem. Staff determined to meet or beat the budget will sign off on procedures they did not do and considerations they did not reckon with. As long as continuance with the firm is based on the ability to meet or beat the budget, this problem will continue. The first and perhaps most important recommendation in Chapter 9 attacks this issue directly.

Work programs and checklists exacerbate the problem because it is much easier to sign off on a planning checklist than to create a planning memorandum. Checklists and work programs, then, cannot be relied on completely to increase engagement effectiveness. Firms must bolster these guides by requiring that one or more procedures be duplicated on every engagement. This policy will deter premature sign-offs, cursory reviews, and the like. Staff who sign off on procedures they did not do need to be censured. Staff who sign off on procedures they misunderstood need additional training and, perhaps, counseling on the meaning and importance of due professional care. Maybe some partners, managers, or in-charge personnel also should be chastised about the pressure they exert to do the impossible.

The need for efficiency in this competitive environment cannot be overemphasized, however. The elimination of the encroachment rules, the economic slowdown, and the use of audit and accounting services as loss leaders in certain instances each contribute to a fiercely competitive environment. Certainly the insistence of governmental entities and others that accounting and auditing services go to the low bidder reinforces this competitive atmosphere. A governmental entity's claim that it is representing the public interest when it makes an audit selection based on the low bid is indefensible. Unfortunately for financial statement users and the public, accounting and audit services have become a commodity. As long as this is the case, there will be pressure to provide substandard service. However, if firms use the guides to compilation, review, and audit, they will be more competitive and still be able to maintain professional-quality service.

Firms that do adopt one of the well-known guides to compilation, review, and audit often go through a predictable learning process. At first, many experience inefficiencies. It takes more time for the staff to complete the new work programs and checklists contained in the guides, so overall engagement time goes up. Also, partner time increases because they are now preparing reviewer checklists in addition to doing their usual meticulous workpaper review. The partners become disgruntled, to say the least. Eventually, they realize that review time could be reduced if they relied on properly completed programs and checklists. The end result is that staff do spend more time on engagements, but the partners spend less time. Because of the disparity between partner billing rates and staff billing rates, overall profitability does increase.

Greater compliance with SSARS, changes in those standards, better education, and the use of guides to compilation, review, and audit are just four of the issues that must be contended with in order to limit the number of points in the letter of comments. Another common problem occurs in the disclosure area.

AVOID DISCLOSURE DEFICIENCIES

There are some common disclosure deficiencies on client financial statements. Most, if not all, are associated not with particularly complex areas, but, rather, with simple oversights that often could have been avoided by using disclosure checklists. Typically, the disclosure inadequacies fall into one of five categories: accounting policy disclosures, debt disclosures, related-party disclosures, detailed pension disclosures, and elaborate income tax disclosures.

Accounting Policy Disclosures

The accounting policy note often fails to include all the required disclosures. These can include inadequacies in depreciation disclosure, basis for valuation of inventories, revenue recognition methods cases, the statement of cash flows, and off-balance-sheet risk.

For depreciation, the cost of the major classes of depreciable assets, accumulated depreciation in total or by class, and methods used must be disclosed, as well as the amount of depreciation recognized in the period. Although it is not required, disclosure of the average useful life or range of years of useful life by class of depreciable assets is very helpful to financial statement readers.

In inventory, it is important to disclose the flow of cost assumption (such as first-in, first-out) and the valuation bases (such as lower of cost or market).

One firm's accounting policy note in a client's financial statement said the inventory was valued at cost. Thinking this was perhaps a departure, it was written up as an MFC. The workpapers, however, showed that it was recorded at the lower of cost or market, so while the financial statement note was incorrect, it was not a departure from GAAP. The financial statements, however, were misleading.

The method of recognizing income must be disclosed, particularly for long-term contracts, real estate transactions, and lease arrangements. Since these methods are complex, appropriate disclosures must be provided.

For leases, the most common disclosure deficiency involves the failure to disclose the future minimum rental payments for each of the next five years. In addition, the aggregate rental obligation must be shown.

SFAS 95, Statement of Cash Flows, requires disclosure of the items treated as cash equivalents. This disclosure is usually part of the accounting policy note.

SFAS 105, Disclosures of Information about Financial Instruments with Off-Balance-Sheet Risk and Financial Instruments with Concentrations of Credit Risk, covers disclosures now being missed. For example, it requires disclosure of forward exchange contracts, financial guarantees, and commitments to extend credit. In addition to these somewhat unique situations for nonfinancial entities, it also requires some common disclosures. A retailer, for instance, "of family clothing that has three stores in the same town and that grants credit to customers generally should disclose that its credits is [sic] concentrated among local residents" ["Recurring Peer and Quality Review Comments," 1991: 4i].

Debt Disclosures

The disclosures most often missed include the nature of the debt, maturities, collateral, guarantees, and interest rates on long-term debt. Maturities should be disclosed in the aggregate and for each of the next five years.

Contingency disclosures also are often missed. When a loss contingency is probable or estimable, but not both, the nature of the contingency and an estimate of the loss generally must be disclosed. A loss contingency that is estimable, but not probable, should be disclosed if the loss is reasonably possible.

Related-Party Disclosures

Since most CPAs work with small and medium-sized businesses, they often find transactions between owners and the business that must be disclosed. These include renting facilities when the owner is also the landlord and borrowing from the business. Inadequate related-party disclosure is a frequent cause of lawsuits.

Detailed Pension Disclosures

For defined benefit plans, SFAS 87, Employers' Accounting for Pensions, requires, among other things, a description of the plan and the amount of the required cost components making up net pension expense. It also requires a reconciliation of the plan's funded status with the amounts reported in the balance sheet. In addition, it requires disclosure of the discount rate and the rate of compensation increase used to calculate the projected benefit obligation. Further, the long-term rate of return on assets must be reported.

Elaborate Income Tax Disclosures

SFAS 96, Accounting for Income Taxes, the much-maligned income tax pronouncement, has finally been superseded by SFAS 109, Accounting for Income Taxes. SFAS 109 is effective for fiscal years beginning after December 15, 1992, and, like its predecessor, SFAS 96, it takes a liability approach for accounting and reporting on income taxes. SFASs 109 and 96 require disclosure of the types of temporary differences that make up significant portions of a deferred tax liability or asset. They also require a reconciliation of tax expense on income from continuing operations to tax expense based on applying the statutory rates on that income. Further, the amounts and expiration dates of carryforwards, including operating losses and credits, must be disclosed. Finally, the amount of current and deferred tax expense, the effect of credits and operating loss carryforwards, and adjustments due to changes in tax laws or rates must be disclosed. SFAS 109 differs in allowing easier recognition of deferred tax assets and makes the tax computation simpler.

In addition to disclosure deficiencies, letters of comments frequently indicate problems that reflect a failure to thoroughly review the engagement workpapers.

COMMON PLANNING AND SYSTEM-RELATED DOCUMENTATION DEFICIENCIES

The most common deficiency in peer and quality reviews is lack of documentation. As discussed previously, in many cases it is not possible for the reviewer to know for certain whether the deficiency is lack of documentation or lack of performance. As a result, the reviewer will generally conclude that it is a documentation error unless the preponderance of evidence indicates otherwise.

At the account level, one frequent technical accounting problem is lack of documentation for needed inquiries about compensated absence liabilities. Also, tax lives and methods often are used in the depreciation calculation for both tax and book purposes. The materiality or immateriality of these differences must be documented. This documentation also should show evidence that future differences are not expected to be material.

Failure to Adequately Document Audit Planning Considerations

Documentation should include evidence of the auditor's understanding of the client's industry, background, related parties, and legal obligations. Evidence about the client's industry might include reference to AICPA audit and accounting guides and trade journals. It also might include notes about prior-auditor responses and reviews of prior-year working papers and permanent files. The documentation should cover industry accounting practices and prevailing economic and industry conditions. Finally, it should include an evaluation of the effects of governmental regulation and technological change on the audit.

The firm's background investigation of new clients should include communication with the predecessor auditor and others about client integrity. The discussion with the predecessor must cover why an auditor change occurred and any disagreements between the predecessor and the client. For example, the predecessor should be asked about any client-imposed scope limitations and disagreements about accounting principles or auditing procedures. In addition, the predecessor should be asked about complex and troublesome engagement areas.

Audit planning also includes review of the client's policies, such as its code of conduct, personnel policies, compensation plans, and so on. Evidence should show that analytical procedures were performed in the planning stage. Specifically, this should include comparisons of the client's current data with prior-period industry data and auditor-predicted data to identify possible errors and irregularities and to test account balance reasonableness.

The client's legal obligations must be identified in the audit planning process. This means reviewing the client's corporate charter, bylaws, and minutes of the board of directors and audit committee meetings. The planning phase also must include a review of contracts such as lease agreements, pension plan amendments, major acquisitions, bond indentures, and the like. Recurring engagements require similar procedures.

Audit planning documentation must include inquiries about the reasons for the audit and an evaluation of the responses. The auditor must continuously reconsider why an audit is needed since the answer has a major effect on firm engagement risk. For example, an audit undertaken because the business is for sale greatly increases the firm's engagement risk. This increased risk significantly reduces acceptable audit risk, which leads to expanded audit procedures.

Audit planning also must include consideration of engagement staffing. Auditing standards, professional ethics, and the quality control standards require the firm to assess its competency to carry out the engagement. Finally, though not required, a firm should always get a signed engagement letter.

Failure to Make Preliminary Judgments about Materiality Levels

SAS 47, Audit Risk and Materiality in Conducting an Audit, provides the authoritative guidance on this matter. It requires the auditor to make a preliminary materiality judgment. Fortunately or unfortunately, depending on your point of view, there is little guidance on determining what is or is not material. GAAP defines materiality as a misstatement or omission that would influence a reasonable user's decision. The auditor has to assess both quantitative and nonquantitative factors. This includes making a judgment about the magnitude of an error that would qualify as material. In addition, the accountant must judge the importance of specific disclosures that will or will not be made. Many firms base the quantitative dimension on a relationship with income before taxes. Some firm managers use a criterion of 3 percent of net income because GAAP uses 3 percent as the cutoff for requiring dual reporting of earnings per share. Evidently, the Accounting Principles Board (APB) felt 3 percent was a useful cutoff for determining materiality. This criterion also probably reflects some risk adversity. Managers of small firms may be more risk adverse because an allegation of misstated financial statements poses a greater threat. Most small firms do not have the resources to defend themselves from litigation, let alone survive an adverse judgment.

Once the auditor has made his or her preliminary materiality judgment, the tolerable misstatement must be decided. This is the amount of error an auditor is willing to accept and still conclude the statements are not materially misstated. The tolerable error amount must be allocated to the individual account balances and cycles, and this allocation should be documented.

Failure to Document That Consideration Was Given to the Client's Control Structure

The control structure includes the control environment, accounting system, and control procedures. "The control environment represents the collective effect of various factors on establishing, enhancing, or mitigating the effectiveness of specific policies and procedures" [AICPA Professional Standards, Volume 1, 1992: AU 319.09]. In assessing the control environment, the auditor must document his or her perception of management's honesty and attitude toward risk. He or she also must include an assessment of management's attitude toward financial reporting, budgets, and performance measurement. For example, a company that ties its performance-reward system to unrealistic budgets puts the auditor in a difficult situation. The audit risk in such a situation may be so great that the engagement should be declined.

In assessing the control environment, the auditor must assess management's attitude toward its control policies and procedures. He or she must consider the effect of the client's internal audit function on the control environment assessment. Further, he or she needs to consider whether the client has policies on conflict of interests and conduct and an audit committee made up of outside directors. Finally, the auditor must evaluate the adequacy of the client's reporting relationships. The control environment and inherent risk assessments are, in essence, an evaluation of the tone at the top.

The auditor must assess the other two control structure components. He or she should document an understanding of the accounting system in the context of its objectives. The auditor should base his or her conclusions on how well that system achieves the objectives of validity, completeness, timeliness, valuation, cutoff, mechanical accuracy, and presentation.

Accounting system tests and evaluation should cover the control policies and procedures. Specifically, the auditor must evaluate the appropriateness of the client's segregation of duties and the adequacy of its documentation. In addition, the auditor needs to evaluate the adequacy of the client's asset safeguards, authorization procedures, and independent performance checks.

Failure to Provide a Summary of the CPA's Evaluation of the Internal Control and Its Effect on the Audit Procedures

This has been a pervasive finding on reviews. Some firms carefully document their understandings of the control structure and the results of their tests, but fail to relate these findings to their assessed control risk. The auditor must assess control risk for each significant account and address the financial statement assertions of existence and occurrence. He or she also must address the assertions of completeness, rights and obligations, valuation, and presentation. Assessed control risk directly affects the nature, timing, and extent of subsequent substantive tests.

On some reviews, firms meticulously document control risk and find it to be below the maximum level for some assertions. They then proceed to do substantive tests as if the control risk were maximum. Perhaps if these engagements had been supervised better, they would have been completed more efficiently.

Many peer reviews show that firms do not test the control system and simply set the control risk at maximum. The rationale for doing this, such as poor controls or greater efficiency, should be stated.

Failure to Use Audit Programs

Far too frequently, firms fail to use written audit programs. Written programs are a requirement under the standards of field work [*AICPA Professional Stan-*

dards, Volume 1, 1992: AU 311.05]. They should detail the audit procedures necessary to accomplish the general audit objectives.

Failure to Justify Sample Sizes

This is another prevalent finding. Professional judgment is permissible in selections, but the rationale should be documented. For example, one reviewed firm used a sample size of thirty items for every compliance test for every audit client. When asked why, firm members said that that was the way they had always done it.

Attribute sampling is an effective and efficient approach to evaluate control risk. In addition, it provides the firm protection from allegations that the audit was not conducted in accordance with professional standards. While it also requires considerable professional judgment, it is defensible for two reasons. First, the sample size is determined statistically. Second, the computed upper deviation rate can be logically related to control risk. (Attribute sampling requires the auditor to make a professional judgment about tolerable error rates and acceptable risk of overreliance. It also requires the auditor to estimate the population error rate.)

The auditor's sample sizes for tests of details can be based on his or her professional judgment. Dollar-unit sampling or other sampling proportional to size methods, however, are defendable and often more efficient. Whether the auditor relies on judgment or statistical methods, the rationale for the sample size needs to be documented.

Failure to Document Inquiries and Evaluation of Related-Party Transactions and Subsequent Events

Related-party transactions are a troublesome area on peer and quality reviews. Often firms do not make appropriate inquiries about their existence. Related-party transactions easily enable a company to misstate earnings. Companies that have optimistic earnings forecasts, excess capacity, problems with obsolescence, and the like can be tempted to use them to change their earnings substantially. The auditor needs to ask appropriate management personnel the names of all related parties. The auditor also should make a list of the client's officers, directors, major stockholders, and pension or profit-sharing plan officers. This list should also include the names of officers, directors, and principal stockholders of the client's major customers and suppliers. Further, it should include the names of officers and directors of companies in which the client has significant financial interests as a result of, for example, loans and leases. Finally, the auditor must possess the interpersonal skills necessary to interview nonmanagement personnel, who often can provide interesting background information on these transactions.

Evaluating related-party transactions is the most difficult part. The issue is whether the transaction was carried out on terms similar to those that would occur with an arm's-length party. For example, if real estate was sold or purchased, the auditor may be required to get an appraisal in order to evaluate the recorded exchange price. SAS 45, Related Parties, and its interpretation provide important guidance for this high-risk area [*AICPA Professional Standards*, Volume 1, 1992: AU 334 and 9334].

Failure to Document Subsequent-Event Inquiries and the Related Responses

A subsequent-event checklist is particularly useful in documenting subsequent-event inquiries and responses. These questions must be supplemented with a review of the latest available financial statements and the minutes of meetings of stockholders, directors, and appropriate committees, and with interviews with the client management about the current status of items in the financial statements being audited [*AICPA Professional Standards*, Volume 1, 1992: AU 560.12].

Failure to Obtain a Letter from the Client's Outside Counsel

To corroborate management's responses to questions about litigation, claims, and assessments, the auditor must obtain a letter from the client's legal counsel. It should, among other things, evaluate pending or threatened litigation [*AICPA Professional Standards*, Volume 1, 1992: AU 337.09].

Failure to Obtain a Letter of Representation

SAS 19, Client Representations, requires firms to get a letter of representation from client management [*AICPA Professional Standards*, Volume 1, 1992: AU 333]. It is customarily signed by the chief executive and chief financial officers.

Sometimes a firm will obtain a representation letter, but neglect to tailor it to the engagement's specific needs. For example, on one reviewed engagement, the letter referred to the disclosure of options and warrants when the client did not have any outstanding. Lapses like this make one wonder about other aspects of the exercise of due professional care.

Documentation Deficiency Causes

It is difficult to pinpoint with any certainty the underlying causes of these recurrent documentation deficiencies. It may, in part, be due to inappropriate or inadequate professional education. This is compounded by a lack of intermediate and advanced CPE courses appropriate for partner-level practitioners. In addition, many practitioners try to be expert in accounting, audit, tax, and consulting services. There are hardly enough hours in a year to be expert in one area, let alone several. To practice professionally requires specialization, and the AICPA is someday going to have to acknowledge that fact. A proposal in Chapter 9 addresses this issue.

Documentation deficiencies also may be due to a commitment to past practices. CPAs are taught to perform audits in a certain manner, and their habits often are difficult to change. Many of the audit advances in the past several years have introduced different and more efficient approaches. These advances are, however, sometimes expressed in terms that are new and, therefore, possibly difficult to grasp. For instance, the auditor's assessment of inherent and control risk is new language, not a new audit consideration.

Whatever the reasons for documentation deficiencies, many of them can be prevented by the firm's quality control system. Reviews, however, show some common weaknesses in the functional areas as well.

FUNCTIONAL AREA DEFICIENCIES

Independence

Many firms fail to require a check of the client receivables before report issuance, or, if they do, they fail to document it. Putting this procedure on the reviewer's checklist would limit such documentation lapses.

Most firms require staff independence confirmations, but reviews sometimes find that a few have been lost and others not obtained. Since it is most often new staff who fail to get these confirmations, perhaps a staff orientation checklist including this requirement would be the answer.

Firms frequently fail to document distribution of the list of clients to which the independence rules apply. Maybe retention of master copies of internal memoranda would reduce such findings.

Assigning Personnel

Many firms require the engagement partner to approve assignment of personnel to engagements. Unfortunately, many of these same firms fail to document this approval. If this step was included on a planning checklist, the documentation problem would not occur as often. The planning checklist should include questions about the engagement partner's consideration of engagement complexity, the planned level of supervision, and the need for staff training, rotation, and so on.

Consultation

Firms or offices of firms often take on engagements that require specialized expertise or involve complex matters. It is troubling how many times the engagement partner and staff fail to consult on these situations. To reduce these instances, perhaps firms should consider requiring concurring partner review on all new engagements.

Sometimes firm libraries are found to be incomplete. This is lamentable because the cost of maintaining an adequate accounting and audit library for firms that do not have SEC clients is far less than most tax services.

Many firms require proof of consultations and then fail to insure such proof is obtained. This requirement could be eliminated from the firm's policies. In an accounting or audit failure, however, the firm will probably be sorry it did not document its consultation.

Supervision

The most common problem is the use of outdated audit, review, and compilation programs and manuals. Requiring periodic evaluation of the appropriateness of the firm's materials would resolve this problem. One small firm hired an accounting professor to serve as a technical specialist and comment on "programs and checklists used on various accounting and auditing engagements" [Pivoz and Wirtz, 1992: 86]. Some firms develop consultation relationships with others that include periodic evaluation of each other's professional materials.

Another common supervision issue is a lack of guidance on accounting or audit objectives. For example, validity and completeness are opposite audit objectives. Validity deals with overstatement and completeness with understatement. If a staff person misunderstands this distinction, then the possibility of drawing the wrong conclusion increases. Some of the packaged work programs exacerbate this problem because they do not adequately incorporate the step's objective and leave inexperienced staff unsure of what financial statement assertion they are testing. This confusion leads to incomplete or incorrect conclusions.

Lack of compliance with the firm's supervision policies is a common problem. Examples include incomplete sign-offs on audit steps and accounting engagement procedures. Also included are engagement review issues. Staff and partners sometimes neglect to initial workpapers and sign off on review checklists. Occasionally, the engagement partner does not indicate the scope of his or her review, such as the client's permanent file, proposed adjusting entries, memoranda on consultation, and so on. The engagement partner also sometimes neglects to document his or her analytical review, a step that is required by GAAS.

Hiring

Firms frequently fail to give enough thought to the adequacy of their staff orientation programs. New staff should receive the firm's quality control document along with its work programs, checklists, and manuals. They would then have some understanding of the firm's philosophy and the operation of its quality control system—as well as their roles in it.

Firms often require a check of a candidate's references, but then fail to make such checks. They should either check references or drop this requirement from the hiring policy.

Professional Development

Many firms allow their staff to take whatever CPE courses they like. While this may be an enlightened management approach, it does not necessarily help the firm achieve its goals. Staff must be competent to carry out their assigned responsibilities, which means that firms must take a more active role in determining the nature and extent of staff training.

Certain firms do not require and others just neglect the distribution of summaries of new technical pronouncements such as SASs and SFASs. The continuing explosion in technical pronouncements requires constant updating of firm materials.

Some firms do not carefully document their in-house CPE programs. Once a system is set up, it is simple to comply with. All that is usually required is a course objective statement, an outline, course attendance records, and a course and instructor evaluation. State boards may have additional requirements.

Many firms do not document consideration of staff development in personnel assignment decisions. In addition, some firms cannot prove they have coordinated their professional development plans with their hiring and advancement policies.

Compliance with AICPA and state professional development requirements also is a problem. Frequently, one of two staff people do not meet the minimum CPE hours. The firm must stress the effect of this failure on the quality review.

Advancement

Some firms fail to require documentation of employee evaluations, while others do not comply with their own documentation requirement. Many evaluate their employees later than promised and wonder why staff are disgruntled. Most employees dread personnel evaluations, but firms that are not conscientious about them will lose good employees.

Acceptance and Continuance of Clients

"The most prevalent problem, reflected in 20% of the filings, was associated with client acceptance and retention policies" [Wallace and Wallace, 1990: 48]. Doing business with reputable clients is probably the most important quality control element of all.

The worst thing a firm can do is fail to have a formal acceptance and continuance policy. Failure to contact the predecessor auditor, bankers, attorneys, and others can be disastrous for the firm's long-term well-being. As important, the engagement partner must take the responses to these inquiries seriously. Certainly, the firms associated with the Lincoln Savings & Loan fiasco may now wish they had listened more carefully or asked more perceptive questions. Another concern is the predecessor's openness. Those that fail to provide full disclosure to the successor should be barred from the profession.

Some firms have acceptance procedures, but do not require that the inquiries be documented. This element is far too important to leave to someone's memory.

In addition, firms should seriously consider declining clients that lack audit committees made up of outside directors. Nonpublic entities must be apprised of the need for audit committees. A proposal dealing with this issue is included in Chapter 9.

Some engagement partners can forget to follow firm policy on client acceptance. Many firms require the concurrence of the partner-in-charge when the engagement requires specialized expertise or has questionable risks to the firm. If partner compensation is affected by total billings or number of new clients, some may overlook the firm's consultation requirement.

While most firms do document their acceptance decisions satisfactorily, fewer show they have made client continuance decisions. A formal procedure for continuance is as necessary as one for client acceptance.

Inspection

The Colorado Society of CPAs reports that failure to do an inspection is a common problem in quality review [1991: 11]. Firms that do an inspection often do it late. If quality control is to be effective, it has to be monitored regularly. As noted above, one firm has an accounting professor perform the annual inspection. Others have firm-on-firm inspections.

The most common review problem is failure to amend quality control policies when circumstances change. The following events should trigger a reevaluation of the firm's policies and procedures:

1. Significant growth in firm accounting and audit services. As a rule, a 10 percent change in gross billings or number of clients should trigger a system reappraisal.

2. New offices or acquisition of a practice. The firm's existing system might be transferable when another practice is acquired, but that may be problematic. It is highly likely that a totally new system will have to be designed.

3. Addition, termination, and retirement of key personnel and changes in employee mix. Staff come and go, including partners. Whenever the person is crucial to the firm's quality, the system must be amended.

4. Addition of clients in high-risk industries or those that require specialized expertise. Firms that accept new financial institution or SEC clients or the like must, at a minimum, amend their supervision standards.

5. Issuance of new professional pronouncements. New SASs often change the way we practice, so amendments must be made to firm supervision and professional development policies.

6. Audit or accounting failure or threatened or actual litigation alleging a failure. This would require a total reappraisal of the firm's system.

7. Downturns in the economy, decreased financial health of significant clients, or increased threats of regulation. Economic slowdowns increase audit risk; thus, the firm's system may have to be reevaluated.

8. Lack of coordination of system elements. For example, firm supervision policies must be coordinated with assignment, hiring, professional development, and consultation policies. The firm's independence policies must relate to those on hiring and personnel assignment. Professional development must consider the firm's hiring, advancement, and supervision policies. The acceptance and continuance policies must be coordinated with the firm's consultation and supervision policies. When system elements are not coordinated, problems occur.

THE BIGGEST PROBLEM

There is one major reason for all letter-of-comments findings. Noncompliance with SSARS and the firm's quality control system is simply a symptom of the real cause. The real cause underlies disclosure deficiencies and incomplete workpaper reviews. It also is behind all quality control system deficiencies. The cause is the wrong tone at the top or, in plain language, partners who do not care. These so-called professionals do not value their clients or their profession.

Some might argue that quality control is too complicated. We are not talking rocket science here, so this contention really has no basis. Designing and installing a quality control system that fits a firm is relatively easy. What is not easy to design and install is the commitment to make it work.

Firms argue, and rightfully so, that the competitive environment requires them to be efficient to survive. They also correctly argue that quality control contributes to inefficiencies. Efficiency, however, cannot come at the cost of effectiveness. If it does, there ceases to be a need for our services. The public would be better off with the services of non-CPAs because at least those services would not cost so much.

College graduates enter the profession with a sense of wonder and reverence for its ethics. Why? Because auditing textbooks include glowing examples of the profession's high standards. These graduates may then find workpapers that do not indicate appropriate inquiries and that fail to provide evidence of preliminary judgments about materiality, control risk assessments, or justification for sample sizes. These workpapers are being reviewed, and are too frequently accepted, by the firm's top people, its partners. In these instances, one message young staff receive, whether it is intended or not, is, Why do it if you don't need to document it? Maybe another message is being sent as well, that efficiency is paramount. To prevent these problems, the profession and CPA firms must rethink their priorities.

Firms also need to reevaluate whether it is in their long-range best interests and the profession's to use simplistic and dangerous employee performance measures, such as the ability to beat the budget and bring in clients. New staff people quickly figure out that the road to the top is, in many cases, based on rainmaking and not technical competence. Firms now believe they should "stop looking for only good future technicians and start seeking people with personalities. Those of above-average intelligence can be trained to be good technicians" [Boress, 1991: 44]. I can see the headlines now: "Lee Iacocca Elected AICPA Chair."

Most readers of this book do not have a minute chance of becoming partners in firms with the wrong tone at the top. The vast majority of CPAs do have an interest in making the profession better, care about it, have at least a modicum of technical competence, and are not primarily rainmakers. Fortunately for all, most firms are led by people who have the right tone at the top.

The profession needs to admonish firms that use accounting and audit services as loss leaders, reward the rainmakers, and put growth and profits ahead of quality. The profession's leaders and all its members also must realize that happiness comes only from serving others. When quality service becomes each person's goal, ample rewards follow. When this happens, we can indeed require others to call us professionals.

Chapter 9 offers over twenty recommendations that would turn the accounting business back into the accounting profession. Peer and quality reviews have done much to limit the likelihood of inferior quality service. More needs to be done. Professional standards, quality review, and quality control all need to be strengthened.

REFERENCES

AICPA Professional Standards, Volume 1. "Planning and Supervision," AU 311. New York: AICPA, June 1992.

———. "Audit Risk and Materiality in Conducting an Audit," AU 312. New York: AICPA, June 1992.

———. "Communications between Predecessor and Successor Auditors," AU 315. New York: AICPA, June 1992.

———. "Consideration of the Internal Control Structure in a Financial Statement," AU 319. New York: AICPA, June 1992.

———. "Analytical Procedures," AU 329. New York: AICPA, June 1992.

———. "Client Representations," AU 333. New York: AICPA, June 1992.

———. "Related Parties," AU 334 and 9334. New York: AICPA, June 1992.

———. "Inquiry of a Client's Lawyer Concerning Litigation, Claims, and Assessments," AU 337. New York: AICPA, June 1992.

————. "Subsequent Events," AU 560. New York: AICPA, June 1992.

AICPA Professional Standards, Volume 2. "Compilation and Review of Financial Statements," AR 100. New York: AICPA, June 1992.

Beasley, M. S., J. M. Sherinsky, and D. M. Guy. "When Do the Provisions of SSARS No. 1 Apply?" *Journal of Accountancy* (February 1992): 62–71.

Boress, A. S. "Building Rainmakers." *Journal of Accountancy* (February 1992): 42–46.

Bremser, W. G. "Peer Review: Enhancing Quality Control." *Journal of Accountancy* (October 1983): 78–88.

Colorado Society of CPAs. *NewsAccount*, October 1991, 11.

McCabe, R. K. "A Quality Review Checklist." *Journal of Accountancy* (September 1990): 69–74.

Ostling, P. J. "Under the Spreading Chestnut Tree—Accountant's Legal Liability—A Historical Perspective." In *Auditing Symposium VIII, Proceedings of the 1986 Touche Ross/University of Kansas Symposium on Auditing Problems*, edited by R. P. Strivastava and N. A. Ford, 1–23. Lawrence, Kans.: School of Business, University of Kansas, 1986.

Pivoz, M. A., and P. T. Wirtz. "The Part-Time Technical Reviewer." *Journal of Accountancy* (March 1992): 85–86.

Quality Review Executive Committee, American Institute of Certified Public Accountants. *AICPA Quality Review Program Manual*. New York: AICPA, 1991.

"Recurring Peer and Quality Review Comments." *The CPA Letter*. New York: AICPA, November 1992.

Wallace, W. A., and J. J. Wallace. "Learning from Peer Review Results." *The CPA Journal* (May 1990): 48–53.

9

Summary, Conclusions, and Recommendations

This chapter begins with a brief synopsis of the revolution that has occurred in the accounting profession. The next section discusses the matter of substandard service quality. Seven recommendations are given that, if adopted, would limit inferior-quality service. Several of these proposals, such as the recommendation to expand the scope of peer and quality review to include an assessment of the tone at the top will assuredly prove to be contentious. There also are recommendations about lengthening the experience requirement for a CPA certificate and strengthening the CPE requirement.

The third section discusses society's expectations and the problem of the continuing expectation gap. Nine recommendations are presented, with several suggestions for changes in professional standards.

Section four reviews two influences on society's expectations: the judiciary and government. In many instances, plaintiffs have nothing to lose in suing professionals except for the anticipated windfall. A proposal in this section would change that.

The discussion of quality review in the fifth section includes several recommendations, some of which will be controversial, that would improve the review process. It begins with the contention that review results must be publicly available and ends with a useful summary of the ten steps to a successful review and a brief description of what happens on a review.

The next section, on quality control, identifies two additional elements that must be included in control systems. The section following asserts that large multi-office firms must allow individual practice offices to develop control systems that fit their practices.

THE CONDENSED VERSION OF THE REVOLUTION

A revolution has occurred in the profession. The repeal of the encroachment rules helped change the accounting profession into the accounting business. Public accounting quickly became the home of the slick marketing executive. Firms try to differentiate themselves by designing and distributing marketing brochures and newsletters, as well as by developing elegant proposal packages and long mailing lists. To compete, they entice rainmakers to join their ranks and reward them abundantly.

Accounting and audit services, like other professional services, are viewed as commodities. They are price sensitive because of the intense competition and because what it is that accountants and auditors do cannot be observed. Some firms "lowball" their audit fees and use accounting and audit services as loss leaders. Underbidding often leads to unattainable engagement time budgets. To meet these demands, staff resort to undiscussable behaviors, such as accepting weak explanations to inquiries. These actions and others lead to substandard service.

Peer and quality reviews have done much to limit the likelihood of inferior-quality service. More needs to be done. This chapter makes over twenty recommendations that, if carried out, would turn the accounting business back into the accounting profession. Some of these proposals will be controversial. As mentioned above, review will have to assess the tone at the top to limit instances of substandard service. Professional standards and quality review also must be changed. Further, quality control systems should be strengthened. If these proposals are implemented, the profession will show that it deserves the right to regulate itself. If they are not, the profession may indeed just go away.

SUBSTANDARD SERVICE

Substandard service has existed in the profession since the earliest times. It existed well before the repeal of the encroachment rules. The elimination of these rules has, however, exacerbated the problem.

Mandatory quality review came about primarily because the accounting profession recognized that too many of its members were providing substandard service. In 1988, the AICPA membership approved the Anderson Committee recommendations, *Restructuring Professional Standards to Achieve Professional Excellence in a Changing Environment*. These recommendations included, among others, a requirement for mandatory quality review.

Substandard service exists mostly because some firms place profits and growth ahead of quality. The adverse consequences of inappropriate priorities can be avoided by expanding the scope of peer and quality review to assess the tone at the top.

To limit instances of substandard service, firms also should be required to have and follow statements of philosophy and written quality control documents.

Obviously, a requirement for practice monitoring must become a condition for licensing. In addition, education in general, and accounting education in particular, must be improved to limit the likelihood of providing services that fail to meet professional standards. To do this, firms will need to take more active roles in improving the quality of education. The profession also has to consider lengthening the experience requirement, requiring additional CPE, and amending and expanding the scope of quality control to cover all services.

Improving the Tone at the Top

"The National Commission on Fraudulent Financial Reporting commonly known as the Treadway Commission considers the tone set by top management—the corporate environment or culture—to be the most important factor contributing to the integrity of the financial reporting process" [Evers and Pearson, 1989: 97]. Just like CPA firm clients, firms have been and will continue to be run by management with the wrong tone at the top. Firms that focus on growth or profits as their primary goal while sacrificing quality service harm the profession. Firm leaders who prize the rainmakers, shun those with technical competence, and turn a blind eye to unattainable time budgets damage our reputation. How many scandals do we need before we decide that the profession should no longer tolerate people who do substandard work? National Student Marketing, ZZZZ Best, and Equity Funding are some examples of the work of too many accountants. Firms that use audit and accounting services as loss leaders cheapen the profession's image. This leads to the first recommendation, and perhaps the most important suggestion in the book.

Recommendation 1
The scope of peer and quality review must be expanded to assess the firm's tone at the top.

Improving the Tone at the Top—Part II

Firms can show the proper tone at the top in several ways. The first step is to provide professional-quality service. Engagement deficiencies should be the result of human error alone, not the consequence of staff pushed to meet unattainable time budgets or partners who put profit ahead of quality. Second, firms must adhere to their own statements of philosophy. SECPS firms are already required to have a statement of philosophy explicitly addressing the importance of quality service within their firm goals. Third, all firms, except sole practitioners without professional staff, must be required to have and adhere to written control documents. Without such documents, the notion of providing professional-quality service is just a phrase. Unless firms give thoughtful consideration to each control element and put those considerations in writing, substandard service will continue. A written document enhances firm commitment. These considerations prompt the next remedy.

Recommendation 2

All firms, except practitioners without professional staff, shall develop, maintain, and comply with a statement of philosophy and a written system of quality control.

Arguments against Assessing the Tone at the Top

Some argue that the tone at the top is too difficult to measure. Is it more difficult to assess than inherent risk and the control environment? Don't we already make audit judgments based on our perceptions of management's attitudes toward control policies and procedures, financial reporting, and budgets? Actually, we have extensive experience at assessing the tone at the top in our audit and review engagements, and maybe it is time we applied it to ourselves.

Requiring Practice Monitoring

The wrong tone at the top is clearly evident in firms that have chosen to opt out of quality review. Too many firms have chosen to drop their AICPA membership and thus avoid review. The leaders of these firms are a disgrace to the profession and to each CPA who takes pride in the designation. They are not professionals and are nothing more than free riders on our reputation. In addition, they do not bear the costs of their behavior. They refuse to undergo review, they probably do not have quality control systems, and they probably render inferior-quality service.

The evidence indicating that review does limit substandard service is persuasive. For example, "since 1979, almost twice as many actions have been brought against firms that have not had SECPS reviews" [Kaiser, 1989: 43]. The GAO found in a review of 150 governmental audits that peer-reviewed firms were charged far less often with standards violations. "The Securities and Exchange Commission studied its 48 enforcement actions against accountants from 1981 to 1986 and reported that the incidence of such actions was 11 times higher for accounting firms which had not undergone a peer review" [Wallace, 1989: 38]. In addition, "there is now statistical evidence that peer-reviewed firms are better liability insurance risks" [AICPA PCPS Executive Committee, 1991].

The free riders cite several arguments to support their indefensible positions. For example, some hold that they are already reviewed by their clients, bankers, and others. This is utter nonsense. Clients lack the expertise and, generally, the time and interest to evaluate the quality of the accounting and audit services they receive. Others argue that review impinges on the right to practice as they wish. Review does require firms to practice in a way that will provide reasonable assurance that they are following professional standards, which is an inherent part of being a professional. If some CPAs do not want to provide quality service, then let them give up their licenses. Each of us should fully support an initiative requiring practice monitoring, which brings us to the next suggestion.

Recommendation 3
State laws must be changed to require practice monitoring as a condition of licensing.

Improving Education

The complexity of transactions and the countless standards that must be followed contribute to substandard service. Some call this situation standards overload. Not too many years ago, GAAP consisted of fifty-one Accounting Research Bulletins. Now the practitioner also must follow thirty-six APB Opinions and well over a hundred SFASs. Each seems to be more complex than the previous one. This problem can be alleviated by improving education. In addition, professional education requirements need to be strengthened. Finally, some things cannot be taught in the classroom, which is why I propose requiring additional experience to earn the CPA designation.

Our educational system and professional development programs have not kept up with the increasingly complex business environment. As discussed in Chapter 2, not too long ago the world was, in a sense, much larger. Many businesses we take for granted today did not exist, and Wall Street was not nearly so inventive.

Passing the CPA examination has become a formidable task and practicing accounting an almost impossible one. In the meantime, we still require just an undergraduate degree to take the CPA examination and, in most jurisdictions, even fewer years of experience than before. Yes, the profession has approved the 150-hour requirement, but its passage by all fifty states cannot be taken for granted. Also, many in the profession argue, and rightfully so, that the additional hours ought to be spent in developing students' oral and written communication skills, analytical ability, interpersonal skills, and the like. Under such a curriculum, we would still graduate students who cannot assess control risk, make materiality judgments, use regression analysis, and, in some instances, keep a set of books.

The justification for allocating more hours to liberal arts courses ultimately rests on the premise that primary and secondary education has failed. In all too many instances, students enter college unable to communicate or analyze. They often leave college much the same way, but they do know enough to pass the CPA examination. Universities, then, are failing as well.

One answer is to teach accounting at the graduate level only. Presumably, the graduate entrance requirements would prohibit entry to those who cannot show some minimum skill in communication and mathematics. This would probably result in a lower supply of graduates and, thus, greater demand, which ultimately would increase the cost of professional services.

Another alternative would be to hold undergraduate educators accountable for demonstrating that their students do have minimum communication and mathematical skills. This option has several pitfalls. Presumably it would involve some testing and evaluation before students could graduate, but cases alleging test discrimination would fill the courts. In addition, education is a complex societal question. Are we to provide higher education to anyone who desires it? This is the prevailing view. Or should higher education be limited to those who have always done well?

One important question is, Who is to control education? It is principally controlled by professional politicians, not, as some might think, by educators or parents. Politicians almost always support education. Most, however, have not and will not vote an additional dollar for it. Education is not high on their priority lists and will not be until parents (voters) demand it.

Additional dollars for primary, secondary, and postsecondary education would help. New programs could be developed, more attention could be given to students, and graduation standards could be strengthened. The dollars would help, but they will not solve the problem entirely. The real problem is that, once again, we have the wrong tone at the top, but this time it is the parents. Education is simply not a high priority in most families, and, until it is, it will not get significantly better. Accounting practitioners, however, should appreciate the importance of education, and as professionals we have an obligation to improve it. This leads to the next prescription.

Recommendation 4

Firms must encourage and support participation of their personnel on local school boards, university trusteeships, accounting department groups, and so on.

CPAs can participate in the education of accounting students in many ways. For example, most accounting departments already encourage practitioner participation. Many universities have an advisory group made up of practitioners and professors. CPAs are kept informed of what is going on at the university and in the accounting department and the accounting curriculum. Professors are apprised of practice issues and are delighted to have practitioners as guest speakers.

Lengthening the Experience Requirement

To join the profession, a person must pass the CPA examination and serve an apprenticeship of maybe up to two years. This apprenticeship period is too short. Much more experience is needed to assess inherent risk, perform meaningful analytics, make judgments about what will influence a user's decisions, and so on. It is also needed to plan and review engagements and to understand the role and responsibility of accountants in society—to function as a professional, in other words. The current requirements to become a CPA can push people into roles they cannot competently fulfill. CPAs with two and three years of experience are planning, supervising, and reviewing engagements. Under most state laws, they can even have their own firms. These realities lead to the next prescription.

Recommendation 5
   To earn the CPA designation, a person shall obtain at least five years' experience in accounting and auditing.

Strengthening the CPE Requirement

The AICPA requires members in public practice to complete, during each three-year period, a minimum of 120 hours of CPE courses, with at least 20 hours taken each year. The weakness in this requirement is that it does not specify the areas that one should study or the courses that one should take. For example, a person who has primary responsibility in accounting and auditing should take at least 120 hours in accounting and audit-related CPE. Those with primary responsibilities in tax should take their tax courses. Individuals who do auditing and tax work should have a 240-hour requirement.

Unfortunately, the reality of professional practice is such that we are expected to be experts in many fields, including accounting, auditing, tax, and systems. Few people are expert in any area.

Firms regularly violate their personnel assignment policies. This is not done intentionally. Many CPAs believe that meeting the profession's licensing and professional education requirements results in expertise. As a consequence, firms assign people to accounting and audit engagements who do not have the competence to carry them out properly. The same problem occurs on tax and MAS engagements. To be capable, one must have many years of experience and appropriate current training in the specialty, which is what inspires the next suggestion.

Recommendation 6
   The AICPA bylaws must be amended to require 120 accounting and audit CPE hours for each three-year reporting period, with a minimum of 20 hours a year for those who provide these services. State board of accountancy regulations also should be changed.

There is persuasive evidence of the need to strengthen the CPE requirements. For example, engagement deficiencies frequently stem from a lack of appropriate CPE. One common engagement deficiency is failure to adequately document planning considerations. Planning omissions include failure to appropriately appraise the client's control structure and resulting control risk. They also include disclosure deficiencies, failure to justify sample sizes, and failure to inquire about related parties and subsequent events. These deficiencies and others often are attributable to inappropriate and inadequate professional education. Certainly using the available guides to compilation, review, and audit would help. However, some practitioners are so far behind in their knowledge of professional standards that even the guides will not suffice. It is imperative, then, that the CPE requirements be strengthened.

Also, individuals who provide tax services should be required to complete tax courses to retain AICPA membership. The era of specialization is here—and has been here for some time.

Expanding Quality Control to Cover Other Services

The accounting profession, unlike other professions, has chosen for the most part to overlook the need for specialization. The AICPA did recognize the accounting and auditing specialties by requiring firms to have systems of control over them. The profession needs to take a further step and require a quality control system over each service firms offer, which is covered in the following suggestion.

Recommendation 7
   Firms must develop, maintain, and adhere to a quality control system for each service they offer, such as tax, client advice, and litigation support.

Many firms have already implemented control systems over the other services they offer. In the main, they follow SQCS 1, but drop the independence requirement.

SOCIETY'S EXPECTATIONS

The expectation gap between how society and accountants perceive our role and responsibility has not been significantly narrowed, even by the expectation-gap standards. Further changes are required.

The average person still thinks a CPA firm guarantees an entity's viability. Business failures trigger undue criticism of the profession because we have not satisfactorily addressed the going-concern issue. What follows are recommendations surrounding the need to disclose the nature and implications of the going-concern assumption. In addition, a proposal is offered on the additional research that is needed into how to predict business failure.

A wide expectation gap also exists in limited-scope engagements. As a starting point, all engagements should be supported by written engagement letters that specify the accountant-auditor's scope and responsibility. In addition, a proposal is made to reconsider unaudited reports.

On reviews and audits, CPAs use analytical procedures extensively, often without access to industry databases. CPAs need greater access to these databases to improve the effectiveness of analytical procedures.

Users also think auditors are and always have been responsible for detecting irregularities and illegal acts. Our role, they believe, is to serve as their eyes and ears and, in a sense, act as the sentry on duty. We do not reject this role, but we do not have all the tools we need to do it. This chapter will recommend that the ASB provide additional guidance on how to detect errors and irregularities. In addition, sponsored audit research should focus on detection of irregularities.

These recommendations are steps toward narrowing the expectation gap. The issue of independence in appearance also must be resolved. This chapter includes a proposal that confronts that issue directly.

Going Concern

On every audit, auditors must assess the client's viability as a going concern. As discussed in Chapter 1, a paragraph questioning the ability of the client to continue as a going concern may assure the client's demise. Is that what society wants? Also, what time horizon should CPAs use? Should it be longer than the present one year?

As a starting point, financial statement readers should be informed that the statements assume the entity is a going concern, and they should be told the implications of that assumption. Financial statement users believe accountants are better able to predict circumstances and recognize situations that foretell of impending disaster than they are. Disclosing the basis (i.e., the going-concern assumption and its implications for balance sheet measures) could be done either as the first required note to the financial statements or in the accountant-auditor's report. The disclosures also should note that the accountant-auditor has not evaluated the appropriateness of that assumption. These considerations guide the next proposal.

Recommendation 8

The notes or the accountant-auditor's report shall state that the financial statements have been prepared under the assumption that the entity is a going concern and should explain the implications of that assumption. The notes or report also shall state that the accountant-auditor has not evaluated the appropriateness of that assumption.

Going-Concern Research and Substantial Doubt

Little guidance exists on how to make the going-concern assessment. The evidence suggests that we are not very good at it, except after a Chapter 11 filing. However, "research in the area of bankruptcy prediction is very encouraging, and indicates that potentially useful models are available for the purpose of at least the initial continued-existence assessment'' [Akresh et al., 1988: 31–32]. These models are not very useful yet because they require complex multivariate analysis. Also, additional guidance must be provided on the meaning of substantial doubt because it is vague, at best. This suggests the following.

Recommendation 9

Research must be performed on the application of bankruptcy decision models to the audit process. Guidance also is necessary to determine the attributes of substantial doubt.

In the meantime we should get out of the business of providing the going-concern warning.

Limited-Scope Engagements

Society, through the courts, also suggests that we have full responsibility for limited-scope engagements, such as compilations and reviews. The following suggestion to the ASB and the AICPA Accounting and Review Services Committee is in order.

Recommendation 10

Firms shall get a signed engagement letter before rendering accounting or audit services. The letter shall detail the scope of the services and the firm's responsibility.

Complicating the limited-scope issue are the standard writers, who do not seem to appreciate fully the circumstances that lead to such engagements and the services rendered. As discussed in Chapter 8, some CPA firms do not comply with the SSARS requirements in all material respects, and this is inexcusable. At the same time, they also do much more than what is required in some areas.

Typically, on compilations, the financial statements and report are the product of a bookkeeping service, which often involves classifying the client's transactions into the proper accounts, reconciling the bank accounts, and totaling client-provided receivable and payable schedules. It includes calculating and recording necessary compensated absences, wages, interest and tax accruals, prepaids, and depreciation. But management does not provide the last information. Most would not have the vaguest idea how to calculate the correct amounts. The firm, thus, does much more than the compilation report says. In the report we correctly say that we have compiled the information management supplied. We do not say that we have created certain information, which we should. This disparity between what we say and what we do prompts the public to assume we carry more responsibility than we would like.

Review engagements have similar problems. The report says that the accountant used inquiries and analytical procedures. Frequently, much more is done. Yes, ratios and changes are calculated, which results in questions being asked. Usually, audit procedures, such as vouching, physical examination, and observation, also are completed because they are efficient and effective. Small companies that have reviews often have poor internal controls and not very capable accounting staff. They frequently need the review because of a lending requirement.

In such cases, the auditor knows that until the accounts are corrected, analytical procedures are a waste of time. He or she fully expects to uncover many errors, and usually does. The auditor may write the inventory procedures, observe inventory taking, and take a few test counts. He or she must provide these audit services because the client often does not know how to perform them. To say that management provided the information for a compilation or that a review is limited to analytics and inquiries is incomplete and possibly just wrong.

The disparity between what the compilation and review reports say and what accountants do is inexcusable. Another review issue is the financial statement user's perception of the differences between the assurance level intended in a review report and that conveyed in an audit. One remedy is to eliminate compilations and reviews, and return to unaudited statements. The following recommendation deserves consideration.

Recommendation 11

The accountant's report accompanying unaudited financial statements shall detail the services rendered and the procedures performed on the engagement. It also shall state that audit procedures sufficient to render an opinion on the statement's conformance with GAAP or OCBOA were not performed. Finally, the report shall state that no assurance can be provided.

The main advantage of this recommendation is that the reader will be informed of what the accountant-auditor did. This report and the user's knowledge of management's integrity enable the users to draw their own inferences about the reliability of the financial statements.

For investors, lenders, and others needing assurance, the only alternative would be an audit. The profession should not continue to provide negative assurance when sufficient procedures have not been performed.

Returning to unaudited reports also would increase the profession's integrity. Telling the reader that certain procedures were performed and that no assurance can be provided without an audit is an honest report. What we offer now is not.

Analytics and inquiries do not provide a sufficient basis to render negative assurance, as is now done in review reports. In many cases, the analytical procedures can be, at best, simplistic. In addition, most firms do not have access to computerized industry databases, which could significantly enhance analytics, because of their high cost. This inspires the following proposal.

Recommendation 12

The AICPA must lead an initiative to help obtain cost-effective access to computerized industry databases.

Errors, Irregularities, and Illegal Acts

Auditors now accept responsibility for designing audits that will detect material errors, irregularities, and illegal acts under SAS 53, The Auditor's Responsibility to Detect and Report Errors and Irregularities, and SAS 54, Illegal Acts by Clients. The average person thought we had that responsibility all along. If it were not for the SEC's 1985 push for auditor responsibility for fraud detection, we would still be trying to avoid the responsibility for irregularities, and understandably so. As discussed, detecting fraud is, at best, mystifying.

There is not much guidance to aid the auditor in the detection of irregularities and illegal acts. For example, distinguishing between direct-effect illegal acts and those that are indirect is a difficult exercise at best. Further, one has to question whether an auditor is qualified to make judgments about violations. Is he or she familiar with all the applicable laws and regulations? There are myriad questions to answer about the auditor's responsibility to detect material irregularities and illegal acts. The new SASs' main accomplishment was to increase the auditor's responsibility. They did not provide the tools necessary to detect or evaluate irregularities or illegal acts. This leads to the following propositions.

Recommendation 13

The ASB must provide auditors with additional guidance on detecting irregularities and illegal acts. In addition, the existing guidance must be clarified.

Recommendation 14

Audit research must be performed to identify signs of possible irregularities.

Much of the sponsored audit research is designed to improve audit efficiency. While this is a worthwhile goal, almost no research has been done on identifying conditions that suggest the existence of irregularities. The chairman of the board of directors of the National Association of Certified Fraud Examiners says, "it is a mystery why no in-depth research has been conducted in the fraud area . . . " [Wells, 1992: 2]. We know very little about what motivates those who engage in irregularities and what clues they leave behind.

Audit Committees

Peer and quality reviews show frequent functional area deficiencies. Client acceptance and continuance issues deserve particular comment. No matter how deficient a firm might be in complying with professional standards, it can still avoid disaster if it designs and implements a satisfactory acceptance and continuance policy. Some clients are just not worth the risk. Clients ought to be required to have audit committees, which leads to the following recommended change to professional standards.

Recommendation 15
Audit engagements shall be accepted only if the client has a functioning audit committee made up of outside directors or their equivalents.

The responsibility for designing an audit to detect material irregularities and illegal acts requires such a change. There are, however, entities controlled by single shareholders for which such a requirement would be a burden. These entities will have to reevaluate their needs for audits. If the audit is needed to provide assurance to a lender, then the entity's board of directors should be expanded and an audit committee created. There is no other way to fulfill our obligation.

Independence

The independence standards should be reassessed. The profession's leadership does not adequately consider the importance of independence in appearance and, instead, requires members to comply with what are, for some, myriad incomprehensible rules. Currently, the AICPA requires its members to abide by many independence rules, each of which is stated negatively. These are the "thou shall nots" of the profession. But we do not prohibit accountant-auditors from providing MAS. While MAS does not necessarily impede firm independence, it just does not look good. The main issue, independence in appearance, remains.

One alternative is to give firms a choice of doing accounting and audit services or something else. Another option is to disclose the existence of relationships that could impair independence, which is covered in the following proposal.

Recommendation 16
The accountant-auditor's report shall disclose the nature of any other services the firm furnishes to the client and the amount billed for those services for the past fiscal year. In addition, it shall include a positive assertion about the firm's independence.

Most practitioners will challenge this recommendation. Some might say that use of the word "independent" in the auditor's report is sufficient. It is doubtful that most readers of auditors' reports are aware of the word or its significance. It is time for the profession to become more forthright. A positive assertion about the firm's independence is long overdue.

Additionally, most practitioners will object to disclosing the nature of other services and related billings. However, the profession requires clients to make disclosures that they would rather not make so that financial statement users can make informed decisions. Many users already believe that CPAs are not independent. Disclosure of the firm-client relationship and affirmation of independence would challenge the doubter's perceptions.

INFLUENCES ON SOCIETY'S EXPECTATIONS

The judicial system, government, and the belief that someone else should be held responsible when things go wrong have each helped reshape society's attitudes about the role of the accountant-auditor.

Judicial Influences

More cases were filed against accountants between 1972 and 1987 than in the entire history of the profession [Mednick, 1987]. U.S. accountants now face 4,000 liability suits—double the number in 1985—and more than $30 billion in damages [AICPA, "Large Firms Unite," 1992: 4]. These suits were made possible, in part, by the class-action doctrine and attorneys' contingent fee arrangements, as well as by the doctrine of joint and several liability. In addition, firms are required to practice essentially as partnerships, which make partners attractive targets because of the accessibility of their personal assets. Those assets combined with malpractice insurance do indeed make accounting firms the deep pockets. (While the AICPA prohibition against practicing in the corporate form has been repealed, it will be some time before it has an effect because state laws must be changed as well.)

The legal assault also came about because there are too many attorneys, which makes loss recovery easier for plaintiffs. When a business failure occurs, plaintiffs have nothing to lose in suing the surviving accountant because it is simple to find an attorney to take the case on a contingent fee basis.

As long as there are too many attorneys, contingent fee arrangements, the class-action doctrine, and joint and several liability, the legal assault will continue.

Users of financial statements expect to be reimbursed for losses incurred, even when they have not relied on the financial statements. Unfortunately, the courts support this view. "Innocent investors" are not held responsible for their decisions, nor are they accountable for their own greed.

At a minimum, the AICPA should develop an initiative to change state laws so that plaintiffs who lose a malpractice suit have something to lose other than their hoped-for windfall. That brings us to the following recommendation.

Recommendation 17
The profession must spearhead an initiative to change state laws to

automatically award costs and attorneys fees when accountants prevail in malpractice suits.

Government

Government continuously threatens to take over the accounting profession. Using the Metcalf report as a model, government would prescribe GAAP and GAAS, decide what services accountants can and cannot offer, and conduct audits of CPA firms. Fortunately for the profession, the conviction that governmental regulation is the means to solve all problems has subsided. There is, however, a trend in Congress and in the executive branch toward increased federal regulation.

The threat of increased regulation is real. We can let those in Congress determine our destiny, or we can take a more active role ourselves. In 1992, two bills that affect CPAs were introduced in Congress. Representative Ronald Wyden (D–Oreg.) introduced H.R. 4313, a bill that "would transfer the setting of auditing standards from the private sector to the government" [AICPA, "AICPA Tells Congressional Subcommittee It Opposes Wyden Bill," 1992: 8]. This legislation passed the House but the "Senate declined to consider the measure before adjournment" [AICPA, "Many Bills Fall Victim," 1992: 6]. However, Representative Wyden is expected to reintroduce his bill.

Another bill, H.R. 4900, introduced by Representative John Dingell (D–Mich.), "would create a Federal Insurance Commission and grant the commission the authority to set accounting standards, and would permit non-CPAs to perform audits and to express opinions on the financial statements of insurers or reinsurers" [AICPA, "Insurance Bill Would Regulate Accounting Profession," 1992: 8]. This proposal also failed to get the necessary support. These proposals are very similar to what Senator Metcalf offered in the mid–1970s.

While it may be difficult to admit, Congress's many inquiries into the profession have helped improve practice quality. It was Congress that demanded quality review. The SEC used peer review in the early 1970s as part of its disciplinary proceeding settlements. In 1987, the SEC developed a proposal requiring peer review of firms auditing public companies.

The profession does need to be more proactive in working with congressional committees, the SEC, and other regulators. At the moment, the AICPA Washington staff is doing an extraordinarily good job, but much more needs to be done.

Proactive leadership would take the initiative. It would request committee hearings to offer updates on the profession's self-regulatory effort. It would appoint ad hoc committees to investigate public scandals. It would fully support the goals and objectives of the QCIC.

A proactive profession would change its standards to conform with society's expectations. A proactive leadership also would seek to improve accounting education as well as promote changes in state laws in order to make quality

review a condition of licensing and to lengthen licensing experience requirements. In addition, it would design and promote an initiative to change state
laws so that plaintiffs in frivolous malpractice suits have something to lose.

To accomplish these goals, the AICPA will need additional resources, and its
membership should fully support appropriate dues increases. A proactive AICPA
will be more costly because it will take additional full-time professionals to
design and carry out such programs. In these slim economic times, this may be
a lot to ask. It is not, though, if the alternatives are considered, which leads to
the following prescription.

Recommendation 18

The AICPA leadership must develop an initiative to regulate the regulators, monitor society's expectations, narrow the expectation gap, improve
accounting education, promote changes in state laws, and strengthen its
CPE requirements. To do these things, the AICPA membership must approve a dues increase.

QUALITY REVIEW

At the moment, there are two practice-monitoring programs: the AICPA Division for CPA Firms and the AICPA quality review program. Their objectives
and requirements are so similar that it is difficult to tell them apart.

The sections that follow discuss the need to make review results publicly
available. In addition, there is a proposal to combine the Division for CPA Firms
with the AICPA quality review program. Finally, there is a recommendation
that the roles and responsibilities of the POB and the QCIC be expanded to cover
all practice units.

The sections that follow also provide useful summaries of the importance of
getting the right reviewer and the steps to a successful review. The final section
is a brief recapitulation of what happens on a review.

Making Review Results Publicly Available

The major difference between division or peer quality reviews is that division
results are publicly available. Keeping quality review results secret is indefensible
and only leaves the profession open to criticism. Financial statement users have
a right to know about the quality of the firm in which they place their trust.
Users of CPA firm services deserve to know if a firm measures up to the
profession's standards.

Many practitioners, especially those whose clients are nonpublic, will probably
resist any effort to make all review reports publicly available. What they are
saying is that owners, bankers, and other interested parties have no business
knowing the quality of the firm that is reporting on statements on which they

must rely. If that is the profession's position, there is really no good reason for our existence.

The real reason for resisting public disclosure is fear. CPAs' apprehension about passing a review and anxiety about what their letters of comments will say are valid. In time, though, the vast majority of firms will pass easily and receive letters of comments with no damaging disclosures. Some firms will need more time to get their practices up to professional standards. Adhering to the large number of increasingly complex SFASs and SASs is not easy. Also, developing a quality control document and implementing its policies and procedures takes time. The following recommendation recognizes these realities.

Recommendation 19
Review results shall be made publicly available on the firm's third review and thereafter.

Eliminating the Division for CPA Firms

Once the major differences between peer and quality reviews are eliminated, there is no reason for the PCPS to continue. The quality review program could take over all Division for CPA Firms activities. SECPS members have additional requirements that could be easily incorporated into the quality review program.

Recommendation 20
The AICPA shall put the activities of the Division for CPA Firms under the auspices of the quality review program.

This recommendation conflicts with the conclusion drawn in Chapter 3 that the Division for CPA Firms is the best choice. That is true right now because the division makes review results publicly available and provides secondary advantages to its members similar to those of a CPA firm association. There is little reason why the secondary advantages of division membership ought to be restricted to this group. In addition, there may be some cost savings to dropping what are, in many respects, duplicate programs.

Expanding the Scope and Authority of the POB and the QCIC

The POB and the QCIC perform important functions by maintaining and improving the quality of professional practice. But the failure to extend public oversight to all firms suggests that public investors deserve higher-quality accounting service than do private investors.

Similarly, the QCIC provides an important service by investigating alleged instances of accounting or audit failure. This service is important to the entire profession, not simply to those that serve public companies. These committees' activities must be expanded, which leads to the following proposal.

Recommendation 21
   The POB and the QCIC should have authority over all firms.

Getting the Right Reviewer

Obtaining a helpful or value-oriented review depends largely on the person performing it. Fortunately, the profession has many excellent reviewers who are making review work. Research shows that reviewer quality does affect the reviewed firm's attitude toward review. It also shows that reviewers have been instrumental in improving firm members' confidence and the firm's ability to detect material misstatements. Further, it reveals that reviewers generally provide suggestions that help firms improve their efficiency and effectiveness. Reviewers, then, deserve our accolades.

Finding a good reviewer is not easy, but it is absolutely critical. It takes time, persistence, and good intuition. The key, of course, is to get references and conduct a thorough interview.

The profession's policy that allows only peers to carry out reviews should be retained. Some reviewers, however, are more talented than others. It is also probably true that experience raises competence. It may be in the profession's best interest to do the following.

Recommendation 22
   Using reviewed-firm comments and analyses of review workpapers, the
   AICPA and state societies shall identify reviewers with exceptional skill.
   These reviewers shall be encouraged to take on more review assignments
   and provide review courses.

Steps to a Successful Review

Chapter 6 outlined ten steps to a successful review. The first step was a review of the firm's quality control document. Firms without these documents should review the appendix to Chapter 5 for an example they can adopt.

Firms should ask questions during control system reviews. Is the system suitably comprehensive, and does it reflect firm policies and procedures? Do not let the reviewer discover that firm procedures are not followed.

Firms also should perform and document internal inspections to save the reviewer time and the firm money. Before their first review, firms are strongly encouraged to get a consulting review, a confidential, high-spot review that sets the stage for quality review.

Firms should choose the reviewer liaison with care, sign the engagement letter, and contact the reviewer. Communication between the liaison and the review team captain is key. The next steps are to develop a firm profile, assemble administrative and personnel files, and conduct a seminar to prepare staff for the review. If the firm has followed the guidelines for developing a quality control document and the steps to a successful review, the experience itself will only affirm that the firm provides professional-quality service.

The Review: What Happens

As Chapter 7 demonstrates, the review is comprehensive. Engagements selected will cover a cross-section by partner, client and engagement types, large and small undertakings, high-risk engagements, and those covered by GAO standards. Common engagement deficiencies are inadequate documentation, failure to assess audit risk or make preliminary materiality judgments, and noncompliance with SSARS. Chapter 8 discusses the common and not so common deficiencies, so read it thoroughly before your review.

The review encompasses an evaluation of control system design. In addition, inquiries and other tests are made to determine if the system actually operates as planned.

At the end of the review the firm receives a letter of comments and a review report. The chances of receiving an unqualified report are, for most, quite good, but the probability of receiving a letter of comments also is high. One of the purposes of review is educational, and research of Division firms supports the fact that in time there will be a significant reduction in the number of comments.

QUALITY CONTROL

The triennial review focuses on the firm's quality control system. Pattillo says that quality control is only for firms "that wish to retain clients, stay out of court, improve profits, toot their own horn, improve the profession, and avoid professional sanctions" [1984: 3]. Because a well-designed and well-executed system reduces incidents of accounting and audit failure, it will help firms keep clients and stay out of court. It may also lead to improved profits. Firms that use well-designed work programs and checklists are finding their review time decreases, which often increases overall profitability.

A quality control system, as discussed in Chapter 5, is made up of policies and procedures, assignment of responsibilities, communication, and a monitoring requirement. Control systems differ among firms because of cost-benefit considerations, the nature of the practice, firm size, and several other considerations. SQCS 1 and Appendix 5.A contain valuable guidance to developing a quality control document.

Adding a Documentation Requirement

The recommended quality control considerations contained in SQCS 1 are comprehensive. The most common weakness in reviews, however, is lack of documentation. Certainly SQCS 1 implies that firms should properly document their engagements; SAS 41, Working Papers, requires appropriate documentation. Perhaps it is necessary to add an explicit documentation element to SQCS 1, which is covered in the next proposal.

Recommendation 23
    There must be policies and procedures for documenting work at all organizational levels to provide the firm reasonable assurance of meeting professional and firm quality standards.

To assure proper documentation, an individual or group should be appointed to develop firm guidelines and procedures. These guidelines should encompass documentation of planning, supervision, internal control understanding, control and inherent risk assessment, planned detection risk, evidence obtained, procedures applied, and so on. They should include a policy requiring communication of the firm's documentation requirement to all professional staff. Procedures to carry out this policy might require the firm to publish the documentation requirements in manuals or cover them in training programs and planning sessions.

Firms also should have policies requiring periodic monitoring of their compliance with their documentation requirements. An individual should be appointed to select engagements, perhaps randomly, and evaluate the correspondence with the firm documentation policies. As important, the findings should be documented and corrective actions taken.

Adding a Reevaluation Requirement

Another quality control concern is the frequent finding in reviews that firms fail to reevaluate their systems when circumstances change. This could be corrected either by strengthening the firm's monitoring policy or by adding a reevaluation element to SQCS 1, as suggested below.

Recommendation 24
    Firms shall establish policies and procedures requiring reevaluation of quality control system design when circumstances change in order to provide reasonable assurance that their accounting and audit services comply with professional standards.

Events that might cause a reevaluation include firm growth, the addition of practice offices or key personnel, the loss of key employees, changes in types of engagements, new engagements in specialized industries, and new SASs and SFASs. The firm should appoint an individual or group to identify situations or events that require control system reevaluation. In addition, it should communicate the reevaluation criteria to all professional personnel and check compliance with this policy at least annually.

MULTI-OFFICE FIRMS

The road to peer and quality review has been an interesting one. In just a few short years, a revolution has occurred. Without a doubt, the profession's response to substandard service has been exemplary. There remains, however, one more issue for consideration.

When a large audit or accounting failure, or a business failure for that matter, occurs, the entire profession suffers. These failures usually involve large firms because they are the only ones capable of handling big clients. Large failures of any kind attract public attention and invite the scrutiny and wrath of those in Congress. It is much easier for politicians to investigate the accounting profession than to deal with crippling budget deficits.

One issue that large multi-office firms must address is the development of their quality control systems. Most large firms develop all policies at their main offices and then hand them down to the local offices. This approach may not be as effective or as efficient as presumed. To be workable, such policies need to be so generic that they may not be very helpful to the offices that must implement them. National firm policies and procedures cannot consider one office's particular personnel, type of clients, and cost-benefit considerations. More important, getting office personnel to commit to something they did not develop is difficult. The autocrats, of course, may respond that they must. While they must, they probably will not. Without commitment, no system of quality control works. Thus, the final recommendation.

Recommendation 25

Multi-office firms shall require each significant practice office to design and implement a quality control system within the firm's general guidelines.

CONCLUDING REMARKS

Audit and accounting failures have many underlying causes, but they ultimately are due to the wrong tone at the top. Every firm must have the best at the top, or the profession will just go away.

The Code of Professional Conduct says that members have a "continuing responsibility to maintain the public's confidence and carry out the profession's special responsibilities for self-governance" [*AICPA Professional Standards*, Volume 2, 1992: ET § 52.01]. To maintain public confidence, substandard service must be prevented. Peer and quality reviews do prevent inferior service. They also show that the profession can and does govern itself. To prevent substandard service, several other changes need to be made.

We need to make this revolution in the accounting profession work because "self-regulation provides credibility, generates public trust and reduces unnecessary, costly governmental intervention" [Kaiser, 1989: 41]. We must make it work, as the alternative is the loss of the professionalism we strive for and the profession we love.

It would be a shame, then, if we ceased to exist because the public lost confidence in our integrity and usefulness. While CPAs usually rank high in public opinion polls on professional ethics, recent highly publicized audit failures and the S&L debacle have hurt our reputation. It is important that we do whatever is necessary to ensure that we continue to earn the respect and confidence of the public and our clients. That is what prompted AICPA members to take the revolutionary step of mandating peer and quality review. That is what prompted this book. The revolution continues.

REFERENCES

AICPA PCPS Executive Committee. *Meeting Minutes of January 17–18, 1991*. Cited in *Of Mutual Interest*. Gainesville, Fla.: CPA Mutual, June 1991.

AICPA Professional Standards, Volume 2. "Code of Professional Conduct," ET § 52. New York: AICPA, June 1992.

"AICPA Tells Congressional Subcommittee It Opposes Wyden Bill." *The CPA Letter*. New York: AICPA, June 1992, 8.

Akresh, A. D., J. L. Loebbecke, and W. R. Scott. "Chapter Two: Audit Approaches and Techniques." In *Research Opportunities in Auditing: The Second Decade*, edited by A. R. Abdel-khalik and I. Solomon, 13–55. Sarasota, Fla.: American Accounting Association, 1988.

Evers, C. J., and D. B. Pearson. "Lessons Learned from Peer Review." *Journal of Accountancy* (April 1989): 96–102.

"Insurance Bill Would Regulate Accounting Profession." *The CPA Letter*. New York: AICPA, June 1992, 8.

Kaiser, C. "The Mandatory SECPS Membership Vote." *Journal of Accountancy* (August 1989): 40–44.

"Large Firms Unite in Fighting Liability Crisis." *The CPA Letter*. New York: AICPA, October 1992, 4.

McCarroll, T. "Who's Counting?" *Time*, 13 April 1992, 48–50.

"Many Bills Fall Victim to Adjournment Pressure." *The CPA Letter*. New York: AICPA, November 1992, 6.

Mednick, R. "Accountants' Liability: Coping with the Stampede to the Courtroom." *Journal of Accountancy* (September 1987): 118–22.

Pattillo, J. W. *Quality Control and Peer Review—A Practice Manual for CPAs*. New York: John Wiley & Sons, 1984.

Restructuring Professional Standards to Achieve Professional Excellence in a Changing Environment. Report of the Special Committee on Standards of Professional Conduct for Certified Public Accountants. New York: AICPA, 1986.

Wallace, W. A. "A Historical View of the SEC's Reports to Congress on Oversight of the Profession's Self-Regulatory Process." *Accounting Horizons* (December 1989): 24–39.

Wells, J. T. "From the Chairman." In *The White Paper*, 2. Austin, Tex.: National Association of Certified Fraud Examiners, March–April 1992.

Glossary

The Accountant's Guide to Peer and Quality Review contains many references to the profession's standards and the names of influential standard-setting bodies and other organizations. The following abbreviations, used by the AICPA and others, are applied throughout the book. Each abbreviation is introduced when it is first used. For those unfamiliar with the language of accounting, the following list may be helpful.

ASB   Auditing Standards Board. This AICPA committee prescribes what auditors describe as generally accepted auditing standards (see GAAS).

CASB   Cost Accounting Standards Board. The board was established by Congress in 1970 to create uniformity and consistency in cost accounting practices. They have issued standards, rules, and regulations that must be followed by companies doing business with the federal government.

CAR   Commission on Auditor's Responsibilities. In 1977, this committee issued a monograph titled *Report, Conclusions, and Recommendations of the Commission on Auditor's Responsibilities*. It has had a major influence on the practice of accounting and auditing.

CART   Committee-Appointed Review Team. Firms undergoing review can elect to have the AICPA or the participating state society appoint the review team.

CPE   Continuing Professional Education. The profession, through the AICPA and other regulatory organizations, requires CPAs to meet minimum annual CPE requirements.

FAF   Financial Accounting Foundation. This is the sponsoring organization of the Financial Accounting Standards Board (see FASB).

FASB	Financial Accounting Standards Board. This committee formulates what accountants call generally accepted accounting principles (see GAAP).
GAAP	Generally Accepted Accounting Principles. These are the rules, procedures, conventions, and assumptions that accountants use in preparing and presenting financial information.
GAAS	Generally Accepted Auditing Standards. There are ten standards that cover standards of field work, standards of reporting, and general standards. In addition, there are numerous interpretations.
GAO	General Accounting Office. The U.S. General Accounting Office was set up to oversee and advise Congress and the executive branch about matters of efficiency and economy.
MAS	Management Advisory Services. Many CPA firms consider themselves as financial service providers. As a result, they offer services other than accounting, auditing, and tax. These services might include system design and installation, budgeting, profitability analysis, devising and testing pension plan alternatives, and so on.
MFC	Matters for Further Consideration. This is the title of a form used on reviews to note possible control and engagement deficiencies.
OCBOA	Other Comprehensive Bases of Accounting. Bases of accounting other than generally accepted accounting principles, such as tax, cash, and regulatory agency bases.
PCPS	Private Companies Practice Section. This is one of the two sections that make up the AICPA Division for CPA Firms.
POB	Public Oversight Board. This is an independent body of five individuals who oversee the activities of the AICPA SEC Practice Section (see SECPS) within the Division for CPA Firms. Its purpose is to represent the public interest.
QCIC	Quality Control Inquiry Committee. This committee investigates audit practices following allegations of audit failure.
QCSC	Quality Control Standards Committee. This AICPA committee developed Statement on Quality Control Standards (SQCS) 1, System of Quality Control for a CPA Firm, and its related interpretations.
SAS	Statements on Auditing Standards. These statements comprise the authoritative literature which makes up generally accepted auditing standards (see GAAS). They are issued by the AICPA's Auditing Standards Board (see ASB).
SEC	Securities and Exchange Commission. This federal agency oversees matters related to the conduct of the securities markets.
SECPS	SEC Practice Section. This is one of two sections within the Division for CPA Firms. Its primary objective is to improve the quality of practice before the Securities and Exchange Commission (see SEC).

SFAS   Statement of Financial Accounting Standards. These statements, issued
                by the Financial Accounting Standards Board (see FASB), set forth
                mandatory accounting principles.

SSARS   Statements on Standards for Accounting and Review Services. These
                statements, issued by the AICPA Accounting and Review Services Com-
                mittee, cover matters related to unaudited financial statements.

TIC   Technical Issues Committee. This is a committee of the Private Com-
                panies Practice Section (see PCPS). It reviews, evaluates, and responds
                to exposure drafts developed by the various standard-setting bodies. These
                exposure drafts contain proposals to change professional standards such
                as accounting, auditing, and standards of conduct.

Index

About the Author

R. K. McCABE is Professor of Accounting at California State University, Fullerton. He has spent much of his career in public accounting and and has served
as a peer reviewer for the AICPA, a state society, and on a state society quality
review board. He is a widely published author of articles in such journals as the
Journal of Accountancy and *The CPA Journal*.